Thinking Through SCIENCE

Arthur Cheney
Howard Flavell
Chris Harrison
George Hurst
Carolyn Yates

Series editor: Chris Harrison

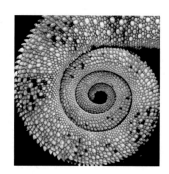

JOHN MURRAY

The cover image shows the coiled tail of a chameleon. The tail is as long as the chameleon's head and body. It acts like a fifth limb, adapted for wrapping around branches to maintain balance and keep the chameleon perfectly still while it waits for its prey.

© Arthur Cheney, Howard Flavell, Chris Harrison, George Hurst, Carolyn Yates 2003

First published in 2003
by John Murray (Publishers) Ltd, a division of Hodder Headline Ltd
338 Euston Road
London NW1 3BH

Reprinted 2003, 2004

Layouts by Stephen Rowling/springworks
Artwork by Oxford Designers and Illustrators Ltd

Typeset in 11/13pt Lucida by Wearset Ltd, Boldon, Tyne and Wear
Printed and bound in Spain by Bookprint S.L., Barcelona

A catalogue entry for this entry is available from the British Library.

ISBN 0 7195 7854 X
Teacher's Book 2 0 7195 7855 8
CD-ROM 2 0 7195 7856 6

Contents

Acknowledgements

Source acknowledgements
The following are sources from which artwork has been taken:

p.33 QCA Enterprises Ltd; **p.186** t © 2002 John Langdon (www.johnlangdon.net); **p.266** t Dave Keeling and Tim whorf, Scripps Institution of Oceanography.

Photo credits
With thanks to Bullfrog Music, Ship Street, East Grinstead for their assistance with the photos on pp110–111.

Thanks are due to the following for permission to reproduce copyright photographs:

Cover Robert Harding; **p.1** tl Science Photo Library/ David Parker, bl Ace Photo Library, tr Science Photo Library/A. Tsiarras, br Ace Photo Library; **p.2** t Science Photo Library/NASA, c Science & Society Picture Library, c John Townson/Creation, b Science Photo Library/ Adam Hart Davis; **p.10** Science Photo Library/EAS/PLI; **p.12** all John Townson/Creation; **p.16** all John Townson/Creation; **p.19** John Townson/Creation; **p.21** all John Townson/Creation; **p.23** all John Townson/Creation; **p.25** all John Townson/Creation; **p.26** tl Corbis, bl Science Photo Library/CNRI, tr Science Photo Library/Deep Light, br Science Photo Library/ David Martin; **p.36** tl, rl Ace Photo Library, bl, tc, tr John Townson/Creation, bc Corbis **p.38** all John Townson/Creation; **p.42** bc, br John Townson/Creation, bl, tl, tc, tr Geoscience Features; **P.43** John Townson/ Creation; **p.44** John Townson/Creation; **p.45** Photofusion; **p.46** Wookey Hole; **p.48** l Oxford Scientific Films, r Rex Features; **p.49** Oxford Scientific Films; **p.50** Geoscience Features; **p.51** John Townson/ Creation; **p.52** l Rex Features, tr, br John Townson/ Creation; **p.55** tl Science Photo Library/David Campione, bl, bc John Townson/Creation, tc Ace Photo Library, r Empics; **pp.56–57** all John Townson/Creation; **p.62** Oxford Scientific Films; **p.65** John Townson/ Creation; **p.70** John Townson/Creation; **p.71** all John Townson/Creation; **p.72** John Townson/Creation; **p.74** John Townson/Creation; **p.77** John Townson/ Creation; **p.79** t Philip Harris Education, b John Townson/Creation; **p.80** Oxford Scientific Films; **p.84** John Townson/Creation; **p.85** all John Townson/ Creation, except bl Science Photo Library/Claude Nuridsany & Marie Perennou, bc Science Photo Library/ James King Holmes; **p.91** t Mary Evans Picture Library, b Derby Museum & Art Gallery/Bridgeman Art Library; **p.92** Science & Society Picture Library; **p.96** all John Townson/Creation, except bl Robert Harding Photo Library; **p.97** tl,tr Photofusion, br John Townson; **p.99** Novosti; **p.100** t Science & Society Picture Library, c Science & Society Picture Library, b John Townson/ Creation ; **pp.101–104** all John Townson/Creation; **p.110–11** all John Townson/Creation; **p.115** John Townson/Creation; **p.117** John Townson/Creation; **p.118** John Townson/Creation; **p.119** Science Photo Library/Vic Bradbury; **p.123** John Townson/Creation; **p.125** Science Photo Library/James King Holmes; **p.126** t Oxford Scientific Films, b Oxford Scientific Films; **p.127** Oxford Scientific Films; **p.131** Science Photo Library/Secchi Lecaque/CNRI; **p.141** Science Photo Library/Geoff Tompkinson; **p.142** Chris Bonnington Picture Library; **p.143** Science Photo Library/George Cornacz; **p.144** Science Photo Library/ Mehau Kulyk; **p.145** Hutchison Picture Library; **p.148** l Science Photo Library/Shelia Terry, r Texas Council for the Humanities Resource Center/Sami Saleh Nawar; **p.151** l,c,r Colorsport; **p.157** John Townson/Creation; **p.158** John Townson/Creation; **p.159** all John Townson/Creation; **p.161** Bridgeman Art Library/National Gallery, London; **p.162** t Science Photo Library/Tek Image, c Science Photo Library/ Adam Hart Davis, b John Townson/Creation; **p.163** Andrew Sloley; **p.164** John Townson/Creation; **p.171** John Townson/Creation; **p.172** Ann Ronan Picture Library; **p.173** Ann Ronan Picture Library; **p.174** John Townson/Creation; **p.176** John Townson/ Creation; **p.179** John Townson/Creation; **p.181** John Townson/Creation; **p.182** t Texas Council for the Humanities Resource Centre/Sami Saleh Nawar, b Mary Evans Picture Library; **p.184** Oxford Scientific Films; **p.186** Rusty Rust Art; **p.187** Science Photo Library/Muybridge; **p.190** John Townson/Creation; **p.191** all John Towson/Creation, except bl Science Photo Library/Dr P Marazzi, bc Science Photo Library/ Damien Lovegrove, br Science Photo Library/Mark Clarke; **p.193** all John Townson/Creation, except bl Ace Photo Library; **p.195** Ann Ronan Picture Library; **p.196** Science Photo Library/Dr P Marazzi; **p.202** Oxford Scientific Films; **p.204** all John Townson/ Creation; **p.210** Wellcome Trust/Punch; **p.214** Roger Scruton; **p.220** Ace Photo Library; **p.222** Rex Features; **p.223** Robert Harding Picture Library; **p.224** Mary Evans Picture Library; **p.226** Oxford Scientific Films; **p.228** tl,tr Geoscience Features, bl, br John Townson/ Creation; **p.233** Mary Evans Picture Library; **p.235** Geoscience Features; **p.236** all John Townson/Creation; **p.237** all John Townson/Creation; **p.238** Mary Evans Picture Library; **pp.56–57** all John Townson/Creation; **p.240** all John Townson/Creation; **p.243** all John Townson/Creation; **p.244** Ann Ronan Picture Library; **p.245** Science Photo Library/Chris Madeley; **p.246** Ann Ronan Picture Library; **p.248** Science Photo Library/ Alex Bartel; **p.260** Science Photo Library/Eye of Science; **p.261** l Science Photo Library/Andrew Syred, c Science Photo Library/Eye of Science, r Science Photo Library/ Claude Nuridsarry & Maria Perennou; **p.262** Science Photo Library/Eye of Science; **p.263** Oxford Scientific Films; **p.264** Oxford Scientific Films; **p.270** Rex Features; **p.277** Geoscience Features.

l = left, r = right, t = top, b = bottom, c = centre

The publishers have made every effort to contact copyright holders. If any have been overlooked, they will be pleased to make the necessary arrangements at the earliest opportunity.

Introduction

→ ## _Science and society_

Science plays an important role in our lives. It helps us to explore, investigate and understand how things work, and to develop new materials and products to make our lives easier and more pleasant. Life would be very different without electricity, and more difficult without antibiotics, plastics or telephones. Science allows us to control our environment to suit our needs and to look beyond our own planet. It encourages us to keep challenging what we already know and to keep looking for new ideas. Today, many people are able to live normal lives even though they have serious conditions, such as diabetes and haemophilia, which would have caused death one hundred years ago. One day we may have a complete cure for cancer.

NASA launch control.

Medical technology.

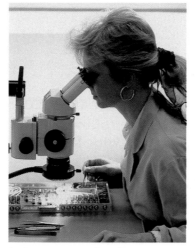

Laboratory scientist.

Geologist.

It is important that society is aware of what is happening in science and of the direction in which research is going. While some people are fascinated and excited by scientific advances, not all people share this feeling. Some people have a negative view about certain aspects of science. Some people worry that new processes pollute the planet; some have concerns about the long-term effects of using mobile phones and microwaves; some people do not think it right to do experiments on animals; some feel that genetic engineering is wrong.

Decade	Some scientific inventions	
1960s	audio cassettes, colour television, lunar spacecraft	
1970s	pocket calculator, videos, personal computer, supersonic plane	
1980s	compact discs, hepatitis B vaccine, video games, soft contact lenses	
1990s	world wide web, DVDs, hydrogen fuel cells, genetically engineered clones	

Your views on science

1 Answer the following questions.
   a) What is your favourite scientific invention? Why?
   b) Would you say that you had a positive or negative view about science? Explain.
   c) Can you name any scientists and what they invented?

   Share your ideas about these three questions with others in your group.

➡ *Working in a school science laboratory*

You should now be familiar with working in a science laboratory and be aware of the health and safety issues.

Imagine that a new pupil joined your class and that he or she had never had a science lesson in a school laboratory.

2 Write out your school lab safety rules and give an explanation of those you think are most important, with reasons.

3 Explain what you have to be careful about when:
- lighting a bunsen burner
- using acids or alkalis
- crushing crystals.

4 Look at the pictures of some pupils doing lab work. Decide who is working safely and who is not. Give advice about how some could work more safely.

5 Make a plan of your school science lab and mark on it where all the safety equipment is kept. List any features of the lab or the equipment that make it a safer place to work in. Can you think of other ways to make it an even safer environment to work in?

→ *Communicating in science*

In the Middle Ages, scientists wrote down their ideas and theories in Latin. Today, English tends to be the language that is used at most international science conferences. Science also has its own special way of communicating by using symbols and units that scientists from all over the world will recognise and understand. For example, scientists measure force in a unit called newtons.

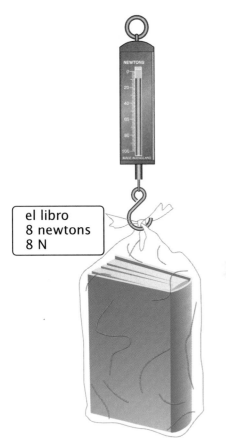

el libro
8 newtons
8 N

une pomme
1 newton
1 N

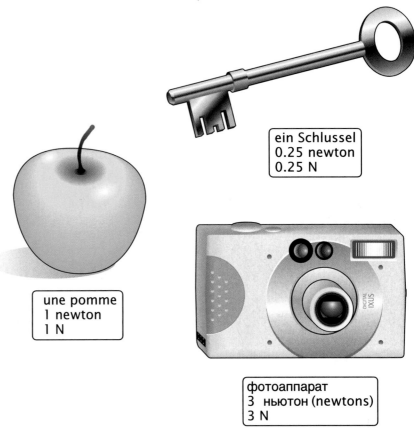

ein Schlussel
0.25 newton
0.25 N

фотоаппарат
3 ньютон (newtons)
3 N

The table below shows some of the units that scientists use.

Measurement	Unit	Symbol
length	metre	m
time	second	s
mass	kilogram	kg
volume	metre^3	m^3
force	newton	N
speed	metre per second	m/s
energy	joule	J
pressure	newton per metre^2	N/m^2
current	ampere	A
potential difference	volt	V
power	watt	W

Sometimes, we use smaller versions of these units. A metre^3 of water would be rather a lot to lift up and pour. In most experiments, we would use about 100 centimetre^3 (cm^3) in a beaker or about 5 centimetre^3 (cm^3) in a test tube.

Scientists also have a shorthand way of drawing apparatus. It would take too much time to draw all the apparatus in an experimental set-up in 3D and so scientists use 2D instead.

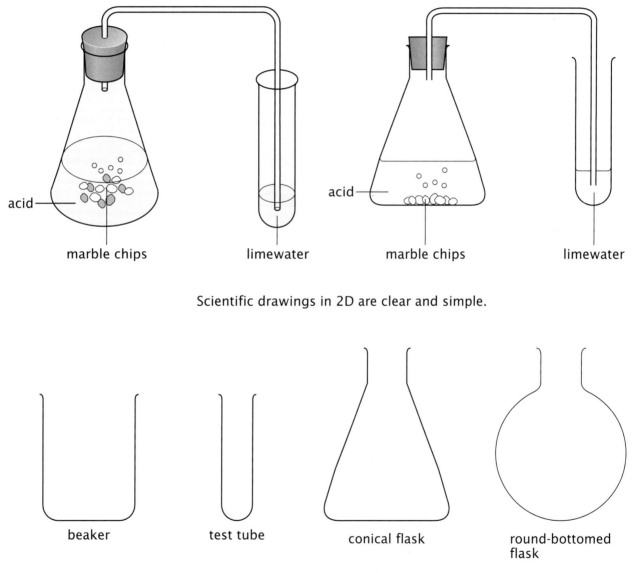

Scientific drawings in 2D are clear and simple.

beaker   test tube   conical flask   round-bottomed flask

Glassware is drawn like this in 2D.

In the topic of electricity, the apparatus is drawn as symbols. The wires that join the pieces of apparatus are drawn as straight lines.

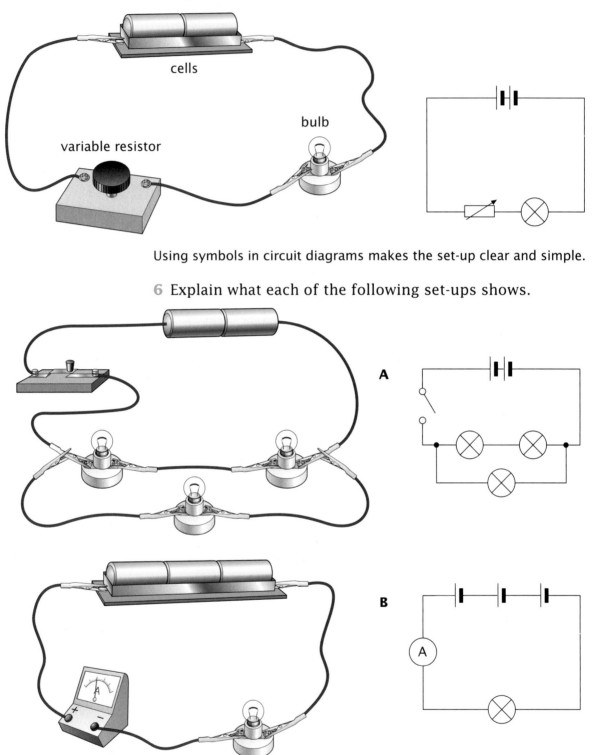

Using symbols in circuit diagrams makes the set-up clear and simple.

6 Explain what each of the following set-ups shows.

A

B

7 A pupil has written up an experiment that she did on testing the strength of three different types of plastic bag, but she has forgotten some of the amounts and units she used. Write out and complete the method for her by adding sensible amounts and the correct units.

C/W   6/10/03   Gina T.

Strength of Plastic Bags

Apparatus

3 plastic bags, scissors, metre rule, string, mass holder, masses.

Method

We cut strips from the three plastic bags, each measuring 10 long and ? wide. We then carefully hung each strip and added ? masses until the strips stretched and tore.

Results

Bag type	Force on bag
Q-shop	5 masses
Toggleby	6 masses
Simpsons	4 masses

Conclusion

Toggleby bags are strongest.

8 Can you draw the set-up that she used for her experiment?

Information processing   ## Scientific data

Scientists are data collectors. Sometimes they collect data in a survey, like that in Table A below showing shoe sizes of a Year 8 class. Sometimes they use observations like those in Table B. In both these cases, the scientists are looking for patterns in their data.

Table A

Shoe size	Number of pupils
1–2	3
3–4	8
5–6	12
7–8	7
9 or larger	1

1 What is the most frequent shoe size from this Year 8 class data?

2 What is the range of shoe sizes from this Year 8 class data?

3 Why do you think the class decided to collect the data in this way? Why did they not list all the shoe sizes?

4 Two new pupils join the class. One takes size $4\frac{1}{2}$ and the other size $5\frac{1}{2}$. Add them to the data in Table A and construct a new table in your book. Draw a bar chart of the data in your table.

5 Compare your bar chart with the one below which shows the data on shoe size for a Year 11 class. How are they similar and how are they different?

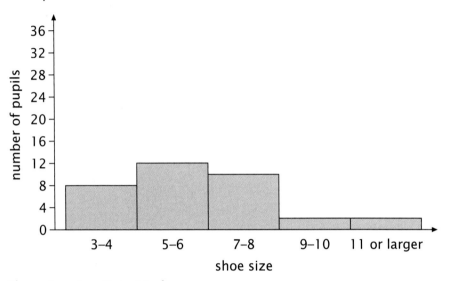

Shoe sizes in a Year 11 class.

Table B

Element	Metal or non-metal?	How it burns
sodium	metal	orange-yellow flame and makes a creamy colour solid
sulphur	non-metal	blue flame and makes dense fumes
calcium	metal	yellowish-red flame and makes a white solid
carbon	non-metal	glows red and makes a colourless gas
magnesium	metal	glows bright white and makes a white solid

6 Write out Table B in your book but put all the metals together and all the non-metals together.

7 Is there anything that the metals have in common when they burn?

8 Is there anything that the non-metals have in common when they burn?

9 Which metal or non-metal would you like to test next to see if it fitted your pattern? Why?

10 When phosphorus burns it produces white fumes and some solid. Do you think phosphorus is a metal or a non-metal? Why?

Information processing *Variables in a test*

Often scientists investigate by carrying out a fair test. This is when they look at how changing one variable can affect another variable. The variable that is changed is called the input variable. The variable that is affected is the outcome variable. The change in the outcome variable can usually either be observed or measured. All other variables stay the same in a fair test and are called fixed variables.

Jack and Ian found this recipe for making bulk quantities of yoghurt from boiled milk and a pot of yoghurt culture.

They wanted to find out the smallest amount of yoghurt culture that would successfully make yoghurt. Here are the results of their investigation.

> ### Yoghurt
>
> 3 pints milk
> 1 pot (200 g) yoghurt culture
>
> #### Recipe
>
> • Sterilise yoghurt pots and a teaspoon with boiling water.
> • Gently boil milk, allow to cool and fill yoghurt pots.
> • Add yoghurt culture to cooled milk and stir with teaspoon.
> • Place in warm conditions for 12 to 24 hours while yoghurt sets.

A
2 tsp

B
1 tsp

C
1½ tsp

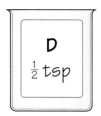

D
½ tsp

E
¼ tsp

F
1 spot

A	thick
B	thick
C	thick
D	runny
E	runny
F	runny

The variables in the 'Recipe for Yoghurt' investigation are:

- volume of boiled milk
- type of jar
- amount of yoghurt culture
- age of yoghurt culture
- temperature of boiled milk + culture
- length of time left
- thickness of yoghurt.

1 Which is the input variable? What values does it have?

2 Which is the outcome variable? How is the outcome variable being judged?

3 Which are the fixed variables?

4 What would be a conclusion for Jack and Ian's investigation?

Information processing   ## Strength of glue

Gill, Tariq and Suzie wanted to find out which type of glue stuck the strongest. They decided to use four types: Sticko, Superstick, Bondeaze and Gluepot. They cut several strips of card measuring 5 cm × 3 cm and stuck the cards together in pairs so that they overlapped by 1 cm. They then tested the strength of the glues by hanging 100 g masses from the bottom card in each pair.

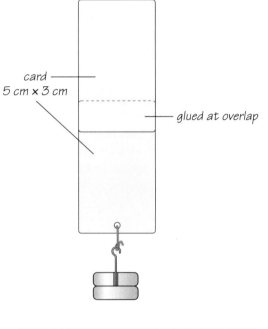

card
5 cm × 3 cm

glued at overlap

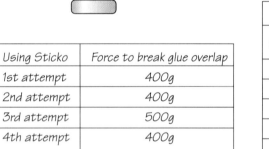

Using Sticko	Force to break glue overlap
1st attempt	400g
2nd attempt	400g
3rd attempt	500g
4th attempt	400g

Superstick	
Exp.	No. of 100g masses
1	6
2	1
3	6
4	5
5	5

Bondeaze results

Try	1	2	3	4	5
Mass	300g	400g	300g	400g	300g

Gluepot

Repeats	1	2	3
Mass (g)	700	700	700

1 Which is the input variable? What values does it have?

2 Which is the outcome variable? How is the outcome variable being judged?

3 Which are the fixed variables?

4 How did Gill, Tariq and Suzie make this investigation a fair test?

5 Can you make a single table to include all the results that Gill, Tariq and Suzie collected?

6 Results that are odd and do not seem to fit in with the rest of the data are called anomalous. Which result was anomalous in this investigation?

7 Why did Gill, Tariq and Suzie repeat their test several times with each type of glue?

8 Write a conclusion for Gill, Tariq and Suzie's investigation.

Information processing *Reacting magnesium and hydrochloric acid*

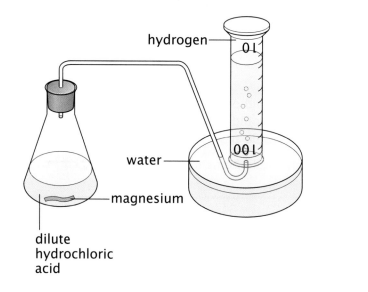

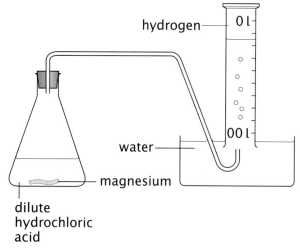

When magnesium is dropped into hydrochloric acid it reacts and produces hydrogen gas. The graph shows how the amount of hydrogen gas changes when different lengths of magnesium ribbon are used.

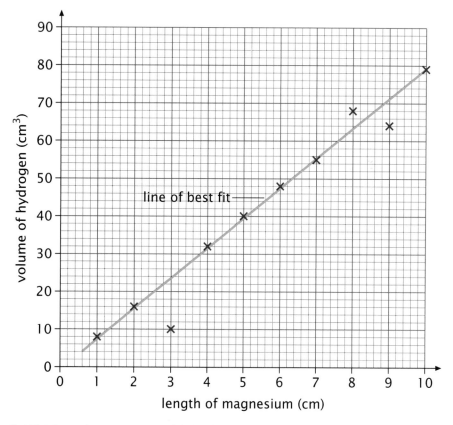

1 Which is the input variable? What values does it have?

2 Which is the outcome variable? How is the outcome variable being measured?

3 Which are the fixed variables?

4 Is this a fair test? Why?

5 Which result was anomalous in this investigation? How did you decide?

6 What is the relationship between the input and the outcome variables?

7 From the graph, estimate the volume of gas that:
   a) 5 cm of magnesium would produce
   b) 3.5 cm of magnesium would produce
   c) 9 cm of magnesium would produce.

8 How much magnesium would be needed to produce 60 cm^3 of hydrogen gas?

Information processing

Problem solving

Science sometimes requires us to look at things differently. Look at this beaker. Is it half full or half empty? Is it half full of liquid or half full of air? Or, is it full of liquid and air?

   Working in groups, look at the shapes below.

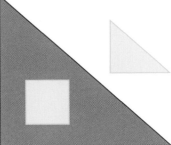

1 What are the variables?

2 Is there a relationship between any of the variables? Can you put this in an 'if it is . . ., then it is . . .' statement?

3 Some more shapes were added to the data set:

- large red circles
- small yellow squares
- large yellow circles
- medium blue diamonds
- tiny green triangles.

a) Which of these would support the relationship that you have decided on?

b) Which would disprove the relationship?

➡ *Developing new ideas*

Science is about explaining why things happen in the way that they do. It is about ideas and theories. Collecting data helps us to form these ideas because we begin to see how one thing affects another. Sometimes our ideas change as we begin to collect more data or a new set of data is found. 2500 years ago people used to believe that the Earth was flat but today we know that it's a giant ball hurtling through space. Ideas started to change when Pythagoras and other scientists began to explain why boats gradually disappeared over the horizon. Today of course, we have photographs of the Earth taken from space.

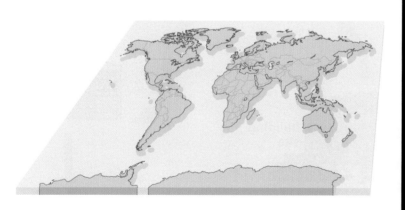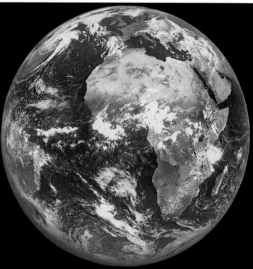

Space photographs prove that the Earth is not flat.

In science, it is important to carefully analyse the data that we collect and use the information that it gives us to try and work out what is going on. It is rather like putting together a jigsaw. It is only when you have a few pieces in position that you can work out what the picture might be. Then it becomes easier to search for new bits of the puzzle to put in place. Sometimes certain pieces do not seem to fit or, as you add more pieces, you realise that the blue piece that you put into the sky is actually part of a pond. So we need to keep questioning what we are doing in any investigation and checking our data carefully.

Sometimes we do experiments to check on ideas that we know. We are trying to prove that our idea works in this particular situation. At other times, we can use data to disprove an initial idea. If we find a way of disproving an idea, then it might mean that we have a new way of looking at something. This is why science is always seeking answers to new questions.

9 If someone believed that 'the higher a leaf is on a tree, the larger it is because it is in the best place to collect sunlight', what investigation could they do to:
   a) prove their idea
   b) disprove their idea?
10 Which evidence do you feel would be stronger – that proving or that disproving the idea?

Models and theories

Key word
* analogy

Sometimes we use models to help us explain how things work in science. The 'particles in a box' model in Book 1 helped us understand about solids, liquids and gases. It helped us explain the way that solids, liquids and gases behave differently. So we could explain why solids stay where you place them, but liquids run away and gases seem to disappear into the air.

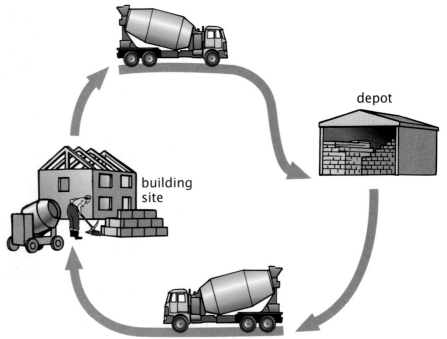

Sometimes we use the term **'analogy'** instead of model. In Book 1, electric current was explained using the analogy of a lorry carrying concrete from a depot to a building site and then returning to the depot. The depot is the battery. The energy is the concrete. The lorry is the moving charge. Another analogy for understanding electric circuits is that of cross-country runners racing across bridges to cross a river. In this one, it is easier to imagine how the pace is faster for the runners if there are two bridges in parallel, and we can use that idea to help us see why parallel circuits have brighter bulbs than series circuits. While the supply of concrete is a good way of explaining how energy travels round a circuit, the analogy of the cross-country runners is better for explaining the difference between series and parallel circuits.

11 use the 'particles in a box' model to explain:
  a) why it's easier to squash a gas than a solid
  b) why two solids do not mix together but two liquids or two gases do
  c) why balloons slowly deflate
  d) why gases tend to be smellier than solids.
12 In the concrete analogy for electricity, what represents
  a) the wires
  b) the bulbs?
13 Which analogy for electricity is best for explaining why the more batteries that you have, the higher the current?
14 You studied friction in Year 7. Can you think of a model or analogy to explain friction?
15 Some people talk about white blood cells being the 'soldiers of the body'. Can you explain why this helps them understand the functions of white blood cells?

→ *Getting started*

In this book, we will help you:

- identify variables and values
- find relationships between variables
- present data in a useful way
- read and interpret data
- recognise anomalous results
- draw graphs
- find the 'line of best fit' on line graphs
- solve problems
- share ideas with others
- learn and use key words
- link ideas using concept maps
- use models to help scientific understanding

but most of all, we will help you THINK!

1 Food and digestion

> **In this chapter you will learn:**
>
> → to describe a balanced diet
> → to name the major food groups and recognise foods and meals that contain these
> → to explain the job that each food group does in the body
> → to describe where digestion takes place in the gut
> → to explain the processes of digestion and absorption
> → to describe how enzymes work
>
> **You will also develop your skills in:**
>
> → interpreting and communicating information
> → interpreting data from bar charts, line graphs and tables
> → identifying variables
> → evaluating experiments

→ → → WHAT DO YOU KNOW?

Word list

* amino acids
* carbohydrates
* digestion
* enzyme
* fat
* starch
* gut
* ileum
* intestine
* liver
* oesophagus
* protein
* saliva
* stomach
* teeth

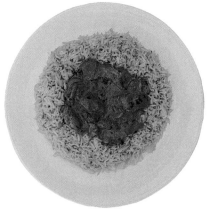

Which is the healthy choice?

1 Look at the pictures of the meals and the list of words. Use them to remind yourself of what you know about this topic already.

2 Decide which words you know in the list and use these to write some sentences or paragraphs about food and digestion.

3 Write down those words in the list that you do not know and keep them aside for later.

4 Share your ideas with others in your group.

Food groups

carbon
hydrogen
oxygen
nitrogen
calcium
phosphorus
iron
sodium
chlorine
sulphur

The list alongside shows the main elements that make up the human body. This does not provide a recipe, however, because humans continuously need new materials. We need proteins to make new cells and repair tissue. This helps us grow. We need carbohydrates and fats as fuel to keep all the chemical reactions working in the cells. This also helps keep our body temperature at 37 °C. We need all three of these food groups to make up our meals each day.

The body also needs small amounts of other food groups. Vitamins are needed to keep healthy. Vitamin C, which is found in fruits like oranges and mangoes, helps keep lining tissue healthy in the body. This will keep gums healthy and help prevent viruses, like the cold virus, breaking through the lining tissues and into the body.

Another food group that we need is the mineral salts. Iron is used to make haemoglobin in red blood cells. Calcium and phosphate are important for strengthening teeth and bones.

Humans also need a regular supply of water. About two-thirds of the human body is made of water (see the pie chart on the next page). Some water gets lost in sweat and urine, so the water needs to be replaced on a daily basis. We obtain water from our food as well as from drinks. Lettuce and other leafy vegetables are about 95% water.

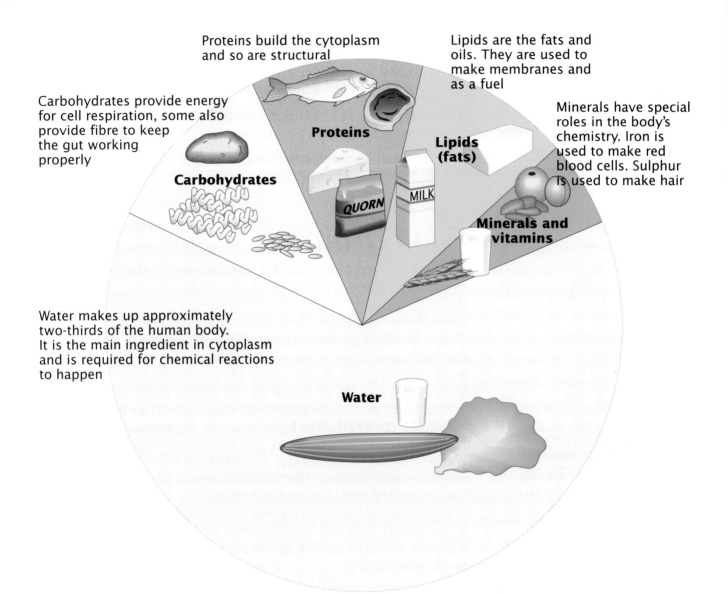

Proteins build the cytoplasm and so are structural

Proteins

Lipids are the fats and oils. They are used to make membranes and as a fuel

Lipids (fats)

Carbohydrates provide energy for cell respiration, some also provide fibre to keep the gut working properly

Carbohydrates

Minerals have special roles in the body's chemistry. Iron is used to make red blood cells. Sulphur is used to make hair

Minerals and vitamins

Water makes up approximately two-thirds of the human body. It is the main ingredient in cytoplasm and is required for chemical reactions to happen

Water

The human body's chemical contents.

1 Use the information in the picture to make a table listing the food groups and examples of food where they are found.
2 Try and add two or three more examples to each food group in your table.

Food labels

Food labels are useful in helping us to find out what is in our foods. The label for baked beans at the top of the next page tells us how much energy is provided and how much of each food group there is in both 'a serving' and 100 g of the food. It also informs us how much of the carbohydrate in the food is sugar and how much of the fat is 'saturated'.

NUTRITION INFORMATION

TYPICAL VALUES (heated as per instructions)

	per ½ CAN	per 100g
ENERGY	760 k J.	362 k J.
	178 k cal	85 k cal
PROTEIN	10.3g	4.9g
CARBOHYDRATE	32.5g	15.5g
of which sugars	13.2g	6.3g
of which starch	19.3g	9.2g
FAT	0.8g	0.4g
of which saturates	0.2g	0.1g
FIBRE	7.8g	3.7g
SODIUM	1.1g	0.5g

per ½ CAN	178 CALORIES	0.8g FAT

GUIDELINE DAILY AMOUNTS

EACH DAY	WOMEN	MEN
CALORIES	2000	2500
FAT	70g	95g

OFFICIAL GOVERNMENT FIGURES FOR AVERAGE ADULTS

If you are not entirely satisfied with this product please let us know on Sainsbury's Careline. Freephone 0800 636262

3 Which food group occurs in the largest amount in baked beans?

4 If 0.2 g of the fat in a serving (half a can) of baked beans is saturated, how much is unsaturated fat?

5 How much protein is there in a serving of baked beans?

6 This can of baked beans contains two servings. How much energy is contained in the whole can of beans?

Baked beans also contain fibre. Some people call this 'roughage'. It is plant material; the cells of the bean have cellulose walls and this is the fibre. It is a useful food group because it gives our food bulk and so makes it easier for the gut muscles to grip the food and push it along the gut.

Sodium is also listed on the food label. The body needs sodium to keep its nerves working correctly. The reason why it is listed on the food label is because it gives us an idea of how much salt is in the food. Salt is sodium chloride. Some people need to keep salt to a minimum in their diet, especially if they have a condition such as high blood pressure.

Food groups in the diet

Look at these four food labels for milk, margarine, bread and tinned pineapple.

Milk (semi-skimmed)

NUTRITION INFORMATION

TYPICAL VALUES	PER 200ml SERVING	PER 100ml
Energy	408kj	204kj
	98kcal	49kcal
Protein	6.8g	3.4g
Carbohydrate	10.0g	5.0g
of which sugars	10.0g	5.0g
Fat	3.4g	1.7g
of which saturates	2.0g	1.0g
Fibre	nil	nil
Sodium	0.12g	0.06g
Calcium	244mg	122mg

Margarine (reduced fat)

INGREDIENTS

VEGETABLE OIL, WATER, OLIVE OIL, WEY POWDER, SALT, EMULSIFIER, STABILISER

TYPICAL VALUES	PER 100g
ENERGY	2205kj
	536kcal
PROTEIN	0.1g
CARBOHYDRATE	1.2g
of which sugars	1.2g
of which starch	0.0g
FAT	56.0g
of which saturates	13.0g
of which mono-unsaturates	33.0g
of which polyunsaturates	10.0g
FIBRE	0.0g
SODIUM	0.6g
VITAMIN A	800µg
VITAMIN D	5µg

Wholegrain bread

INGREDIENTS

Wheatflour, Water, Cut wheat, Oats, Dried gluten, Yeast, Malt flour

NUTRITION INFORMATION

TYPICAL VALUES	PER 100g	per slice
ENERGY	988kj	247kj
	235kcal	60kcal
PROTEIN	11.0g	2.8g
CARBOHYDRATE	42.8g	10.7g
of which sugars	3.0g	0.8g
FAT	2.0g	0.5g
of which saturates	0.4g	0.1g
FIBRE	5.6g	1.4g
SODIUM	0.42g	0.11g
VITAMIN B₁₂	0.2µg	0.05µg

Tinned pineapple

INGREDIENTS

PINEAPPLE, PINEAPPLE JUICE

NUTRITION INFORMATION

TYPICAL VALUES	PER ½ CAN	PER 100g
ENERGY	562kj	260kj
	132kcal	61kcal
PROTEIN	0.9g	0.4g
CARBOHYDRATE	31.8g	14.7g
of which sugars	31.8g	14.7g
of which starch		
less than	0.1g	less than 0.1g
FAT	0.2g	0.1g
of which saturates		
less than	0.1g	0.1g
FIBRE	1.5g	0.7g
SODIUM		
less than	0.1g	less than 0.1g

7 Match one of the foods with each of the statements below.
a) This food is high in fibre and carbohydrates but low in sugars.
b) This food contains all the food groups including the mineral salt calcium.
c) This food is mainly a source of sugars and some fibre.
d) This food is high in fat.
e) This food would be beneficial for children, to help them develop strong teeth and bones.

8 Which vitamin is found in pineapple but is not shown on the label above?

9 Now write six questions that you would use to check if someone could interpret the information on the food labels for milk, bread, margarine and tinned pineapple.

10 Why is the information on the food groups given per 100 g of food as well as per serving or per item?

Sometimes the information about a food is given in the form of a bar chart or a pie chart.

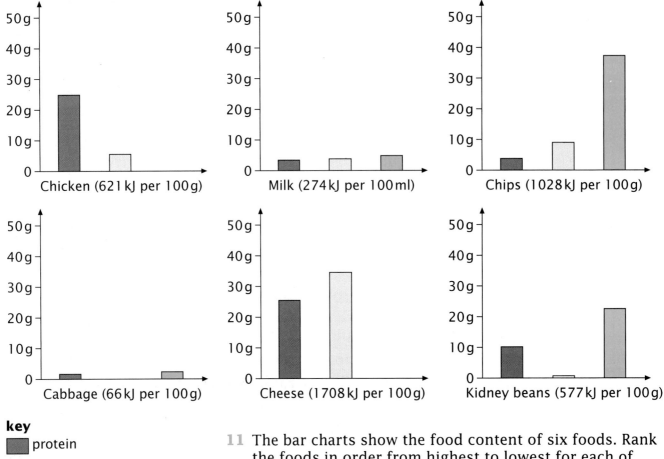

key
- protein
- fat
- carbohydrate

11 The bar charts show the food content of six foods. Rank the foods in order from highest to lowest for each of carbohydrate, protein and fat.

12 Which food(s) would be a good protein source for a vegetarian diet?

13 You may have done food tests on some foods or seen these demonstrated. The table below lists the main food tests and the results you would get with each test. Imagine doing food tests on chicken, milk, chips, cabbage, cheese and kidney beans. What results would you expect with each of the food tests described?

Food	Example	Test	Positive result
starch	bread	add a drop of brown iodine solution	iodine changes from brown to blue/black
sugar	sugar	put food in blue Benedict's solution and warm gently	blue colour changes to bright orange
protein	meat	add Biuret A and B solution	clear liquid turns a lilac colour
fat	butter	add some water and a few drops of ethanol, and shake	liquid should go whitish and oil drops appear

A healthy diet

There are a lot of people willing to give advice about a healthy diet. The difficulty is in making sense of it all. To help you make sense of the advice on the next page, study this page and make a table to summarise the information.

Nuts are high in fat but also contain carbohydrate and protein. A 50 g serving contains as much as 1200 kJ of energy. Some people are allergic to nuts.

Breads are starchy, high fibre foods, with a little protein and almost no fat. Two slices for your sandwich provide around 500 kJ of energy, but butter more than trebles the energy intake.

Fruits are low energy foods, providing around 200 kJ a piece. They provide fibre, some carbohydrate and vitamins, especially vitamin C.

Fish is a high protein food that has very little carbohydrate. The fat content depends on the type of fish. A portion for a main meal provides about 1000 kJ of energy.

Vegetables like broccoli are high in fibre, mineral salts and vitamins. They are low energy foods. A portion of broccoli provides less than 100 kJ of energy.

Meat is high in protein and can be high in fat. A chicken portion provides around 600 kJ of energy while a steak might provide over 1500 kJ. There is no fibre and little carbohydrate in the meat. Some red meats are a rich source of iron.

Evaluation Advice for a healthy diet

A vegetarian diet gives you a low fat, high fibre, healthy diet with plenty of vitamins and mineral salts in a wide variety of fruits, vegetables, seeds and nuts.

A balanced diet is a healthy diet and you achieve this through varied meals that include all the food groups. But you should avoid too much high fat or high protein food. Eating at least five portions of fresh fruit and veg each day also helps promote good health.

On average these days we eat about 1 kg of sugar a week. A hundred years ago that's how much a person would eat in a whole year! Most of our sugar is in convenience foods. In a can of fizzy drink there can be up to 10 teaspoons of sugar. If you want to eat a healthy diet, cook fresh food and keep away from packets and tins and ready-made meals.

I lost 10 kg in 6 months just by cutting out some of the fat in my diet. There's fat in red meat, sausages and cheese, so I chose chicken or fish mostly for my main meals. I kept butter and margarine to a minimum and changed to skimmed milk. I cut down crisps and biscuits to a treat once or twice a week. If you want a healthy diet, eat less fatty foods.

1 Describe the sort of foods and meals that you would imagine each of the four people in the picture would eat.

2 For each person, explain the healthy aspect of their diet.

3 Use the information to decide how healthy your diet is. How could it be made healthier?

4 A friend says that she wants to eat more healthily and so is thinking of going without breakfast because she has found out that her cereal has a lot of sugar. What would your advice be and why?

Reasoning Diet diary

1 Keep a diary of all that you eat and drink for a whole day. Put each item or part of an item on a single line. For example, a cheese and tomato sandwich might be listed as:

    two slices of wholemeal bread
    margarine
    cheddar cheese
    tomato

2 From your knowledge of food groups, identify whether the food on each line is carbohydrate, protein, fat or a mixture of these food groups.

3 Look at one another's food diaries and see if you agree with the way that the foods are categorised into the three food groups.

4 A balanced diet should contain all three food groups but fats should be minimised wherever possible. Think about your diet diary. Do you have a balanced diet? Explain your reasoning to your partner and see what they think.

Time to think

- Go back to the work that you completed in *What do you know?*, the first activity in this chapter, and find the list of unknown words that you made. Check how many of these you now understand.
- Construct a concept map of your understanding in this topic so far.
- Compare your concept map with at least two others in your class and be prepared to justify how you have linked some of the words together.
- Look at your concept map again and make any changes or additions to it, having learned from looking at others' work.

Digestion

Key words
* digestion
* soluble
* enzymes
* ileum
* peristalsis
* oesophagus

Digestion is the process that gets food into our body systems. The gut breaks the food into small, simple molecules so that these can pass through the gut wall and into the blood. For example, carbohydrates such as starch are broken down into **soluble** sugars. The soluble food can then travel to all the cells and organs of the body.

Starchy foods are insoluble but sugars are soluble.

The gut has mechanical ways and chemical ways of breaking down food. The teeth are the first mechanical means of breaking down the food. At the front of the mouth are the incisor and canine teeth. At the back are the premolars and molars. The incisors chop and cut the food while the large premolars and molars grind the food into much smaller pieces. These actions increase the surface area of the food. This is useful as it helps the **enzymes** to break down the food chemically. In the mouth, starch is also broken down chemically by saliva.

The gut is really a giant tube, measuring about 8 metres in length. It begins at the mouth where food is taken in. Digestion takes place from the mouth to the beginning of the **ileum** (small intestine). This is about 1 metre of the tube. Digested food is absorbed through the small intestine wall into the blood. The large intestine (or colon) is responsible for absorbing water into the bloodstream and finally for getting rid of any food that cannot be digested. The left-over food is made into faeces in the rectum.

Study the diagram of the gut and construct a table to explain the role each part plays in digestion.

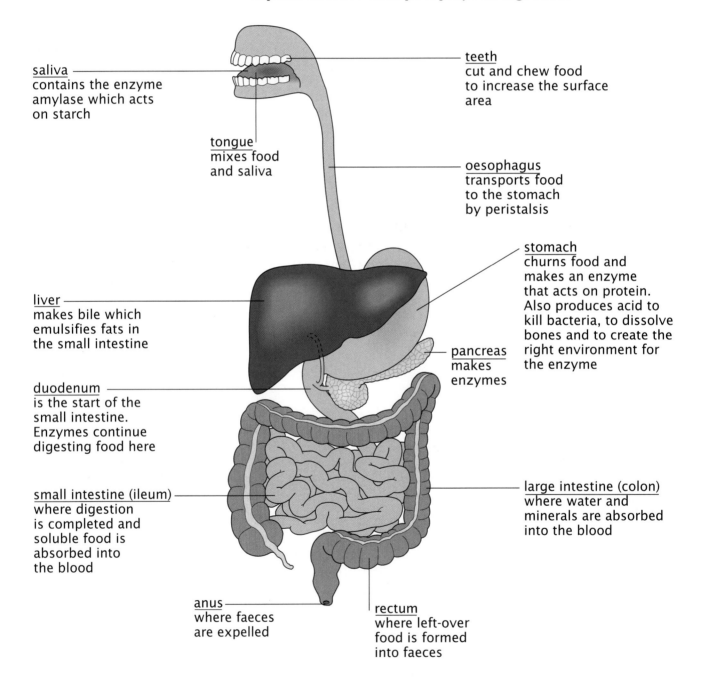

saliva
contains the enzyme amylase which acts on starch

teeth
cut and chew food to increase the surface area

tongue
mixes food and saliva

oesophagus
transports food to the stomach by peristalsis

stomach
churns food and makes an enzyme that acts on protein. Also produces acid to kill bacteria, to dissolve bones and to create the right environment for the enzyme

liver
makes bile which emulsifies fats in the small intestine

pancreas
makes enzymes

duodenum
is the start of the small intestine. Enzymes continue digesting food here

small intestine (ileum)
where digestion is completed and soluble food is absorbed into the blood

large intestine (colon)
where water and minerals are absorbed into the blood

anus
where faeces are expelled

rectum
where left-over food is formed into faeces

Food is pushed through the gut by muscles in the gut wall. This process is called **peristalsis**. Imagine the food in a ball, passing into the **oesophagus**. Muscles in the wall behind the gut squeeze and push the ball of food towards the stomach, rather like a marble being pushed along a flexible tube.

muscles squeeze here

In the stomach, the muscles in the wall churn the ball of food and turn it into a liquid, rather like a thick milkshake. Food is held in the stomach for a few hours because proteins are digested here. Then the food is passed into the start of the small intestine to finish off the digestion process. Again peristalsis is responsible for pushing the semi-digested food along.

14 Name two ways in which the gut breaks down food.
15 How is food moved along the gut?
16 In which parts of the gut does digestion take place?
17 a) What happens to the digested food in the small intestine?
   b) What happens to the food that is not digested?
18 What job does the large intestine do?
19 If you had to link parts of the gut to kitchen tools that had a similar role, which part is most like:
   a) a food mixer
   b) scissors
   c) a sieve?
   Explain your reasoning for each part.

Creative thinking ## Gut facts and figures

Look at the table below.

Part of gut	Approximate length	Approximate time food remains there
mouth	10 cm	1 minute
oesophagus	25 cm	10 seconds
stomach	15 cm	2–3 hours
small intestine	5–6 m	3 hours
large intestine	1–1.5 m	2 days

Think how you might combine these facts and figures with the information in the text and diagrams to produce either

- a poster, pamphlet or PowerPoint presentation on the human gut, or
- a story that describes the journey of your breakfast through your gut.

Medical knowledge of the gut

Captain William Beaumont attending
Alexis St. Martin

Captain William Beaumont was an American
army surgeon in the early part of the nineteenth
century. In 1882 he was called to see a patient,
Alexis St. Martin, who had been accidentally
shot in the stomach. The wound healed in a few
weeks but left a hole leading right into the
man's stomach. In fact, the hole had to be
plugged with a rolled-up bandage to stop the
stomach contents leaking out. Beaumont was
able to advance his knowledge of how the
stomach worked by watching the movements of
the stomach directly. He also took samples from
the stomach and did tests on the foods and the
stomach juices. He discovered new knowledge
about the digestive system, which he published.
One of the interesting facts that he discovered
was that the stomach contains a very strong
acid that could burn a hole in thick cloth.

X-ray systems now allow
doctors to see the gut and how
it is working. X-rays pass
through soft tissue, so to get
an X-ray image the gut needs
to be made denser. This is
achieved by giving the patient
a 'barium meal'. The patient has
to swallow a solution of barium
sulphate. This spreads through
the gut and so the shape of the
gut appears on the X-ray. If the
gut is blocked or twisted, this
can be seen on the X-ray.

Another medical technique that
allows doctors to see inside
bodies is the use of optic fibres.
These tiny tubes can carry light
along them into the gut. The light
can then bounce back inside the optic
fibre cables and an image of the inside of part
of the gut is seen. This method allows the
doctors to look closely at the lining and
contents of the gut.

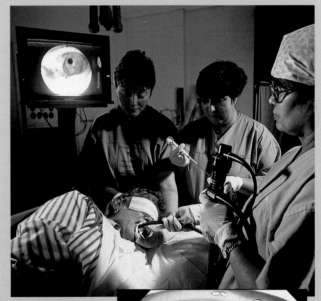

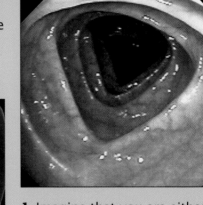

Endoscopy
and the image
obtained of
the inside of
the gut.

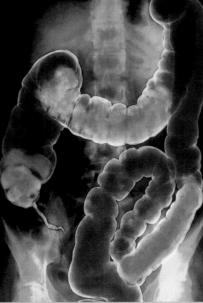

Barium X-ray of the gut.

1 Imagine that you are either
   the surgeon William
   Beaumont or his patient,
   Alexis St. Martin. Write your
   diary entries from when you
   first met in hospital until
   after Beaumont's discovery
   about acid in the stomach.
2 What is a 'barium meal'?
3 How do optic fibres help
   doctors diagnose problems
   in the gut?

Enzymes

Enzymes help speed up reactions. In the gut, enzymes help break down food. Starch is a long molecule made up of lots of smaller sugar units. The enzyme **amylase** helps break the large starch molecule into smaller sugar units. Other enzymes, called **protease**, help break proteins into **amino acids**. Yet another group of enzymes helps break down fats into smaller units.

Key words
* amylase
* protease
* amino acids
* carbohydrases

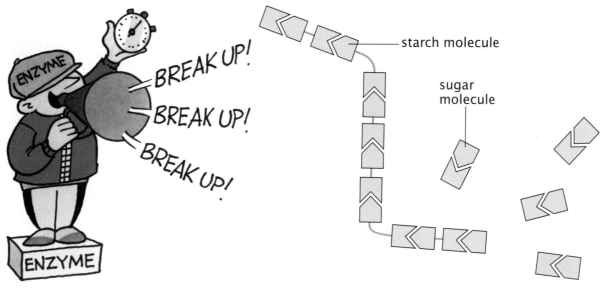

starch molecule

sugar molecule

Bread is mainly starch. By the time that the bread reaches your small intestine, all of the starch in it has been broken down into sugars. The enzyme amylase, and other **carbohydrases**, have broken down the large starch molecules into smaller, simpler sugar molecules.

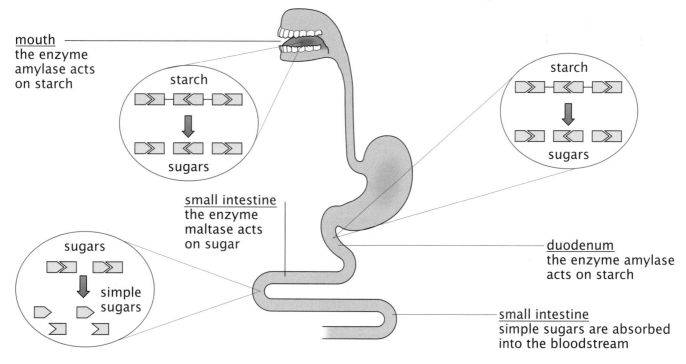

mouth
the enzyme amylase acts on starch

starch

sugars

small intestine
the enzyme maltase acts on sugar

sugars

simple sugars

starch

sugars

duodenum
the enzyme amylase acts on starch

small intestine
simple sugars are absorbed into the bloodstream

Enzyme action on starch and sugars in the gut.

Reasoning ## Starch breakdown

Adrian, Julia and Lee carried out an experiment to show that starch breaks down into sugars when a particular enzyme is added. They selected three enzymes – protease, amylase and catalase – to test which was the best enzyme at breaking down starch into sugars. They set up three tubes, each containing 20 cm^3 of starch solution. They added 2 cm^3 of one of the enzymes to each tube of starch solution. Every 2 minutes they tested a drop of their starch and enzyme mixture to see if the starch had been broken down into sugar. Here are their results:

Time in minutes	Colour of starch + enzyme + iodine		
	Protease	Amylase	Catalase
0	black	black	black
2	black	black	black
4	black	black	black
6	black	brown	black
8	black	brown	brown
10	black	brown	black
12	black	brown	black

1 What was the input variable in this experiment?

2 What were the fixed variables in this experiment?

3 What piece of apparatus do you think the pupils used to measure the volume of the starch solution?

4 How do you think the pupils tested for starch?

5 What do the results show about the breakdown of starch by these three enzymes?

EXTENSION 6 Julia was concerned that Lee sometimes forgot to clean the glass rod that they were using to collect a sample of the starch and enzyme mixture. Do any of the results confirm Julia's concerns? Explain why you think this.

7 If your school ran out of iodine solution, how else could you test that starch had been broken down by one of the enzymes?

8 Starch is broken down in the mouth and the duodenum. Both of these areas are slightly alkaline. How could you redesign the experiment to see if one of the enzymes works better in alkaline conditions than it does in neutral conditions?

DID YOU KNOW?

Pineapples produce a protease enzyme. This makes it impossible to make an orange jelly with pineapple fruit in it for dessert.

Absorption

Proteins and fats get broken down in a similar way to starch. Protein digestion starts in the stomach where a protease enzyme is released onto the food. By the time the large protein molecule reaches the small intestine it is broken down into small amino acid units. Fats do not start to be broken down until they reach the small intestine but once there the fat enzyme gets to work.

So digestion is the breakdown of large food molecules into small food molecules. Large food molecules, like starch, are **insoluble**. This means that they do not dissolve. However, small food molecules, like sugar, are soluble. So these can dissolve in water. In solution these small food molecules can **diffuse** through the wall of the small intestine. The sugars, amino acids and tiny fat molecules can then be transported to all the body cells. The process of the foods dissolving and passing through the gut wall is called **absorption**.

20 What do we mean by 'digestion'?
21 Why does the gut need to digest starch?
22 Which process describes how soluble food passes through the gut wall?

Word play

Enzyme names always end in -ase and the first part of their name usually tells you what is being broken down. So a carbohydrase breaks down carbohydrates. What do you think the following enzymes break down?
a) sucrase
b) cellulase
c) nuclease

Information processing

Absorption

Look back at the two drawings on pages 24 and 27, and make your own drawing to show what happens in absorption. Annotate your drawing to give some of the detail of what happens.

Time to think

- Look back again at the list of unknown words that you made at the start of this chapter. Check that you now understand them all.
- Divide a piece of paper into four sections. In each section, put one of these words in a box in the centre: starch, protein, fat, enzyme. Draw four lines spreading out from the word in the box and write a different fact about the word at the end of each line. Can you add any more facts?

Enquiry   *Model gut*

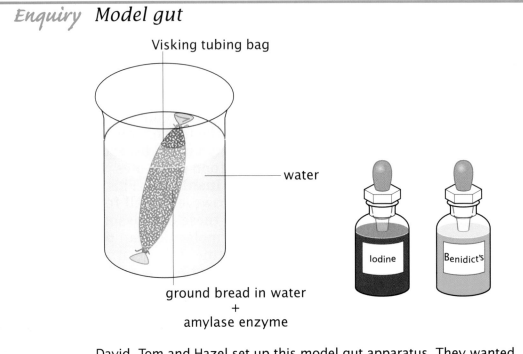

David, Tom and Hazel set up this model gut apparatus. They wanted to model what happens to a slice of bread in digestion and absorption.

1 Their teacher suggested that they grind up the bread before adding it to the water in the Visking tubing. Why do you think she suggested this?

2 David and Tom had an argument about the experiment. David wanted to add amylase enzyme and then 10 minutes later test a drop of the bread solution with iodine. Tom agreed about the enzyme and the time but wanted to do a sugar test. Hazel said she thought they were both correct. What do you think?

3 Unfortunately, they forgot to add the enzyme. What result do you think they got after 10 minutes with
a) iodine solution
b) Benedict's test?

4 When they realised their mistake, they added the enzyme, waited 10 minutes, then tested a sample of the bread solution with
a) iodine solution
b) Benedict's test.
What results do you think they got? Why?

5 Why did they wait for 10 minutes before doing the test?

EXTENSION   **6** Later, their teacher told them to take a drop of the liquid from just outside the Visking tubing and test for sugar. She said this would show that absorption was taking place. They found that the sample went yellow/orange after the test.
a) Which test did they do?
b) Did the sample contain sugar?
c) How did this show that absorption was taking place?

7 Their homework was to draw a diagram of the apparatus and annotate it to show what was happening. Here is their work.

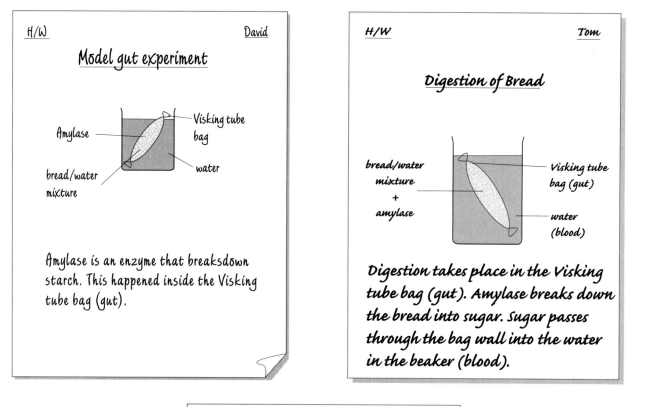

H/W David

Model gut experiment

- Visking tube bag
- Amylase
- bread/water mixture
- water

Amylase is an enzyme that breaksdown starch. This happened inside the Visking tube bag (gut).

H/W Tom

Digestion of Bread

- bread/water mixture + amylase
- Visking tube bag (gut)
- water (blood)

Digestion takes place in the Visking tube bag (gut). Amylase breaks down the bread into sugar. Sugar passes through the bag wall into the water in the beaker (blood).

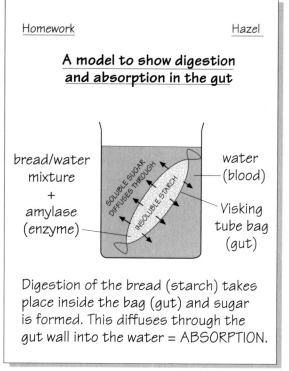

Homework Hazel

A model to show digestion and absorption in the gut

- bread/water mixture + amylase (enzyme)
- SOLUBLE SUGAR DIFFUSES THROUGH
- INSOLUBLE STARCH
- water (blood)
- Visking tube bag (gut)

Digestion of the bread (starch) takes place inside the bag (gut) and sugar is formed. This diffuses through the gut wall into the water = ABSORPTION.

Discuss the quality of each one. What comments could you make to each pupil to help them improve their homework?

Word play

Copy and complete the word puzzle using the clues below.

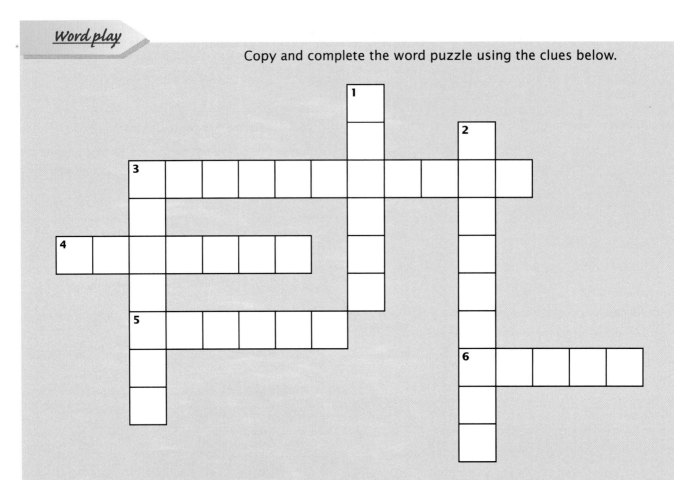

Across

3 The process that moves food through the gut (11)
4 Part of the gut that turns the food into liquid (7)
5 A chemical that helps break down food (6)
6 Digestion ends here and absorption starts (5)

Down

1 A complex carbohydrate (6)
2 The process of breaking down food (9)
3 Type of food found in meat (7)

EXTENSION Can you add some more words to the puzzle and think up suitable clues for them?

DID YOU KNOW?

There is enough energy in a meal of salami pizza, ice cream and cola to supply a person's energy needs for a whole day.

Time to think

Carefully read through the work that you have done on this topic and then through the chapter of this book.

Here is the type of question that might appear in a test on this topic.

---

8. The following are important parts of a balanced diet.

    carbohydrates
    proteins
    fats
    vitamins
    water

    A pupil has a sweet, juicy orange to eat.

    (a) Complete the following sentences using words from the list above.

        (i) An orange is a good source of

        _____ and _____   *2 marks*

        (ii) An orange is a poor source of

        _____ and _____   *2 marks*

    (b) Give the names of **two** parts of a balanced diet which are **not** shown in the list above.

                                                          2 marks
        1. _____

        2. _____

    (c) In order to obtain the nutrients, food must be chewed.
        Give **two** reasons why it is important to chew food.
                                                          2 marks
        1. _____

        _____

        2. _____

        _____

                                                maximum 8 marks

    KS3/00/Sc/Tier 5-7/P2   14

Imagine that you were a teacher and had to set a 30 minute test on this work. Write some questions to go in the test. What are the correct answers to each of your questions?

Try your questions out on other people in your group, to:

- see if they can answer your questions
- check what they think of your questions and the answers you expect
- help you to work on any questions that need to be improved.

2 Rocks and weathering

In this chapter you will learn:

→ how grain size and rock type affects the properties of different soils
→ to classify rocks based on appearance, texture, hardness and porosity
→ the key properties of igneous, sedimentary and metamorphic rocks
→ how rocks are weathered and how erosion occurs
→ how eroded rocks are carried long distances and settle down on the sea bed

You will also develop your skills in:

→ analysing data
→ planning and predicting the outcome of experiments
→ using keys
→ creative writing

→ → → WHAT DO YOU KNOW?

Farmers and gardeners try to improve their soil to grow better crops and plants.

1 The table below gives the features of a good soil. The explanations have been mixed up. Try to match them up correctly.

Features of a good soil	What it provides
humus (dead plant material)	provide air pockets which contain carbon dioxide and water
spaces between the grains	enriches the soil and, when broken down, provides important nutrients for the plants
minerals	lets the plants get the right amount of water
drainage	when dissolved, provide essential nutrients for plant growth and health

2 There are four main types of soil:
- sandy
- chalky
- loam
- clay

Read these descriptions carefully and match each of them up to one of the types of soil:

A The grains are very small; it is difficult to dig through and easily becomes waterlogged.
B This is the best soil for growing plants as it contains a large amount of humus and has good drainage.
C Grasses grow well on this soil but because it is alkaline heather does not grow well there.
D This soil has grains just big enough to see. The soil is easy to dig and water drains through it very quickly.

3 Lucy says that big grains have bigger spaces between them than small grains, which helps to explain drainage. What does she mean? Use diagrams to help explain Lucy's idea. Add notes to your diagrams.

→ *Rocks and their uses*

Key words
* minerals
* elements
* compounds
* properties
* construction
* ores

Rocks are naturally occurring materials that are made up of one or more **minerals**. Some minerals are **elements** but most minerals are **compounds** (see Chapter 7). Minerals can usually be identified by simple **properties** such as colour, hardness, acid test and the shape of their crystals. Rocks are a mixture of the different minerals.

Rocks can be valuable raw materials that provide us with very useful chemicals and fuel sources. Some rocks and minerals can be used almost in the condition they are dug from the ground. For example, sand, gravel and clay are used for **construction** of buildings, road and bridges, and for brick manufacture. Others require only some 'dressing up' to make them suitable for their intended uses. Examples are the sawing of sandstone into blocks and sheets for building construction, or the cutting and polishing of granite for decorative cladding and bench tops. Many other rocks are used for buildings and their interiors, for example limestone and marble.

Some minerals, for example coal and limestone, as well as being used straight from the ground, can be changed into different materials by chemical reactions. Some minerals may be compounds of a useful metal such as iron or aluminium. If the rocks contain enough of the metal to be worth mining they are called **ores**. Large amounts of electricity are needed to separate aluminium from its ore, aluminium oxide (bauxite), but once separated the metal is highly resistant to corrosion and lasts a very long time. Some metals, such as gold, platinum, and occasionally copper and silver, occur in the Earth as native elements, requiring no treatment other than separation from their host rocks.

Quarrying gravel.

Bricks.

Paving slabs.

Granite.

Bauxite mining.

Aluminium extraction plant.

There are a great number of different rocks and they vary in many different ways. Many rocks contain tightly packed crystals, others contain fossils that are the remains of living things preserved in rock layers. They can tell us a lot about what sorts of plants and animals lived on Earth over a time scale spanning about 3000 million years.

1 What is a mineral?

2 Try to classify (sort out) the different rocks mentioned in the passage under the following headings:

Rocks used straight from the ground	Rocks that are changed into different materials

3 Were any rocks difficult to classify?

4 Discuss in your group how you would classify rocks and minerals.

5 Why do you think that studying fossils in rocks can be useful?

6 Gold and platinum are described in the passage as 'native elements'. What do you think this means?

7 Aluminium is a very common element (making up 8% of the Earth's crust by weight). However it is still very expensive. Look through the passage again and find a reason why.

Information processing ## Using minerals

Based on current consumption, it is estimated that every person in the United States will use more than 460 000 kg of rocks, minerals and metals during their lifetime, including those in the table below.

Mineral	Amount used (kg)	Uses
lead	360	primarily used in the construction of batteries; also used as radiation shielding during X-ray treatment by doctors and dentists
zinc	340	mainly used to stop steel rusting in the construction of cars, buildings, bridges, ships and trains
aluminium	1 640	used in the manufacture of cans, aircraft and cars, sports equipment, electronic equipment and electrical appliances
iron	14 550	used to make steel for cars, subways, ships and cans, and in building construction, for heavy equipment, appliances, power transmission turbines, towers and bridges
clay	1 230	used to coat the pages of newspapers, magazines, stationery, brochures and boxes (so that the ink used in printing on them will be bright and will not run); also used as a brightener and abrasive in toothpaste, and in medicines to provide a smooth coating for the stomach
salt	12 730	used in food preservation (almost all canned and frozen food contain salt) and to melt the ice on streets and motorways during the winter; also used in the manufacture of many chemicals, soaps and detergents, for water treatment, papermaking, and in petroleum refining
sand, gravel and cement	455 000	used in the construction of houses and other buildings, in particular in the foundations, and as decorative materials for patios and gardens; also used in water purification

The population of the USA is about 285 million. The UK population is about 60 million.

1 What is the total mass of metals used per person in the USA during their lifetime?

2 What percentage of the metals used is aluminium?

EXTENSION

3 To the nearest whole number, how many times bigger is the USA population than that of the UK?

4 What is the total mass of sand, gravel and cement that will be used by the current UK population in their lifetime, assuming the same uses as in the USA?

Creative thinking *Metal crisis*

What if a family in the USA woke up to the following news?

> There is a resource crisis. The country has run out of iron, aluminium and lead.

Imagine that family a few years later. How would their lives have changed? What materials would they be using? Which gadgets and appliances would no longer be in use? Write a report for the local newspaper.

Research

To resolve the resource crisis, someone suggests using plastics instead of metals. Find out from which natural material plastics are made. Find out the properties of plastics. Explain why using plastics is not going to be a complete, long-term answer.

➡ # Describing rocks

Some children were playing at the seaside and noticed lots of different pebbles on the beach.

Key words

* Mohs' scale
* porous

8 Look carefully at the photographs. How many differences can you spot between the different pebbles? What other differences might there be between the different boulders and pebbles?

9 Calcite is a mineral, which fizzes when hydrochloric acid is added to it. The gas produced turns limewater milky.
   a) What gas is being produced?
   b) What type of compound is calcite?
   c) Can you remember the names of any other materials that are attacked by acid?

Hardness is a measure of how much a mineral resists scratching. The scale for hardness is known as **Mohs' scale** and values on the scale can be any number between 1 and 10.

Using this scale, a mineral with a higher number will scratch a mineral with a lower number. We often use simple objects to give us a rough guide (or estimate) of the hardness of a material: a copper coin, a penknife blade or a fingernail may be used.

10 Look carefully at this table showing a hardness scale for some well known minerals.

Mineral	Hardness
diamond	10
garnet	6–7
magnetite	5–6
calcite	3
talc	1

   a) Diamond is used for drilling through rocks and engraving/cutting metals. What makes it suitable for these uses?
   b) Magnetite is a mineral that can be used to make compasses. What special property does it have? Which metal might it contain?
   c) Which minerals do you think could be scratched using a penknife?
   d) Which mineral(s) does a penknife not scratch?
   e) Which minerals do you think could be scratched using your fingernail?

Enquiry **Studying rocks**

A group of pupils were studying the properties of a selection of rocks. Here is a list of the equipment they used:

magnifying lens, needle, top-pan balance, teat pipette, dilute hydrochloric acid

1 a) What do you think the magnifying glass was used for?
   b) A steel needle can be used to get some measure of how hard materials are. Describe what would happen if you scratched a soft pebble and a very hard rock with the needle.

2 Read this information carefully.

Rocks that soak up liquid are said to be **porous**. They have spaces between the grains where water and acid rain can pass through. Rainwater will soak through most soils and even some rocks. Many types of sandstone are porous and have spaces between the grains for the water to pass through.

A group of pupils wanted to find out which rocks were porous.
a) Which of the apparatus in the list on page 39 would they need to use?
b) What measurements would they need to make for their investigation?
c) How might they present their results?
Discuss these questions in your group, then feed your ideas back to the class.

Rock groups

Key words
* geologist
* igneous
* sedimentary
* metamorphic

A **geologist** is a scientist who studies rocks. As you have seen, rocks can be different in many ways, but geologists classify them into groups depending on how they were formed.

Rock type	Properties
igneous	formed in volcanoes and underground from cooling liquid rock (magma); usually quite hard and made of crystals
sedimentary	formed when sediments settle and harden; usually laid down in layers; sometimes contain fossils; often soft
metamorphic	produced from existing rocks as a result of high pressure and/or high temperature; usually hard; contain crystals in layers or bands

The next table gives descriptions of a number of different common rocks, and their classifications.

Rock	Description	Rock type
granite	grey, speckled with randomly arranged crystals	igneous
limestone	reacts with acid; consists of grains; often contains fossils; made from the mineral calcite	sedimentary
gneiss	contains pink–grey crystalline minerals in bands	metamorphic
basalt	black, fine crystals	igneous
slate	coloured (ranging from grey to green and purple); crystals too small to be seen; splits into sheets	metamorphic
chalk	white; fine grains; no crystals	sedimentary

Information processing ## Classifying rocks

1 Use the information in the two tables to either:
   a) write one or two paragraphs about rock types, or
   b) produce a single table containing the important pieces of information.

2 Read the information in the second table about limestone carefully. What type of chemical do you think calcite is? What evidence is there?

3 Below are brief descriptions of three rocks. Decide which rock type each belongs to, giving reasons for your choice.
   a) Gabbro is a dark-coloured, coarse-grained rock, very similar to basalt in its mineral make-up.
   b) Marble is much harder than limestone, its parent rock, and is formed at high temperature and pressure. The shells that formed the limestone break down and recrystallise.
   c) Sandstone is formed by the cementing together of sand-sized grains, forming a solid rock. Minerals grow as crystals in the spaces around the sand grains. As the crystals fill the gaps, the individual sand grains become changed into a solid rock.

Rock key

Different rock types have different properties. This helps us to classify them. Granite is much harder than chalk, for example.

A key such as the one below can help us to identify rocks.

Rock key

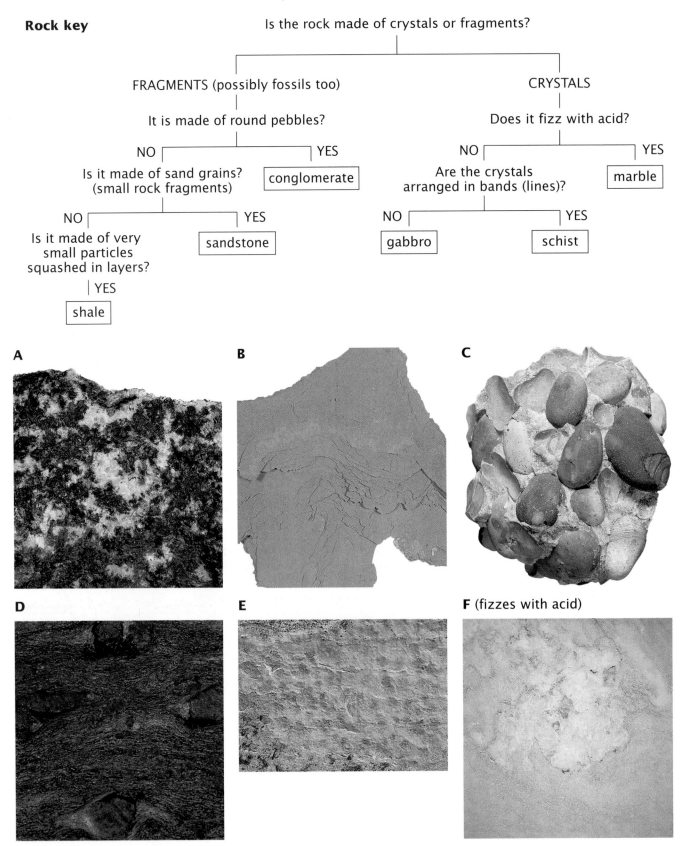

Is the rock made of crystals or fragments?

FRAGMENTS (possibly fossils too)

It is made of round pebbles?

NO — Is it made of sand grains? (small rock fragments)

YES — conglomerate

NO — Is it made of very small particles squashed in layers?

YES — sandstone

YES — shale

CRYSTALS

Does it fizz with acid?

NO — Are the crystals arranged in bands (lines)?

YES — marble

NO — gabbro

YES — schist

A

B

C

D

E

F (fizzes with acid)

11 Use the key to identify the rocks shown.

EXTENSION

Enquiry *Strength of rocks*

Philip had devised an experiment to measure the strength of different rocks. His notes have been ruined by an acid spill and only the apparatus list is left:

200 g mass, long cardboard tube, nylon thread, and these rocks: granite, limestone, chalk, sandstone, slate

1 Copy and complete the following variables table and work out a sensible method of comparing the strengths of the rocks.

Variable	Type	Value(s)
mass		200 g
height of mass (cm)		
	outcome	number of cracks

2 Predict the results you might expect.

Time to think

Use the key words from this chapter so far to write a summary of the work covered. Compare your summary with those of at least two other pupils, and make any changes to yours if necessary.

➡ *Breaking rocks*

Key words
* scree
* weathering
* permanent
* physical weathering
* chemical weathering

Rocks don't stay the same forever. They appear solid, hard and everlasting but even the toughest rocks are slowly broken down into smaller pieces. In mountain areas you might see a pile of rocks, big and small, at the bottom of a steep slope. These fragments are called **scree**. The same thing can happen to manufactured rocks such as concrete, bricks and other building materials. Old gravestones are often difficult to read because many of the letters have disappeared. For most rocks these changes can take thousands of years but some rocks can be affected by wind, rain and ice, and will crumble much sooner, depending on the type of rock and where it is located. These changes are caused by the way the rocks react to the weather. They are known as the forces of **weathering**.

Word play Have you heard the expression 'rock solid'? It is used to describe something that is hard or **permanent**. Can you think of any other words that could be used to describe anything that is rock solid?

Rocks can be broken down into smaller fragments by a number of different processes but these can all be divided into two main groups: **physical weathering** and **chemical weathering**.

Remember that chemical reactions are generally irreversible; that means you can't change them back. You end up with new chemical(s). Physical changes do not result in new chemicals being produced.

12 Write down the main differences between a physical change and a chemical change.

13 Make a list of as many physical changes and chemical changes that you can remember having learnt about.

Physical weathering

Frost damage

Key words
* expand
* contract
* exfoliation

Look at this bottle of milk that has been left out during a very cold day. What has happened to the milk?

When water freezes it **expands**. This means its volume increases because ice takes up more space than water. If water gets into cracks in rocks and then freezes, the force of the expanding ice will make the crack bigger and wider.

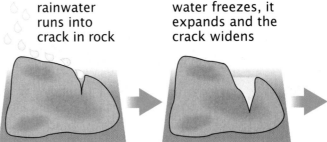

rainwater runs into crack in rock

water freezes, it expands and the crack widens

the widened crack collects more water, further freezing causes further enlargement of crack

This expansion can cause real trouble if your water pipes at home freeze. In winter many homes suffer from flooding caused by burst pipes. This is sometimes called the freeze–thaw effect. It usually happens because the metal pipes have not been properly insulated.

14 What type of material would be used to insulate pipes?

15 Describe what will happen to the pipes if the water in them freezes.

16 The family won't realise that there is a problem until the end of the cold weather. Why do you think this is?

Desert dust

Have you ever broken a test tube by trying to wash up before the test tube has cooled down? The cold water makes the hot glass contract very quickly, breaking the cooled part away from the rest.

In hot deserts the sun heats up rock surfaces during the day. At night the temperature drops dramatically. This causes the rocks to expand (get bigger) in the day and then **contract** (get smaller) at night. Rocks often crack because they contain different minerals that expand and contract at different rates.

Even in the desert, dew is produced at night. This fills the cracks made in the surface of rocks by the repeated heating and cooling. Outer layers will crumble away and expose new rock. This is called **exfoliation**.

17 What happens to the particles when materials are heated and cooled? Draw particle pictures to help your explanation.

EXTENSION 18 Imagine that you are a mineral in a layer of rock in a hot desert. Describe what happens when night falls and the layer above you cools quicker than your layer. The layer below you is cooling even more slowly.

DID YOU KNOW?

Plants can cause physical weathering. Look at this photograph showing the damage to a concrete drive caused by tree roots.

Chemical weathering

Some rocks come under chemical attack, and minerals in the rocks may react with air or water. Pure rainwater is usually acidic although it can be made even more acidic by the release of pollutant gases from the burning of fossil fuels.

Some rocks can be broken down slowly by rainwater alone, for example limestone reacts with the slightly acidic rainwater. The main mineral in limestone is calcium carbonate and this reacts with acids. Limestone has natural cracks, which are easily opened up by the acid in the rain. These cracks will widen and eventually caves are formed.

Limestone caves at Wookey Hole, Somerset.

19 Which gas in air would rocks react with?
20 Name the gas naturally occurring in air that makes rain acidic.
21 Name some of the gases released from power stations that would cause acid rain.
22 Can you name other rocks containing calcium carbonate that will react in a similar way to limestone?
23 Rocks broken down by chemical weathering are sometimes called 'rotten rocks'. Why do you think they have been given this name?

Resistance to weathering

One of the main things that determines whether a rock is **resistant** to weathering is the number of cracks or joints it contains. Granite is an igneous rock, made from the three minerals feldspar, mica and quartz, and their crystals are interlocked together to make a very hard rock indeed.

Key word
* resistant

The rock is resistant to physical weathering but it will break down slowly by chemical weathering. Not even granite is rock solid! Granite breaks down into clay, sand and various soluble chemicals.

The rate of weathering is controlled by a number of key factors, as shown in the table.

Factor	Description
climate	desert conditions and very cold conditions increase physical weathering; chemical weathering can be accelerated by warm, wet weather
living organisms	plants can hold the soil in place, protecting the rock below, but the roots can cause cracks to develop in the rocks
pollution	the lower the pH of the rainwater, the greater the risk of chemical weathering
soil covering	the deeper the layer of soil, the greater the protection from weathering
rock features	the softer the rock, the faster the weathering

24 a) How can chemical weathering be speeded up?
  b) Ella was upset to see so many shrubs being dug up in her local park. She said that they helped to anchor the soil in place. The park keeper argued that the roots damaged the paths. What do you think?
  c) Amy was shocked to find that the pH of the rainwater was 5.5. What effect will this have on the marble statue in the park?
  d) Give one reason why chalk might weather faster than limestone.

EXTENSION
  e) Why should rocks under deep layers of soil weather more slowly? Give as many reasons as you can.

→ What happens to weathered rock?

Key words
* erosion
* sediment
* destination
* gravity
* source
* delta
* deposited

So much for the phrase 'rock solid'! Not only do rocks not stay in one piece for ever but they do not even manage to stay in the same place. Rocks are broken down into smaller pieces by the conditions around them. This is weathering. If these broken pieces are moved away, it is called **erosion**. Erosion takes place when rocks are moved away by the action of:

• streams and rivers
• gravity
• ice
• sea waves and tides
• wind.

You probably remember the damage caused by the terrible floods in recent years. Once the water level has subsided the unfortunate homeowners are left with the task of cleaning up. Their homes are ruined by mud and silt. A river in flood can carry massive amounts of mud and silt such as sand.

25 Can you suggest where all this mud and silt has come from?

Erosion by streams and rivers

Rivers weather (wear away) the rocks over which they pass and carry the debris away. This is erosion. The Mississippi River in North America carries over 1 million tonnes of **sediment** every day to the Gulf of Mexico. You need energy to do work and the river needs energy to carry all this weathered rock stuff to its eventual **destination** – the sea. The amount of debris the river carries depends on how fast it is flowing. The movement of loose pebbles and sand can itself cause more weathering to the rocks they pass over.

Erosion by gravity

Gravity is responsible for the movement of weathered rock pieces down mountain slopes, in rivers, avalanches, landslides and mudflows. What energy change takes place when dislodged boulders roll down a hillside?

A small stream has more force than individual raindrops or melting snow. It begins to stir up larger particles and carry them away. The place where a river begins is called its

Rivers begin high in the mountains.

source. Rivers begin high in the mountains, where melting snow gathers in small streams. The mountain river flows swiftly, with many rapids and waterfalls. It wears away its bed and cuts a narrow, V-shaped valley with steep sides. The roots of plants and trees hold the soil in place when the rain comes, and their leaves break the force of the falling raindrops. Valleys with plants and trees do not erode as quickly as valleys of bare earth, but they gradually change over time.

Rivers cut V-shaped valleys.

Soil is held in place by the roots of plants and trees.

In the last part of a river's journey, it flows through a gently sloping flood plain. The river carries a heavy load of sediment. When the flow of water slows, the sediment settles to the bottom. Sandbars begin to appear. The final stage in the life of a river is its joining with the sea. By now the river is travelling smoothly and carrying a lot of sand and clay. Merging with the sea slows the water flow even more, and the sediment drops out. This often leads to the formation of a **delta**, with many sandbars and water channels.

A river delta.

When all the fragments of rock come to rest they settle and are **deposited** on the seabed. This is a constant process and soon more sediment arrives which buries and squashes the layers underneath. Mud ends up being compressed into shale, and crushed shells form limestone that contains many fossils. These are sedimentary rocks.

Layers of sedimentary rock.

26 Which sediment in the photo is the oldest? Why do you think this?

Creative thinking ## Film making

Imagine you have to make a 3-minute film to explain how rivers carry material from the mountains to the sea. Draw three or four main shots that you would film and write an accompanying script.

Enquiry ## Erosion

Key words
* predicted
* relationship

Matthew and Nisha wanted to investigate whether the size of the rock fragments transported by rivers depends on how fast the water is flowing. Their builder friend, Bob, provided them with a 3-metre length of plastic guttering. He said it would last longer than a cast iron section.

1 Why would the plastic guttering last longer than a cast iron section?

Matthew suggested that the faster the water flows, the bigger the rock pieces that will be transported. He thought they should use a mixture of sand, as well as various sized stones and pebbles.
Nisha **predicted** that the speed of flow depended upon the slope. She suggested they set up the tube at three different angles, 30°, 10° and horizontal.

2 Think about the journey a river takes from mountain stream to the sea.

   a) Which stage of the journey is represented by each angle of slope?

   b) Put each stage in order of energy content.

3 Matthew also predicted that very few large pieces would reach the sea. Do you agree with him? What will happen to the large rock debris as the river carries it along?

The diagram shows the movement of rock debris towards the sea.

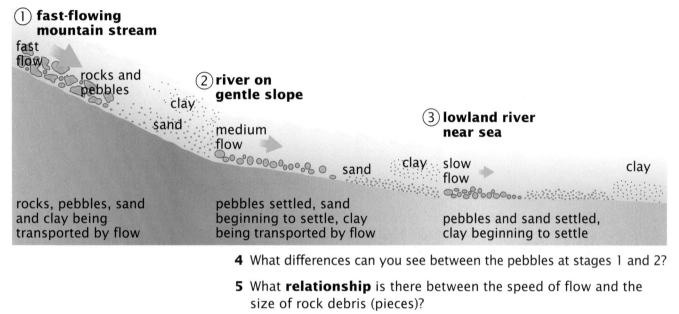

① **fast-flowing mountain stream**

fast flow

rocks and pebbles

② **river on gentle slope**

clay

sand

medium flow

③ **lowland river near sea**

sand

clay

slow flow

clay

rocks, pebbles, sand and clay being transported by flow

pebbles settled, sand beginning to settle, clay being transported by flow

pebbles and sand settled, clay beginning to settle

4 What differences can you see between the pebbles at stages 1 and 2?

5 What **relationship** is there between the speed of flow and the size of rock debris (pieces)?

6 Nisha thinks that once the sediment reaches the sea, all of the rock debris will settle down on the sea bed. Do you agree? What has happened to the river's kinetic energy?

Erosion by glaciers

Key word
* glaciers

Glaciers are huge 'ice rivers' flowing slowly towards the sea. The underneath part of the glacier may have frozen rocks in the ice, and as the glacier moves, it grinds the rocks beneath it. Glaciers move all sizes of rocks, and grind some of the stones to a very fine dust called 'glacial flour'.

A glacier.

Erosion by wave action

Waves move up and down the beach and the waves cause erosion. The rocks and stones on the beach are rounded from thousands of years of being rolled against each other by waves. Careless people leave bottles on the beach. The sharp broken pieces are gradually worn down and made smooth by erosion. Waves also erode cliffs along the seashore. They undercut the cliffs, and eventually the cliffs fall.

Wind erosion.

Wave erosion.

Erosion by the wind

Wind picks up dust and sand. Sandstorms can act like sand blasters if the wind is moving fast enough. Sometimes when people are driving in the desert they drive through a sandstorm which 'erodes' all the paint off their cars! In the desert the wind moves the sand into dunes, piling it up and covering the surfaces with ripples.

Time to think

1 Describe all the possible ways that this once new statue has been changed into what you see now.
2 Layla says that the temperature plays a big part in weathering. What does she mean? Give as many examples as you can.
3 Which type of rock will never contain fossils? Try to explain your answer.

4 A group of pupils wanted to demonstrate how a hard rock could be changed into sedimentary rock. This is what they did.

A A pile of different rocks was placed into a large plastic jar. A liquid was added and it was left for a few weeks.

B The liquid was then carefully poured away and the lid was placed on the jar. The jar was shaken for 10 minutes.

C The contents were sieved into a large bowl full of water. The bowl was left standing for a few days.

D Some heavy weights were put on top of the solid at the bottom of the bowl.

a) Which liquid did the pupils use?

b) Look at their method and match up each lettered stage with the following words:

      deposition   erosion   weathering   burial

Explain your choice.

5 Write clues for this word quiz.

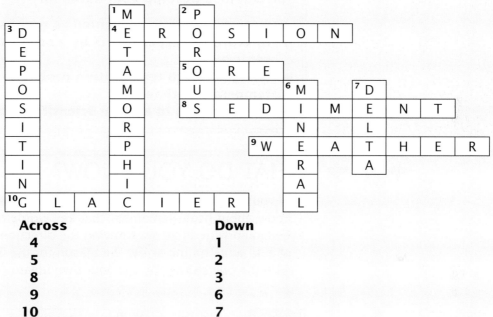

Across	Down
4	1
5	2
8	3
9	6
10	7

6 Rock Wars Annihilator

It is the televised final of the Rock Wars. In the arena are the Basalt Basher, the Slate Smasher, the Marble Mauler, the Chalk Champ, the Granite Grinder and the Limestone Crusher.

Once in the arena the rocks collide with one another as hard as they can. One rock is eliminated at the end of each round.

Write a report for the TV section of a daily newspaper. For each of the contestants, give a brief description under these headings:

- appearance
- hardness
- family background (rock type).

Describe what happens to the rocks as the contest progresses. Decide which rocks are eliminated at each stage. Draw the winner's podium with first, second and third-placed rocks in their positions.

3

Heating and cooling

In this chapter you will learn:

→ **the distinction between temperature and heat**
→ **why objects expand or contract with changes of temperature**
→ **how energy is transferred by the movement of particles in conduction, convection and evaporation**
→ **that energy is transferred directly by radiation**
→ **that although energy is always conserved, it may be 'spread out', making it less readily available**

You will also develop your skills in:

→ **interpreting data presented as graphs**
→ **interpreting experiments by a scientist from another century**
→ **using ICT with temperature probes to record temperature changes**
→ **using models to explain scientific ideas**

➜ ➜ ➜ WHAT DO YOU KNOW?

1 In your group, produce a concept map showing what you already know about heat. Remember that key words or concepts should be linked with an arrow showing the direction of the link, and you should write on the arrow the reason for the link. You could start with the one shown, or use your own ideas.

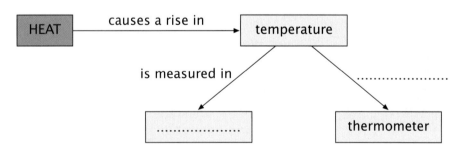

2 In your group do one of the following. Prepare your answers so that one person in the group can feed back what you have discussed to the rest of the class.

  a) Produce a drawing with a temperature line on it and mark in any special temperatures you know. The passage at the top of the next page may give you some ideas. You may find it helpful to produce a table of the various temperatures before you mark them on a temperature line.

Nowadays we measure temperature in degrees Celsius, °C. This is sometimes called the centigrade scale. Temperatures exist that are much colder than the freezing point of ice, 0 °C. The lowest possible temperature is −273 °C. At this temperature all particles have their minimum energy. This is called absolute zero. The coldest place on Earth is Antarctica where a temperature of −89 °C was recorded. Our freezers are designed to keep frozen food below about −18 °C. Room temperature is about 20 °C. The hottest place on Earth is Al Aziziyah in Libya where the temperature has been recorded as high as 58 °C. Although water boils at 100 °C, other liquids boil at different temperatures. For example alcohol boils at 79 °C, while liquid oxygen boils at −183 °C. Wax melts at around 57 °C, whereas tin melts at about 330 °C and gold will not melt until the temperature is over 1000 °C.

b) Produce a poster to show the differences between solids, liquids and gases.

c) Produce a transparency to explain what we mean by the water cycle. (You could use overlays to build up the picture.)

d) Prepare a presentation about how things or people can be affected by temperature. You may get some ideas from these photos.

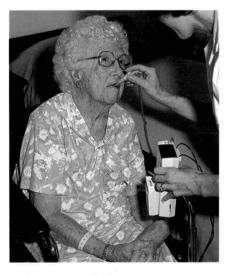

Measuring temperature

Key words
* thermometer
* temperature
* clinical
* Celsius

In 1724 Gabriel Fahrenheit, an instrument maker of Danzig (now Gdansk) and Amsterdam, first used mercury as the liquid in a **thermometer**. Mercury does not stick to the glass, and it remains a liquid over a wide range of **temperature**. Its silvery appearance makes it easy to read.

Today there are many types of thermometer. Some are mercury in glass like Fahrenheit's, others are coloured alcohol in glass. Some are digital, while some have dial scales. They have different ranges and uses. A meat thermometer would have a range of 0–120 °C. A **clinical** thermometer usually has a range of 34–42 °C.

C stands for **Celsius**, since we use the Celsius scale. On this scale the freezing point of water is 0 °C and the boiling point of water is 100 °C.

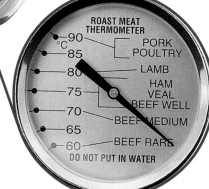

Meat thermometer.

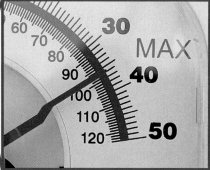

Maximum–minimum thermometer.

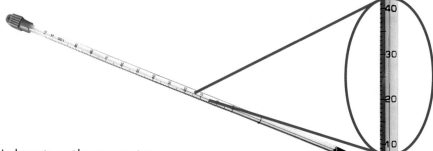

Laboratory thermometer.

1 Where would a meat thermometer be used?
2 What is a maximum–minimum thermometer used for?

The Fahrenheit scale is still used in some countries. On this scale, the freezing point of water is marked 32 °F and the boiling point of water is 212 °F. Another scale that was widely used in Germany and Russia was the Réaumur scale, invented by René Antoine Ferchault de Réaumur, a French physicist born at La Rochelle in 1683. On his scale the freezing and boiling points of water were 0° and 80°.

A clinical thermometer is used for measuring the temperature of your body. It continues to show the measured temperature until reset. A point on the scale has an arrow that indicates normal body temperature. As your body heats the mercury, the mercury expands and rises up the tube. A small kink in the tube prevents the mercury sinking back into the bulb when the thermometer is removed from the warmth of your body. To return the mercury after the thermometer has cooled down, it must be given a shake. Nowadays, we also use digital readout thermometers and temperature strips to measure body temperature.

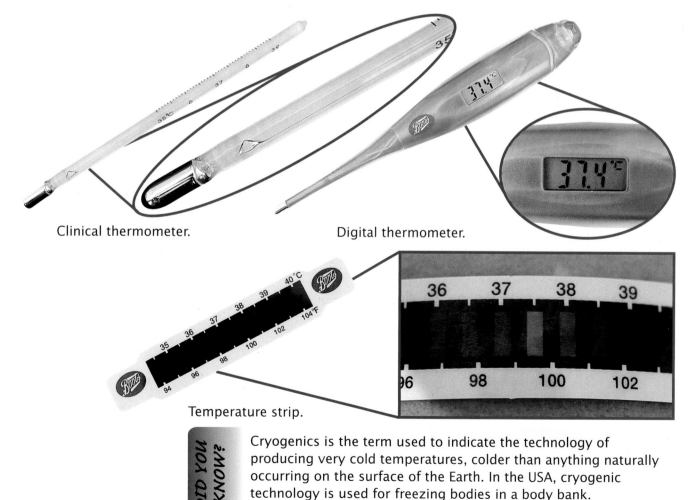

Clinical thermometer.

Digital thermometer.

Temperature strip.

Cryogenics is the term used to indicate the technology of producing very cold temperatures, colder than anything naturally occurring on the surface of the Earth. In the USA, cryogenic technology is used for freezing bodies in a body bank.

➡ *Heat and temperature*

In your group discuss the difference between temperature and heat. For example, if you hold a sparkler and one of the sparks lands on your hand it is unlikely to burn you, although it may be at a temperature of 1000°C. However, if you picked up an iron bar at 100°C you would certainly burn your hand.

3 If you plunged your hand into a bowl of boiling water at 100°C you would give yourself a bad burn, whereas a tiny droplet of water at 100°C on your hand is unlikely to be painful. Why is this?

EXTENSION   4 If you preheat an electric oven to 200°C and then place a pizza inside the hot oven, you are unlikely to burn yourself unless you touch the sides of the oven or a shelf. Discuss why this is.

Information processing   ## *Temperature graphs*

Look at the two drawings of water being heated. Both beakers are filled with water from the tap and heated for 10 minutes. After about 3 minutes the water in the small beaker is boiling; after 8 minutes the water in the larger beaker is also boiling.

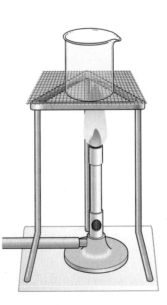 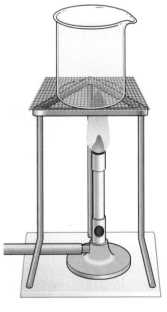

Look at the graphs opposite.

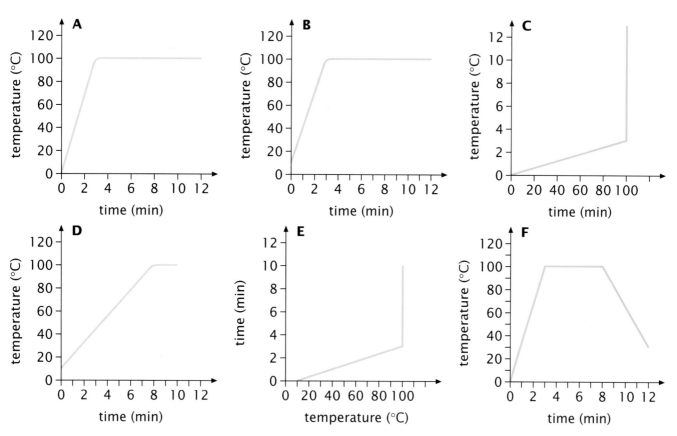

1 Which graph could show the change in temperature for the small beaker?

2 Which graph could show the change in temperature for the larger beaker?

3 Can you explain in words what is happening in the graphs you have chosen?

This third drawing shows a much larger beaker. It is also filled with water and heated with the same type of Bunsen burner for 10 minutes, but the water does not reach boiling point.

4 Sketch a temperature–time graph to show this.

5 What can you say about the amount of energy transferred to the beaker and water after 10 minutes?

6 Which of the three beakers of water are at the highest temperature at the end of heating?

7 What is that highest temperature?

8 If a second Bunsen burner was added below the largest beaker, what effect do you think this would have? Why?

EXTENSION 9 Can you suggest how a graph similar to graph F could be produced?

The temperature of the boiling point of water varies with air pressure. At sea level water boils at the familiar 100 °C, but if you boiled a kettle of water at the top of Mont Blanc, it would boil at 84 °C.

EXTENSION

5 If you take equal volumes of hot water and cold water and mix them together, what can you say about the temperature of the mixture?

6 If you take 1 litre of water at 20 °C and mix it with 1 litre of water at 60 °C, what will be the temperature of the mixture?

7 If you mix 1 litre of water at 20 °C with 3 litres at 60 °C, what do you think will be the temperature of the resultant mixture?

➡ *Thermal energy transfer*

Key words
* thermal energy
* transferred
* conduction
* convection
* radiation
* conductor
* insulator

Heat is often referred to as '**thermal energy**' by scientists. There are a number of ways in which thermal energy is **transferred** from place to place. These include **conduction**, **convection** and **radiation**. Convection and radiation will be considered later in the chapter.

Conduction

When a material is heated, the particles that make up the material begin to vibrate more and each vibrating particle passes on some of its energy to its neighbour. In this way the energy is transferred along the material from the hot region to the cool region. Some solid materials, for example metals, are good at this. Others, for example wood, plastic and glass, are poor at this.

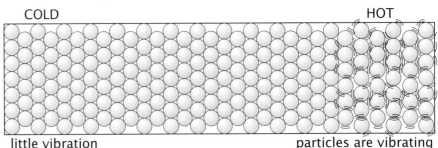

COLD   HOT

little vibration   particles are vibrating
                                                     about a fixed position

The temperature of each end of a metal rod is a measure of the energy of vibration of the particles.

The words **conductor** and **insulator** are used in a similar way here to the way they are used in electricity. A good conductor of thermal energy is a material that will allow the energy to be transferred through it easily. A poor conductor will not allow the thermal energy to pass through easily. A very poor conductor is an insulator.

8 Look at the picture below, which shows an experiment you may have done or watched. Can you explain what happens?

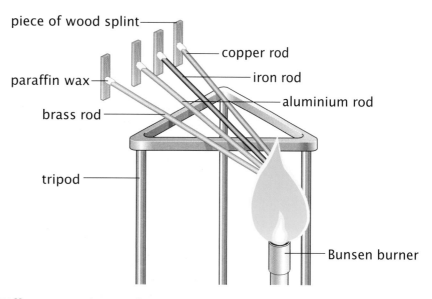

piece of wood splint
copper rod
paraffin wax
iron rod
aluminium rod
brass rod
tripod
Bunsen burner

Different metals transfer energy at different rates.

Liquids are generally poor conductors. The picture below is of a demonstration to show this.

9 Why does the water at the top boil while ice remains at the bottom?
10 Why is the metal gauze necessary?

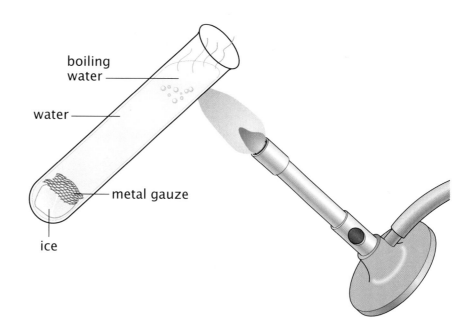

boiling water
water
metal gauze
ice

Air is a very poor conductor. That is why in cold weather birds fluff up their feathers to trap air between them and improve their insulation. Trapped air, which cannot be blown away by draughts, makes a very good insulator. We use air in this way when we wear a woolly jumper to keep warm. As well as the wool itself being a good insulator, air is trapped between the fibres. A duvet acts in the same way.

11 Sometimes we want part of an object to be a conductor and part of it to be an insulator. Give an example of this in the kitchen.

12 Explain why, on a cold day, a metal railing feels colder than a wooden fence.

13 Find out what the 'TOG' rating of a duvet is.

The principle behind the Davy lamp

The passage below is taken from a school textbook published in 1909. It was quite unusual for textbooks at that time to contain so much detail of practical activities. Look at the three activities described.

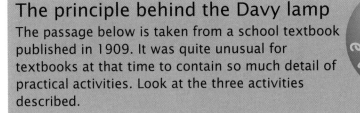

141. The principle of the Davy lamp. When we apply the flame of a lighted match to gas issuing from a jet the temperature of the gas is raised above its temperature of ignition and combustion commences and continues so long as a supply of oxygen is obtainable and the temperature remains above the ignition temperature of the gas.

If, however, a piece of good conducting material be placed in a flame it may conduct away the heat so rapidly that

212   CONDUCTION OF HEAT.

the temperature falls below the temperature of ignition and combustion ceases. This effect is illustrated by the following experiments.

Exp. 94. Take a piece of thick copper wire and coil it into a spiral of about half a centimetre internal diameter. Light a candle, and when the flame is burning strongly lower the coil of copper wire on to the wick of the candle. The flame at once goes out.

Exp. 95. Take a piece of clean copper gauze, not too fine in mesh, and lower it on to the flame of a Bunsen burner or spirit lamp. It will be found that the flame does not get through the gauze. As the gauze is lowered the flame is kept below it and may be extinguished completely by lowering the gauze on to the burner or wick. The gauze conducts the heat away from the portion of the flame in contact with it sufficiently rapidly to lower the temperature below that at which combustion takes place, and the region of combustion is therefore unable to extend above the gauze.

If the gauze is held over the flame until it is heated to the temperature of ignition it ceases to be effective for the purpose of this experiment.

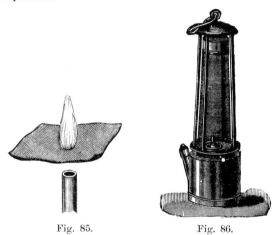

Fig. 85.   Fig. 86.

Exp. 96. Hold a sheet of gauze about an inch above a Bunsen burner and light the flame *above* the gauze. It will now be found that the flame appears only above the gauze and is prevented by the conductivity of the gauze from extending below it (see Fig. 85).

CONDUCTION OF HEAT.   213

The principle illustrated by these experiments has been utilised in the construction of the Davy lamp (Fig. 86). The flame of the lamp is enclosed in a cylinder of wire gauze so that when the lamp is placed in an explosive atmosphere the gases which penetrate to the flame are ignited and burn *inside* the gauze with a peculiar flickering, but the flame produced is unable to extend outwards through the gauze unless the gauze becomes hot. The explosion which would be produced by a naked light is thus averted. As soon as the miner notices the presence of the ghostly fire-damp flame he leaves the working at once and gives notice to his foreman, whereupon the mine is thoroughly ventilated.

It has been found, however, that the Davy lamp is not, in all cases, an efficient protection against explosions in mines.

1 Can you explain in your own words what the experiments are about?

If you were to do the first experiment, you would need to be sure that you didn't burn your fingers. One way would be to push one end of the copper spiral into a cork.

2 Draw an example of what the first experiment would look like.

3 There is no diagram provided for the second experiment, either. Can you supply one?

4 What do the following words from the passage mean?
- issuing
- combustion
- mesh
- ignition
- utilised
- penetrate
- averted
- firedamp
- ventilated

→ *Expansion*

When a solid object is heated it gets bigger. This is called **expansion**. There are many experiments that demonstrate expansion. The diagrams below show a few of these experiments.

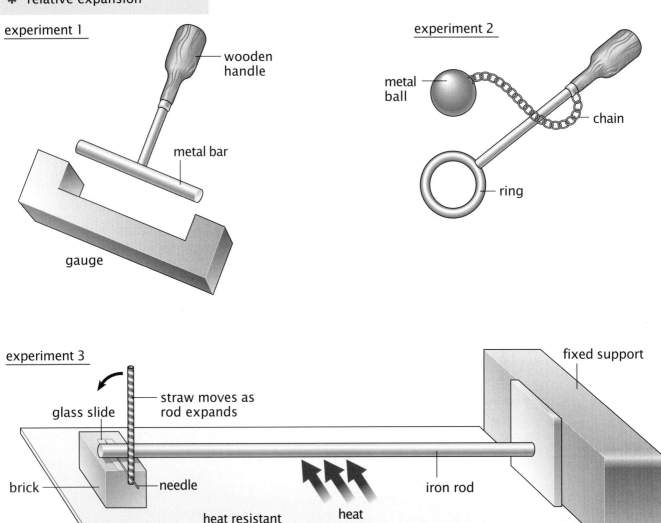

experiment 1

wooden handle

metal bar

gauge

experiment 2

metal ball

chain

ring

experiment 3

glass slide

straw moves as rod expands

brick

needle

heat resistant mat

heat

iron rod

fixed support

In the first experiment, the metal bar will just fit inside the gauge when it is cold. When it is heated it expands and is then too big to fit. Similarly, the ball in the second experiment fits through the ring when cold but when heated it will not pass through. The third experiment shows us that while the expansion is very small, the effect can be 'magnified' using the apparatus shown. Expansion on heating can be a problem where much greater lengths are involved, for example in bridges.

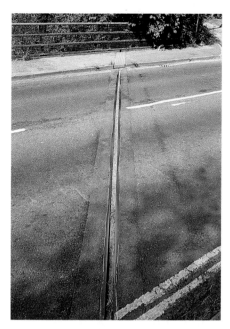

Expansion joints in a road bridge.

There are strong forces involved when a material expands or contracts. One piece of equipment that demonstrates this effectively is shown in the diagram below. It is sometimes called the 'breaking bar' apparatus. When the steel rod is heated, it expands. The heated steel rod is prevented from contracting by placing the iron 'breaking bar' through the second hole, on the other side of the pillar. As the rod cools down, eventually the force of **contraction** on the iron bar becomes so great that the bar snaps.

 SAFETY

If this experiment is observed, eye protection should be worn.

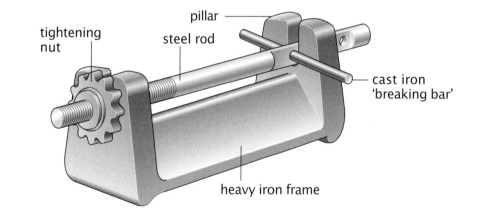

pillar

tightening nut

steel rod

cast iron 'breaking bar'

heavy iron frame

Research

There are many other situations where the effects of expansion have to be taken into account. Find out about and explain some further examples. A few ideas include: pipelines in the chemical industry; overhead power lines; steel tyres on trains; riveting.

Relative expansion

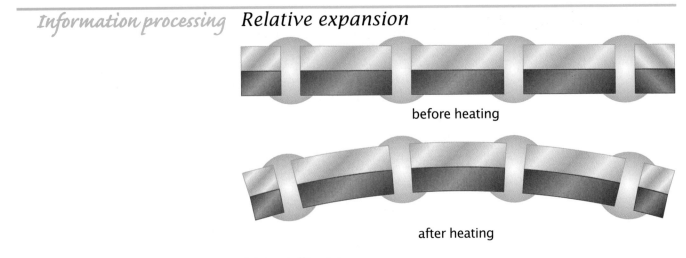

before heating

after heating

A bimetallic strip.

A **bimetallic** strip is used in a room thermostat. It consists of two strips of different metals tightly fixed together. It curves when it is heated because one metal expands more than the other. The table below shows the **relative expansion** of different materials when the same length is heated through the same number of degrees.

Material	Relative expansion
aluminium	26
brass	19
concrete	11
copper	17
glass	9
invar	1
iron	12
lead	28
platinum	9
Pyrex	3
steel	11
zinc	28

1 a) Which two materials could you use for a bimetallic strip? What are the requirements for the two materials?

b) How can the bimetallic strip be used as a thermostat?

2 Ordinary glass jars may crack if boiling water is poured into them. Why would a Pyrex dish be less likely to crack?

3 Steel rods are used to reinforce concrete without any problems caused by changing temperatures. Why is this?

Models of expansion

The expansion of a solid can be explained by using our 'particles in a box' model. In the solid the particles are packed closely together. They are held in position by strong forces. The particles do not move around. They only vibrate about their fixed positions. As the solid is heated the particles vibrate more about their fixed spot and so each one needs a bit more room to move. The solid expands.

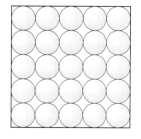 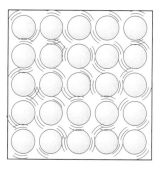

The drawing below shows a group of pupils acting as a solid.

14 Explain what this model is representing. What are the pupils supposed to be? How might they show that they have more energy in **B**?

A **B**

EXTENSION **15** Can you use the particle model to explain the breaking bar experiment described above?

Expansion of liquids

Liquids also expand when heated. A simple piece of equipment to demonstrate this is shown in the diagram. The flask is heated by placing it in a large beaker of hot water. A group of pupils closely watching this demonstration made the discovery that the liquid level in the tube fell slightly before it rose.

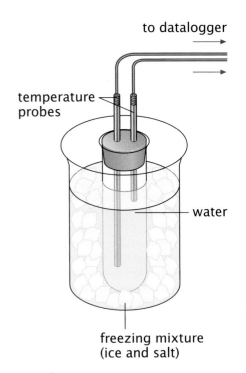

long glass tube

glass flask full of coloured water

hot water

16 Below are some of the statements that the pupils made. Can you use the statements to write a full explanation of what is happening?

Glass expands when heated.
The liquid expands much more than glass.
The water in the beaker is hot.
The liquid in the flask is cold.
Glass is not a very good conductor of heat.

17 Expansion can be used to remove a metal top from a glass bottle. To do this you hold the top under the hot water tap. How does this method work?

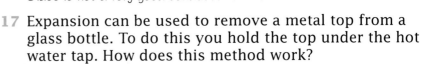

Information processing *Water*

Most liquids expand steadily when heated and contract steadily when cooled. An exception to this is water. The apparatus shown is recording the temperature of water in a boiling tube. Placing it in a mixture of ice and salt cools it. (When you mix ice with salt the temperature of the mixture falls below 0 °C.) The results are shown in the table opposite.

1 Use these results to plot a graph. You can either use a spreadsheet or other graphing program, or plot it by hand on graph paper. There are two sets of results, which should be plotted on the same axes.

to datalogger

temperature probes

water

freezing mixture (ice and salt)

Time (minutes)	Upper temperature (°C)	Lower temperature (°C)	Time (minutes)	Upper temperature (°C)	Lower temperature (°C)
0	15.0	15.0	16	12.0	4.0
1	15.0	14.0	17	11.0	4.0
2	15.0	13.0	18	10.0	4.0
3	15.0	12.0	19	9.0	4.0
4	15.0	11.0	20	8.0	4.0
5	15.0	10.0	21	7.0	4.0
6	15.0	9.0	22	6.0	4.0
7	15.0	8.0	23	5.0	4.0
8	15.0	7.0	24	4.0	4.0
9	14.9	6.0	25	3.0	4.0
10	14.7	5.5	26	2.0	4.0
11	14.5	5.0	27	1.5	4.0
12	14.3	4.5	28	1.0	4.0
13	14.0	4.3	29	0.6	4.0
14	13.6	4.2	30	0.4	4.0
15	13.0	4.1			

2 Did you need to plot all the points? Could you have plotted every fifth point? Try it.

In your group, use your graph to answer the following questions:

3 Describe in words the shape of the two graphs. Make sure you explain the difference between the two graphs and mention any special temperatures.

4 Which temperature probe will first record 0 °C?

5 Where will ice first form in the beaker?

6 Where does ice form in winter when a lake or canal freezes?

7 From what you have already learned about density, you will know that more dense liquids sink to the bottom. Can you say at what temperature water is most dense?

EXTENSION **8** This unusual expansion of water has an important consequence for ponds and the animals in them such as fish. What might happen in winter if water didn't have this unusual behaviour?

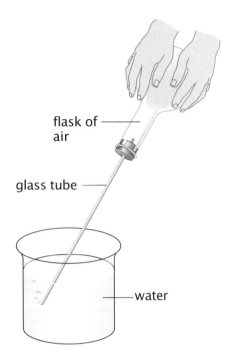

flask of air

glass tube

water

Expansion of gases

Like solids and liquids, gases also expand when heated. In fact they expand much more than liquids and solids. The diagram shows a simple experiment to demonstrate this. As the person's hands warm the air trapped in the flask, the air expands and air bubbles begin to come out of the end of the tube. We can explain this in terms of the motion of the air particles. As described in Book 1, the particles of a gas are moving freely, colliding with the walls of the container and with each other. When the gas is heated, the particles move faster. They have gained energy. They collide with the walls more often and at a greater speed. This means they push harder on the walls of the container. As a result, the gas will expand if it is able to do so. In this case some of the air escapes.

➡ *Convection*

Look at the photos showing convection currents in a liquid. A beaker of cold water has been placed on the tripod. Then a crystal of 'dye' (potassium permanganate) has been carefully dropped down the side of the beaker. As the edge of the beaker underneath the crystal is gently heated you can see the convection currents that are set up. This is explained as follows. The liquid that is heated becomes warmer and less dense. It rises, and colder liquid comes in from sides to take its place. This colder liquid in turn becomes warmed and then rises. In this way there is a continuous circulation of liquid. The circulation of the water spreads the energy throughout.

Convection also occurs readily in gases. The diagram shows a piece of apparatus to demonstrate this.

18 Can you explain what is happening? Your explanation should say why the smoke from the smouldering cardboard is drawn down the one side. You should also refer to how the density of air changes when it is warmed and what happens to warm air.

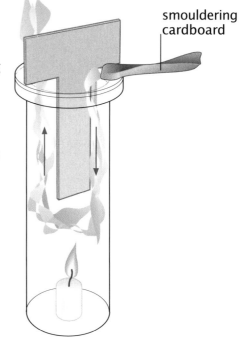

smouldering cardboard

19 The photos show some Christmas decorations. They depend on convection currents to work. Can you explain what happens?

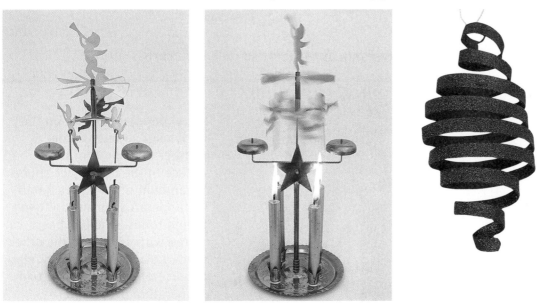

Research   Winds are examples of convection currents on a large scale.

- Find out about the trade winds, where they occur and how they are produced.
- Land and sea breezes are also caused by convection of the air. Find out how they happen and draw diagrams to show sea breezes and land breezes.

→ *Radiation*

Key words
* vacuum
* infrared

If an electric kettle has just boiled you can tell it is hot without touching it. You can feel the warmth on the back of your hand or on your cheek. We know that air is not a good conductor and that convection currents rise, so the energy must be transferred to us by another method. This is called radiation and is how energy from the Sun reaches us. It does not need any material to travel through. Radiation travels through space: it can pass through a **vacuum**. Although some radiation is visible (we see this as light), much of it is invisible but we can still detect it. We can feel **infrared** radiation as warmth. All hot objects give out infrared radiation.

We feel warmth as the infrared radiation reaches us.

Information processing *How much radiation?*

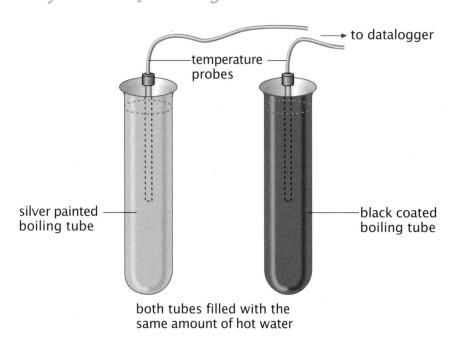

temperature probes

→ to datalogger

silver painted boiling tube

black coated boiling tube

both tubes filled with the same amount of hot water

The experiment shown on the left is used to investigate whether the colour of the surface of the hot object affects the amount of energy radiated. The apparatus consists of two boiling tubes. One has been coated with silver and the other painted black. A kettle provides a source of hot water. The two temperature probes are connected to a datalogger and computer, so that the apparatus can be left to plot the readings for about half an hour. The graph that was obtained is shown opposite.

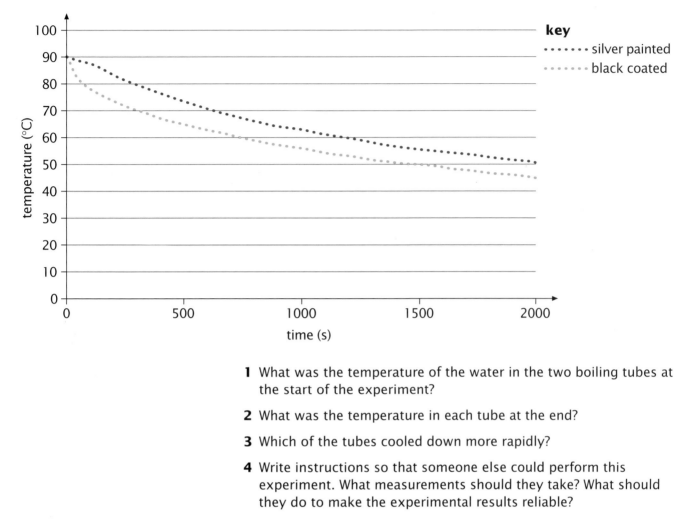

1 What was the temperature of the water in the two boiling tubes at the start of the experiment?

2 What was the temperature in each tube at the end?

3 Which of the tubes cooled down more rapidly?

4 Write instructions so that someone else could perform this experiment. What measurements should they take? What should they do to make the experimental results reliable?

5 What does the experiment suggest about the type of surface that is the best radiator of thermal energy?

This diagram shows an experiment to find out about the absorption of radiation. One of the metal plates is painted black and the other is shiny. Corks are stuck on the back of each plate with candle wax. They are both the same distance from the energy source. After a short time the cork on the back of the black surface falls off while the other cork is still stuck to the shiny surface. This shows that the black surface absorbs the radiation more quickly than the shiny surface.

So a dull black surface is not only a good radiator, it is also a good absorber of radiation.

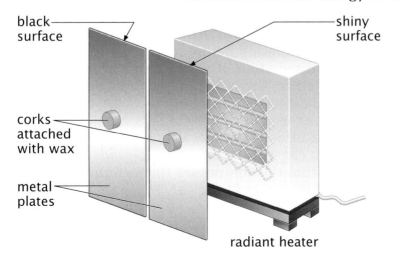

radiant heater

Time to think

Either:

- In pairs, list the key words used so far in this chapter. Arrange them in alphabetical order and write a definition for each to be used in a science dictionary. Compare your definitions with those of another pair. Decide which are the best definitions and why.

Or:

- Choose one of the following topics: conduction, convection, radiation, thermal expansion. Produce a Key Facts card for the topic. An example for temperature is shown here. Compare your card with that of another group. What are the differences and what things do you both have?

KEY FACTS

Temperature

Knowing the temperature of something tells us how hot or cold it is on a temperature scale. The most common temperature scale is the Celsius scale. On this scale the melting point of pure ice is 0 °C and the boiling point of pure water is 100 °C. We use a thermometer to measure how hot or cold an object is.

Here are some temperatures on the Celsius scale.

COLD											HOT
−273°C	−196°C	0°C	37°C		58°C	100°C	900°C	1540°C		6000°C	

absolute zero — nitrogen gas turns to liquid — freezing point of water — normal body temperature — highest air temperature recorded — boiling point of water — Bunsen flame — iron melts — surface temperature of the Sun

Links: expansion, energy.

A mercury in glass thermometer:

narrow capillary tube

temperature

mercury

bulb

100 °C

scale

vacuum

glass tube

0 °C

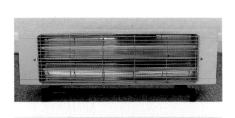
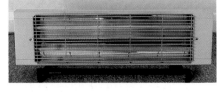

The greenhouse effect

Consider an electric fire. When you first switch it on, you can feel the radiation before it starts to glow red. This is the infrared radiation. If you place a sheet of glass between you and the fire, the radiation reaching you is reduced. The visible radiation is still passing through, but the infrared cannot pass through the glass. This is called the greenhouse effect. It can be dangerous if babies or animals are left in a car with the windows closed. The visible radiation from the Sun passes through the car windows and warms up the inside of the car. The warmed objects inside the car give out infrared radiation, which cannot escape, so the temperature inside the car rises steadily.

Word play

EXTENSION
Read this newspaper article and answer the questions following it.

Saturday, June 30, 2001

Forgotten baby dies in sweltering car

A 6-month-old boy left by his parents in a car for more than five hours Friday died of extreme heat exposure, the second time in six weeks Las Vegas' sweltering desert climate has claimed the life of an infant abandoned in a vehicle. Police said the parents forgot to drop the boy off at a day-care center before they went to work near Interstate 215 and Warm Springs Road about 8 a.m., on what would later be recorded as the hottest day of the year. By afternoon – when the parents discovered their son still strapped into a child-safety seat in their employer's parking lot – efforts at resuscitation were futile, Clark County Fire Department spokesman Steve La-Sky said. "This is about as bad a call as you can get. It was an extremely disturbing scene," La-Sky said. "There was nothing the parents could do by the time they remembered."

Detectives from Las Vegas police's Abuse and Neglect Detail were still questioning the parents, whose names were not released, and taking statements from co-workers Friday afternoon, but police said the baby's death appeared to be an accident. "We are humans, and humans make mistakes," said Lt. Tom Monahan. A recent change in the parents' schedules may have been a deadly factor for the forgotten baby. The parents told police they usually drop the infant off at a day-care center and then take their 4-year-old child to another day-care center. They told police they took the 4-year-old first on Friday, and then drove to work. Police and paramedics were called about 1:20 p.m. to URS Corp., an engineering firm at 7115 Amigo St., where both parents work, Sgt. Mike Thompson said. The mother had called her baby's day-care center to check on him, then realized she couldn't remember dropping him off there. She ran outside and found her child unresponsive inside the car. Thompson said URS personnel tried to revive the infant with cardiopulmonary resuscitation before emergency crews arrived. "The child had been dead for a while, it appears," La-Sky said. He described the scene inside URS as frantic, and said "a lot of tears were being shed." Thompson said the child's seat was one designed to face the rear of the vehicle, which may have prevented passers-by from noticing the dying baby. About an hour after the child was pronounced dead and placed inside an ambulance, several people stood outside the business, embracing and comforting one another. The company let employees go home early, La-Sky said. After police investigators finish their probe, the case will be forwarded to the Clark County District Attorney's office for prosecutors to determine if criminal charges are warranted, Thompson said. An autopsy is scheduled for today.

County prosecutors decided earlier this month not to prosecute Las Vegan Faun Nelson in the death of her 9-month-old son Dallas, who suffered fatal heat exposure May 22 after his mother left him in a sport utility vehicle for about two hours. In 1996, the mother of a 3-month-old Las Vegas girl was not prosecuted after the woman forgot that the baby was in the rear of her car for more than a day.

La-Sky said the temperature inside a white car with dark interior, like the one involved in Friday's incident, can be twice as hot as the temperature is outside. Less than an hour after the baby's discovery, the National Weather Service recorded a high temperature of 108 degrees F (42 °C) in Las Vegas. "Obviously, that's incompatible with a child's life, much less an adult's," La-Sky said.

Pediatric studies show heat stroke can occur in children exposed to 105 degrees F (40 °C) temperatures for prolonged periods, and that temperatures as low as 110 degrees F (43 °C) can be fatal.

By J.M. KALIL, REVIEW-JOURNAL

1 Make a list of all the words you are not sure about. Compare your list with a friend's. Explain to your friend any of the words that he or she has written down that you have not included in your list. Now produce a combined list of the words that neither of you are sure about.

2 Words can be formed from other words. For example, consider the term 'cardiopulmonary resuscitation' from the passage. Cardio means to do with the heart; pulmonary means affecting the lungs; resuscitate means to bring back to life or revive. What do you think a paramedic does if they perform cardiopulmonary resuscitation?

3 An English newspaper would use different words or spellings from some of the ones in this passage from an American newspaper. For example, a post-mortem is called an 'autopsy' in this article. Can you see any other differences?

4 What temperature could the interior of the car have reached, according to the County Fire Department spokesman?

EXTENSION

➡ # *Models of heat transfer*

Key word
✳ analogies

We have used models (or **analogies**) before to explain scientific ideas. Here is a model to explain the differences between conduction, convection and radiation.

20 Can you explain the cartoons? What do the pupils represent? What represents the thermal energy to be transferred?

21 Which cartoon represents conduction and which convection?

22 One cartoon shows a process similar to radiation. The message (energy) is transferred through space without the person (particle) moving. Which one is this?

Think about the model. How good is it in helping to explain the ideas of conduction, convection and radiation?

➡ *Evaporation*

If water is left in a saucer for some time it will eventually disappear. We say that it has **evaporated**. All liquids will evaporate. Some evaporate more easily than others.

Evaporation produces cooling, as you will have experienced. When you get out of a swimming pool or the sea you feel cold, but you would not feel cold if you were dry. Before you have an injection, the area to be injected is often wiped with a cotton wool swab soaked in alcohol. As this evaporates it makes the area feel cold.

23 Look at the photos, which show someone cooling down their tea before they drink it. Can you explain the scientific principles behind this?

We can explain cooling by evaporation in terms of our particle model. In the liquid all the particles are moving around, colliding with each other and with the walls of the container. On **average** they will all have the same speed. After colliding, some may be moving faster than the average and others slower. If one of the faster particles happens to be moving up towards the liquid surface it may escape from the liquid altogether. Because the liquid has lost one of the faster-than-average particles, then those left behind are, on average, moving more slowly. As we have seen, the speed at which they are moving is a measure of their temperature. So as faster particles leave the surface, the temperature of those left behind is reduced.

We can also explain other things that affect the rate of evaporation. The larger the surface area, the more likely it is that evaporation will take place. If there is a draught of air, some of the particles of the liquid will be carried away with the air and will not have a chance to drop back again.

24 Draw a series of pictures to help make this long explanation clearer.

The vacuum flask

The vacuum flask was originally invented to store liquid air, which boils at about −180 °C. The drawing shows a modern vacuum flask, used to keep drinks hot or cold on picnics.

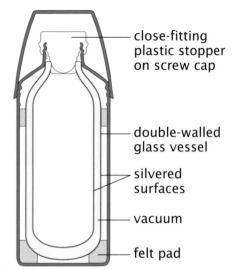

close-fitting plastic stopper on screw cap

double-walled glass vessel

silvered surfaces

vacuum

felt pad

25 Copy and complete the table describing the construction of this vacuum flask.

Construction	Reason
two containers inside one another, separated by a vacuum	a vacuum prevents thermal energy loss by...
the surfaces of both containers are shiny	
plastic insulating screw top	

Energy conservation

We are increasingly concerned about energy **conservation**. We need to reduce energy waste. Look at the diagram below. This is from a French brochure. It describes where the energy losses occur in a typical house. These can be reduced by various types of insulation.

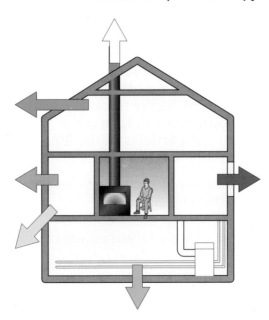

Les déperditions✻ de chaleur

➡ portes et fenêtres ≃ 13%

➡ murs ≃ 16%

➡ toits ≃ 30%

➡ sols ≃ 16%

➡ renouvellement d'air ≃ 20%

➡ ponts thermiques ≃ 5%

✻ Maison non isolée

26 Can you produce your own diagram labelled in English to show these energy losses?

27 Represent the energy losses in a pie chart.

Enquiry ## An investigation

Plan an investigation from one of those suggested below.

1 Decide how you will carry it out safely and what equipment you will use. What readings will you take?

2 What range of measurements do you expect?

3 What do you need to keep constant to make it a fair test?

4 Can you predict any pattern of results before you start?

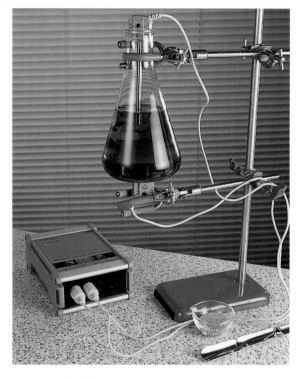

5 How will you present your results?

6 Ask your teacher to check your plan.

Choose one of these:

- Does evaporation produce cooling?
- Which is the best supermarket packaging for transporting ice cream?
- Design a container to keep an ice cube for as long as possible.

EXTENSION
- Design a container to keep a cooked chicken leg hot for as long as possible.

Enquiry ## Why do penguins huddle?

In the Antarctic winter, penguins often huddle together in a large group. Our hypothesis for this is that they do it to keep warm.

An experiment was performed using temperature sensors and 'model penguins' to find out whether huddling together does help them to keep warm.

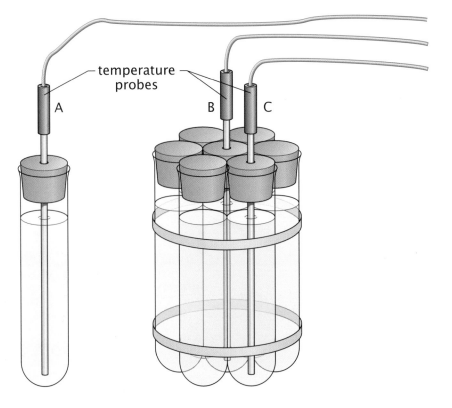

The apparatus was set up as shown in the diagram. The test tubes were filled with hot water from a kettle and the temperatures were recorded for 60 minutes.

1 Explain what the equipment is meant to represent.

2 Predict which penguin will cool down fastest. Explain your prediction using your knowledge of how heat is transferred.

Here is some data obtained from this experiment. Do the results obtained agree with your prediction?

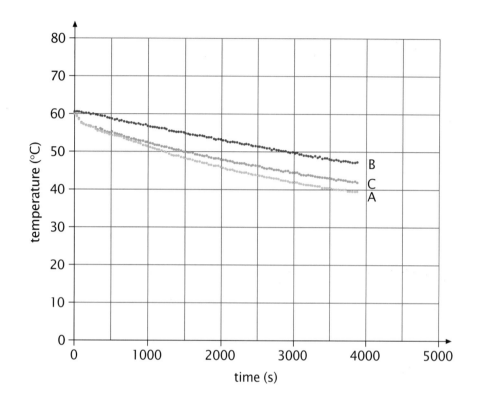

Results analysis

3 Which of the 'penguins' cooled down fastest?

4 Which 'penguin' is best insulated?

Evaluation

5 What would you need to do to ensure that this was a fair test?

6 Are there any changes you might make to improve your results?

7 Can you now answer the question 'Why do penguins huddle?'? Write a few sentences as an explanation.

8 Was this a good model to use to find out why penguins huddle? Explain why you think this.

EXTENSION **9** What effect would the size of the penguin have on the results? What significance does this have for young penguins?

➡ *Change of state*

You already know about the three states of matter: solid, liquid and gas. You will be familiar with experiments on warming solids, liquids and gases, for example warming crushed ice gently in a beaker and noting the temperature. A typical graph obtained is shown below.

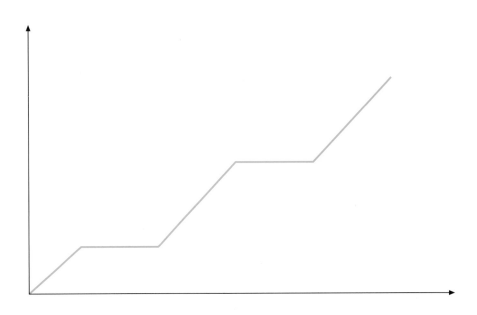

28 The graph has not been labelled. Copy the graph, label the axes and mark in the important features. You should show the three states, solid, liquid and gas; the temperatures at which the solid becomes a liquid and the liquid changes to a gas.

29 Copy and complete the diagram below. Each corner represents one of the states of matter. Write along each side of the triangle the names of the processes involved in changing between the states.

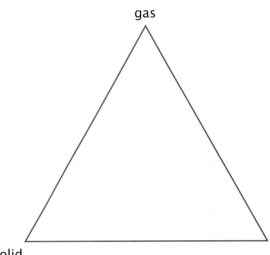

There are a number of simulations available which show animations of solids, liquids and gases changing state. They show not just how they visibly change but also how the particles behave. Some show a temperature–time graph on the screen. If you have an opportunity, you should try to use one of these simulations.

Time to think

Produce a leaflet giving information on one of the following:

- energy conservation in the home
- clothes to keep an elderly person warm
- land and sea breezes
- hot air ballooning
- the greenhouse effect.

Ask someone else to read your leaflet to check that you have used all the key words correctly.

4 Atoms and elements

In this chapter you will learn:

➡ how everything on Earth is made from just 92 simple substances (elements)
➡ that each element is made up of just one type of particle called an atom
➡ how the idea of elements has developed over the past 2500 years
➡ to use the particle model to describe what happens when elements combine to form compounds

You will also develop your skills in:

➡ researching information on different elements
➡ using models to picture how elements react together to form compounds
➡ predicting the names of compounds formed when elements react together
➡ investigating whether a substance is an element or not

➡ ➡ ➡ WHAT DO YOU KNOW?

Key words
* materials
* elements
* chlorine
* substance
* mixture
* pure

There are millions and millions of different **materials** in the world around us. They are made up from just 92 **elements** which combine together in different ways. One of these elements is called **chlorine**. It is added to drinking water and swimming pools to kill bacteria. It is also found in many different materials. Think about where the chlorine is in each of the materials shown on the opposite page.

Chlorine gas.

Synthetic materials

Chlorhexidine (antiseptic).

Polyvinylchloride.

Dichloromethane.

Sodium hypochlorite.

Benzene hexachloride.

Natural materials

Sodium chloride (common salt).

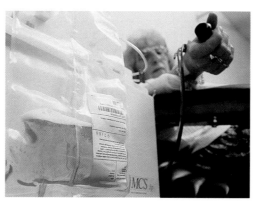

Blood plasma contains sodium chloride.

Hydrochloric acid (human stomach acid).

1 Name one synthetic material and one natural material containing chlorine.

2 How can you tell from the name of a material whether it contains chlorine?

3 Draw a 'particles in a box' picture of:
a) chlorine gas
b) sodium chloride solid
c) dichloromethane liquid.

4 For each of your 'particles in a box' pictures, choose a description of the movement of the particles from the following:
A The particles are slipping past one another.
B The particles are moving very quickly.
C The particles are vibrating from side to side.

The element chlorine was discovered by Humphrey Davy in 1810. He named it after the Greek word for green (*chloros*) because of the colour of the gas.

The names of all of the above materials contain the letters chlor, showing that they contain the element chlorine. However, a few words contain the letters chlor because of a connection with the Greek word *chloros*, meaning green, and not because the material contains chlorine.

5 What natural material in plants has a name containing the letters chlor because it is coloured green?

The scientific use of the word 'material' is applied to any matter or 'stuff' in the world around us. The everyday use of the word 'material' is often connected with something that is man-made (for example, a building material).

A material may be a single **substance**, for example pure water or pure gold. Or it may be a **mixture** of substances, for example sea water contains common salt and many other substances dissolved in water.

In science, **pure** means that the material contains only one type of substance. The word often has a very different meaning when used in everyday language.

Word play

1 For the word 'material'
a) write a sentence as it is used in everyday language
b) write a sentence as it is used in scientific language.

2 Write a sentence containing the word 'pure' in
a) everyday use
b) scientific use.

Look at the sentences that others in your group have written. Compare the meanings of the word 'pure' in science and in everyday use.

Looking for the elements

For more than 2000 years, people have thought that all of the materials on Earth were made from simple substances called 'elements'. However, most of the ideas from long ago have since been proved to be wrong by scientists.

A scientist is someone who:

- makes observations
- tries to classify the observations into groups
- tries to explain the observations with a **hypothesis**
- tests the hypothesis with experiments
- changes the hypothesis according to the results of the experiments.

This is part of the story of how the ideas about elements changed.

In ancient Greece, wise men called **philosophers** tried to explain the world around them.

Aristotle's Four Element Theory lasted for 2000 years.

The ancient Greek philosophers were only interested in ideas. They did not test out their theories.

This is the right mixture to make gold.

LEAD

EARTH

200 BC

The Egyptians learned about the Four Element Theory. They decided to try to make gold by mixing different materials together, changing the proportions of the four 'elements'.

After heating the mixtures in sealed clay pots for days, imagine their excitement, then disappointment, as they broke open the pots!

Which one contains the gold?

THE EGYPTIAN EXPERIMENTERS WERE CALLED ALCHEMISTS. THE OLD EGYPTIAN WORD FOR EGYPT IS KEMI WHICH BECAME AL-KIMIYA IN ARABIC AND THEN ALCHEMY IN ENGLISH.

1 Thales thought that everything was made from water because it was the only material that he knew that could exist as a solid, a liquid and a gas. We now know that many materials can exist in all three states.
   a) What do we call solid water?
   b) How would you change the following materials into a liquid?
     ▪ iron
     ▪ air
2 Aristotle was a great philosopher but his Four Element Theory was eventually proved to be wrong.
   a) Explain why Aristotle was not a scientist.
   b) Can you think of any experiments that you could do to prove that copper is not made out of earth, water, fire and air?
3 In their experiments, the Egyptian **alchemists** learned how to make many new materials, such as dyes, but they failed to make gold.
   a) Explain why the Egyptian alchemists were a little more scientific than the ancient Greeks.
   b) Which branch of modern science has taken its name from the word **alchemy**?

The modern theory of elements

We now know that the vast number of materials on the Earth are made up from 92 elements. Elements are simple substances that cannot be split into other substances. Examples of elements are: chlorine, iron, copper, oxygen, sulphur, silver and carbon.

It's elementary, my dear Watson.

1 Working in a group, make a copy of the table below and complete it after discussion. The first example has been done for you.

	A material?	A pure substance?	An element?
sea water	✓	✗	✗
iron			
pure water			
air			
milk			
carbon dioxide			
concrete			
oxygen			

2 The link between materials, substances and elements can be shown in a Venn diagram:

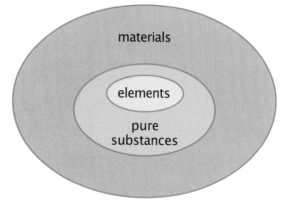

Working in a group, make a copy of the Venn diagram on a large sheet of paper and add the materials from the above table in the correct parts of the diagram.

EXTENSION

3 Can you classify the materials in the room around you into materials, pure substances and elements? Add some of them to the correct parts of the Venn diagram.

4 Explain to another member of the group how the Venn diagram works.

Atoms

Key word
* atom

An element is made up of just one type of particle called an **atom**. The atoms of each element are different. Atoms are incredibly small. If atoms could be lined up side-by-side along the edge of a ruler, there would be 25 million of them every centimetre!

DID YOU KNOW?

The word atom dates back to the fifth century BC, when a Greek philosopher called Democritus developed a theory that all matter was made up of very small building blocks which he called *atomos* (meaning 'cannot be split up'). He was not a scientist and his theory was not based on any experiments or observations. The idea of atoms was rejected by other philosophers but it returned more than 2000 years later when an English scientist, John Dalton, introduced his atomic theory.

Elements and the alchemists

In AD622, the prophet Mohammed began teaching the religion of Islam. His followers built an empire that stretched from Egypt to the borders of China and also included Spain. Islamic alchemists continued the experimental work that was started in Egypt. They improved the equipment for processes such as distillation, and they discovered many more new substances such as sulphuric acid and nitric acid. Some of the names that they gave these substances are still used in English today:

alkuhl   alcohol
sukkar   sugar
al-qali   alkali

One famous experimenter who lived near Teheran in Iran was Abu Al-Razi (865–923). He classified all of the 'minerals' used by the alchemists into the following groups:

- 'bodies' – gold, silver, iron, lead, tin
- 'stones' – iron pyrites (iron sulphide), haematite (iron oxide), malachite (copper carbonate)
- 'vitriols' – blue (copper sulphate), white (zinc sulphate), green (iron sulphate)
- 'salts' – soda (sodium oxide), lime (calcium oxide), al-kali (potassium carbonate)
- 'spirits' – mercury, sulphur

Some Islamic alchemists were beginning to doubt the Four Element Theory. Ali Ibn-Sina Avicenna wrote 'I think it is quite impossible to split up one metal into another.'

Ali Ibn-Sina Avicenna (980–1037) being received by the Governor of Isfahan.

While the Islamic alchemists were discovering many new substances, Europe was in the 'Dark Ages'. In 1144, a book on alchemy was translated from Arabic into Latin and this started the spread of the Four Element Theory to western Europe. The Europeans were excited at the thought of making gold and their efforts continued until the seventeenth century. They discovered many new substances and used some unusual materials. The painting shown here depicts an alchemist making phosphorus by distilling fermented urine. However, as more new substances were made, the experimenters started to question the Four Element Theory. When they compared their results with the theory, they did not seem to fit. Some experimenters gave up trying to make gold and concentrated on finding out more about chemicals and their reactions.

'The Alchemist' by Joseph Wright (1734–1797).

1 Explain why Abu Al-Razi worked more scientifically than the early alchemists of Egypt.
2 The European alchemists added mercury, sulphur and salt to the Four Element Theory. Which of these are now considered to be elements?

EXTENSION

3 Avicenna thought that a metal could not be split up into another metal. What experiments could you do to test his theory?

Symbols for the elements

Key word
* symbols

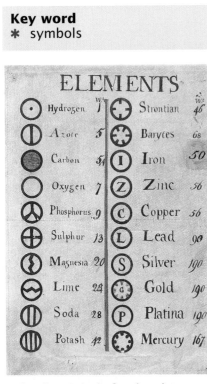

Dalton's symbols for the elements.

In 1808, John Dalton published a book about his atomic theory, using experiments and observations to back up his ideas. He said that all elements are made up of tiny, indestructible particles called atoms, and that the atoms of one element are all alike and different from the atoms of the other elements.

He produced **symbols** to represent the atoms of the elements.

5 In everyday life many types of symbols are used, for example:
   a) Can you think of one other symbol that may be found on a washing label?
   b) Can you think of some other general types of symbols used in everyday life?

As more elements were discovered, scientists agreed to use only letters for the symbols of atoms. Modern examples are given in the table below.

Element	Symbol
aluminium	Al
boron	B
bromine	Br
carbon	C
calcium	Ca
caesium	Cs
cobalt	Co

6 Why do the symbols of some elements have two letters rather than one?
7 Why does the element caesium have the symbol Cs rather than Ca?
8 There are some simple rules for choosing the symbol for an element. One is that the first letter must be a capital letter. Look at the examples in the above table. Can you think of some other rules?
9 Can you predict the two-letter symbols for these elements?
   a) barium
   b) silicon

Hundreds of years ago in Europe, all science books were written in Latin (the language of the Romans). This enabled scientists in different countries to communicate with each other. The symbols of the few elements that were known then were based on their Latin names, for example:

Element	Symbol	Latin name
iron	Fe	ferrum
copper	Cu	cuprum
silver	Ag	argentum
lead	Pb	plumbum
gold	Au	aurum

In more recent times, most symbols have been based on the English names of the elements. The names in other languages are often very similar, for example:

Element	Symbol	Foreign name	Language
nickel	Ni	niquel	Spanish
hydrogen	H	hydrogène	French
oxygen	O	ossigeno	Italian
nitrogen	N	nitrogênio	Portugese
chlorine	Cl	chloor	Dutch
magnesium	Mg	magnesium	German

Some symbols are based on the name of the element in another language, for example:

Element	Symbol	Foreign name	Language
tungsten	W	wolfram	German
potassium	K	al-kali (potassium carbonate)	Arabic
sodium	Na	natron (sodium carbonate)	Arabic

我們可以為光合作用下一個定義：

綠色植物利用由葉綠素吸收的陽光的能量，以二氧化碳和水製造糖。

以下是光合作用的化學方程：

$$6CO_2 + 6H_2O \xrightarrow{\text{光能}} C_6H_{12}O_6 + 6O_2$$

二氧化碳　　　水　　　　　　葡萄糖　　氧

但這方程只顯示了整個過程的開始和結果，並沒有顯示中間眾多的步驟。

Chemical symbols are now universal.

10 Can you think of two reasons why scientists use symbols for the elements?

Elements and the first scientists

An Irish scientist called Robert Boyle took experimental results and used them to prove that the Four Element Theory was wrong. He believed that 'elements' were the simplest substances that could exist, but he wasn't sure which of the many known substances were actually elements.

This Four Element Theory must be wrong. The four elements cannot be combined together to make a new material, and you cannot get the four elements out of any material.

Boyle cast doubt on the Four Element Theory.

A century later the French scientist Antoine Lavoisier took Boyle's ideas further.

Elements are substances that cannot be split up into anything else. I have divided them into four groups.

The four groups of elements:

Vapours: oxygen, nitrogen, hydrogen, light, heat
Solids: sulphur, phosphorus, charcoal
Metals: cobalt, copper, gold, iron, lead, silver, mercury, nickel, tin, zinc
Earthy substances:
lime (calcium oxide),
magnesia (magnesium oxide),
silica (silicon dioxide)

Lavoisier called his elements '_substances simples_' (simple substances).

Lavoisier was not sure that all of the 'earthy substances' were true elements.

However, before Lavoisier could investigate any further, the French Revolution broke out. He was arrested, falsely accused of 'plotting with the enemies of France' and executed by guillotine.

A few years later Humphry Davy tried applying some of Lavoisier's ideas.

Advances in science sometimes happen because of new technology, as well as through new ideas.

Davy made three new metallic elements from potassium carbonate, sodium oxide and calcium oxide by passing electricity through them.

1 Did Robert Boyle work like a scientist? Explain your answer.
2 How did Lavoisier decide whether a substance was an 'element'?
3 Which of Lavoisier's 'elements' are not made of matter?
4 Which of Lavoisier's 'elements' are actually compounds (combinations of elements)?
5 Which three new elements did Davy discover?

Classifying elements: metals and non-metals

Most of the 92 naturally occurring elements can be divided into two groups: metals and non-metals. Each element can be **classified** in this way by looking at its **physical properties** – how it behaves when we do things to it such as heat it, stretch it or hammer it. Metals have many uses because of their physical properties.

Uses of metals

Iron girders.

Brass (copper and tin) bell.

Steel car body.

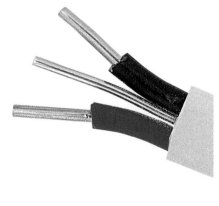
Copper electric cable.

Copper-based frying pan.

Recycling of aluminium cans.

Most metals have very similar properties. A particular metal is chosen for a particular use because it has an advantage in the property required. For example, all metals are good conductors of electricity but copper is one of the best and therefore is used in electrical wiring. However, only iron (and steel), cobalt and nickel are magnetic metals.

Uses of non-metals

Helium is used to inflate balloons because of its very low **density**.

Non-metals do not have as many uses that depend on their physical properties, although helium is an exception. They are mainly used for their **chemical properties** – how they react with other substances.

Summary of the physical properties of metals and non-metals

Metals	Non-metals
solid at room temperature	solid, liquid or gas at room temperature
strong	weak
shiny when polished	dull
sonorous (ring when struck)	not sonorous
malleable (can be beaten into shape)	**brittle** (break when struck)
ductile (can be pulled out into a wire)	not ductile
good conductors of electricity	poor conductors of electricity
good conductors of heat	poor conductors of heat
high melting and boiling points	low melting and boiling points
high density	low density

When we classify elements using these properties, some don't quite fit all of the rules:

- Mercury is a metal with a low melting point – it is a liquid at room temperature.
- Carbon in the form of graphite is a non-metal which is a very good conductor of electricity.
- A few elements have some of the properties of metals and some of non-metals. They are called **semi-metals** – for example germanium is a silvery solid which conducts electricity but is brittle.

11 For each of the following metals and uses, state which physical property is important:
   a) iron for building frames
   b) silver for a mirror backing
   c) steel for a car body
   d) copper for the base of a saucepan
   e) lead for diving boots.

The periodic table

By the end of the eighteenth century just over 20 elements were known. During the nineteenth century increasing numbers of new elements were being discovered. Scientists were looking for a method of classifying the elements so that they could understand their reactions and predict the properties of undiscovered elements.

A Russian scientist, Dmitri Mendeleyev, made data cards of all of the known elements and tried arranging them in different ways. He found that he could position them in an

Mendeleyev's periodic table.

array with horizontal rows in order of increasing mass of the atoms and with vertical groups containing 'families' of elements with similar chemical properties. In 1869 he published his **periodic table**, so called because when going across successive rows, elements with similar properties were repeated **periodically**.

Initially many scientists did not see the significance of the system. However, Mendeleyev had left gaps in his table and had predicted the properties of some elements that had not yet been discovered, and within 20 years three of these new elements had been found and their properties confirmed. All scientists then fully accepted the periodic table as an important classification system. Each element was given a number, its **atomic number**, according to its position in the table.

group:	1	2										3	4	5	6	7	8
				1 **H** hydrogen													2 **He** helium
	3 **Li** lithium	4 **Be** beryllium										5 **B** boron	6 **C** carbon	7 **N** nitrogen	8 **O** oxygen	9 **F** fluorine	10 **Ne** neon
	11 **Na** sodium	12 **Mg** magnesium										13 **Al** aluminium	14 **Si** silicon	15 **P** phosphorus	16 **S** sulphur	17 **Cl** chlorine	18 **Ar** argon
	19 **K** potassium	20 **C** calcium	21 **Sc** scandium	22 **Ti** titanium	23 **V** vanadium	24 **Cr** chromium	25 **Mn** manganese	26 **Fe** iron	27 **Co** cobalt	28 **Ni** nickel	29 **Cu** copper	30 **Zn** zinc	31 **Ga** gallium	32 **Ge** germanium	33 **As** arsenic	34 **Se** selenium	35 **Br** bromine	36 **Kr** krypton
	37 **Rb** rubidium	38 **Sr** strontium	39 **Y** yttrium	40 **Zr** zirconium	41 **Nb** niobium	42 **Mo** molybdenum	43 **Tc** technetium	44 **Ru** ruthenium	45 **Rh** rhodium	46 **Pd** palladium	47 **Ag** silver	48 **Cd** cadmium	49 **In** indium	50 **Sn** tin	51 **Sb** antimony	52 **Te** tellurium	53 **I** iodine	54 **Xe** xenon
	55 **Cs** caesium	56 **Ba** barium	57 **La** lanthanum	72 **Hf** hafnium	73 **Ta** tantalum	74 **W** tungsten	75 **Re** rhenium	76 **Os** osmium	77 **Ir** iridium	78 **Pt** platinum	79 **Au** gold	80 **Hg** mercury	81 **Tl** thallium	82 **Pb** lead	83 **Bi** bismuth	84 **Po** polonium	85 **At** astatine	86 **Rn** radon

The main part of the periodic table.

12 a) How did Mendeleyev try to classify the elements?

b) Why did Mendeleyev call his classification the 'periodic' table?

c) What evidence was needed to convince all scientists that Mendeleyev's ideas were correct?

d) What does the atomic number of an element show?

Research

Use CD-ROMs, reference books or the internet to find out the following pieces of information for five elements:

- symbol
- atomic number
- state (solid, liquid or gas, at room temperature)
- metal or non-metal
- one fascinating fact

Key word
∗ semiconductors

Metals, non-metals and semi-metals in the periodic table

All of the elements in the periodic table can be classified as metals, non-metals or semi-metals. A section of the periodic table is shown below:

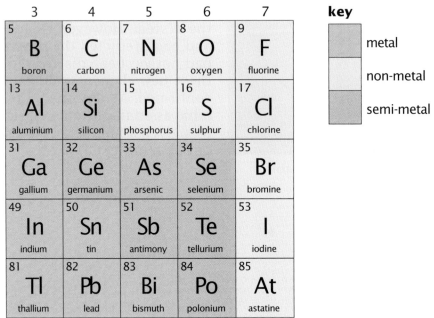

3	4	5	6	7
5 **B** boron	6 **C** carbon	7 **N** nitrogen	8 **O** oxygen	9 **F** fluorine
13 **Al** aluminium	14 **Si** silicon	15 **P** phosphorus	16 **S** sulphur	17 **Cl** chlorine
31 **Ga** gallium	32 **Ge** germanium	33 **As** arsenic	34 **Se** selenium	35 **Br** bromine
49 **In** indium	50 **Sn** tin	51 **Sb** antimony	52 **Te** tellurium	53 **I** iodine
81 **Tl** thallium	82 **Pb** lead	83 **Bi** bismuth	84 **Po** polonium	85 **At** astatine

key
■ metal
□ non-metal
▨ semi-metal

The development of the radio over the last 100 years has relied on knowledge of the properties of semi-metals.

You can see from this that the metals to the left of the table are separated from the non-metals on the right by a diagonal band of semi-metals.

The earliest radios at the beginning of the twentieth century used a 'cat's whisker'. This involved holding a thin wire (the 'whisker') against the surface of a crystal of the element germanium or the mineral galena. The 'cat's whisker' was soon replaced by valves, which are glass vacuum tubes through which electricity is passed. Although better than 'cat's whiskers', valves were easily broken and wore out fairly quickly. Scientists decided to look for a better alternative to the valve and discovered that the crystals used in the early radios were **semiconductors** – materials that conduct electricity at room temperature better than insulators but not as well as metals. They found that, with improved technology, the group 4 element germanium made a good alternative to the valve. In the 1940s and 50s, germanium was the main semiconductor material used for electronic equipment. Semiconductor components are not only stronger and longer-lasting than valves, they are much smaller and lighter.

DID YOU KNOW?

By the late 1960s valves had been replaced by semiconductors in most electronic equipment, but they are still used today in some devices. Guitar amplifiers originally used valves and some electric guitarists still prefer the sound produced by a valve amplifier to that from a semiconductor amplifier.

In time it was found that germanium was unsuitable for some uses and scientists began the search for even better alternatives.

13 Using the diagram of part of the periodic table opposite, which other elements would you choose to investigate as alternatives to germanium? (HINT – remember how Mendeleyev decided to arrange the elements in the periodic table.)

14 Which element is mainly used nowadays as the semiconductor in electronic devices such as computers?

The mineral galena that was used for the crystal in the first radios is formed when the group 4 element lead combines with the group 6 element sulphur.

15 Name three other pairs of elements that you would choose to investigate as alternative combinations to lead and sulphur.

It was later discovered that the group 3 element gallium combines with the group 5 element arsenic to form a semiconductor that emits light when a small electric current is passed through it. This is called an LED (Light Emitting Diode). These components are used for the displays in electronic equipment such as clocks and video recorders.

16 Name two other pairs of elements that you would choose to investigate as alternatives to LED semiconductors.

17 LED semiconductors are sometimes called 'III–V compounds'. Can you suggest a reason for this?

18 From what you have learned in this topic, why do you think that the periodic table is so important to research scientists?

DID YOU KNOW?

Silicon Valley in California, USA, obtained its name from the large number of electronics and computer companies that were built in the area in the 1970s and 80s.

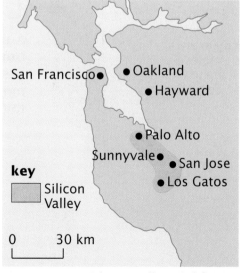

Silicon Valley, California.

Time to think

True or false?

Read the following statements and decide whether each one is true or false.

1 The millions of different materials are made from less than 100 elements.
2 Every material is a pure substance.
3 Elements can be split up into other substances by distillation.
4 Every pure substance is an element.
5 An element is a material.
6 Fresh orange juice is a pure substance.
7 An atom is roughly as big as the nucleus of a human cheek cell.
8 The symbols of all elements have two letters.
9 The symbol for iron is Fe.
10 The symbol for copper is Co.
11 All metals are magnetic.
12 All metals are solids at room temperature.
13 All metals are good conductors of electricity.
14 Lead is made up of only one type of atom.
15 There are many more metals than non-metals in the periodic table.
16 All gases are elements.
17 All non-metals are gases.

- Check your decisions with others in your group. Write all the true statements in your exercise book.
- Can you alter any of the false statements so that they become true? If you can, write the true versions in your exercise book.
- Can you think of three other true statements about the work in this chapter so far? Add these to your exercise book.

Compounds

Key words
* molecule
* bond
* compound

A **molecule** is formed when atoms are joined together by a **bond**. If the atoms are all of the same type, the substance is still an element. For example, chlorine gas consists of molecules made up from two atoms of chlorine joined together.

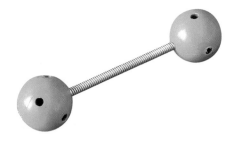

A model of a chlorine molecule. Chlorine is an element.

If the atoms forming the molecule are different, the substance is a **compound**. For example, hydrogen chloride consists of molecules made up of one atom of hydrogen and one atom of chlorine joined together.

A model of a hydrogen chloride molecule. Hydrogen chloride is a compound.

Water contains molecules made up of two atoms of hydrogen and one atom of oxygen joined together.

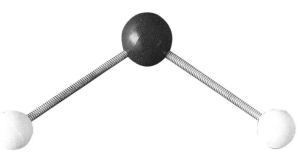

A model of a water molecule. Water is a compound.

A compound is a pure substance that is made up of two or more elements bonded together.

Making some compounds

When different elements react together they form a new substance which is a compound.

Key word
✱ word equation

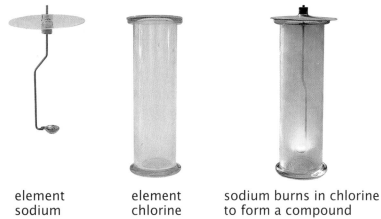

element sodium

element chlorine

sodium burns in chlorine to form a compound

Sodium burns in chlorine, giving out light and heat energy. A chemical reaction occurs, forming the compound sodium chloride from the two elements. The silvery metal (sodium) reacts with the green gas (chlorine) to form the white powder (sodium chloride – table salt).

The reaction can be represented by a **word equation**:

sodium + chlorine → sodium chloride

Note that when chlor<u>ine</u> reacts, it forms a chlor<u>ide</u>.

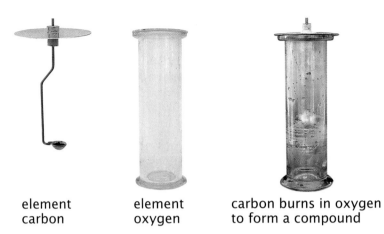

element
carbon

element
oxygen

carbon burns in oxygen
to form a compound

Carbon burns in oxygen, giving out light and heat energy.
The black solid (carbon) reacts with the colourless gas
(oxygen) to form the colourless gas (carbon dioxide). The
word equation is:

carbon + oxygen → carbon dioxide

Note that when ox<u>ygen</u> reacts, it forms an ox<u>ide</u>. The
compound is called carbon <u>di</u>oxide because there are two
oxygen atoms in a molecule of carbon dioxide (see page 106).

element
copper

element
sulphur

copper reacts with sulphur
to form a compound

Copper reacts with sulphur, giving out light and heat
energy. The brown powder (copper) reacts with the yellow
powder (sulphur) to form the black powder (copper
sulphide). The word equation is:

copper + sulphur → copper sulphide

Note that when sulph<u>ur</u> reacts, it forms a sulph<u>ide</u>.

19 Can you work out the names of the missing elements or
compounds **A–E** in this table? Explain to each other how
you did this.

Elements in the compound	Name of the compound
iron and oxygen	**A**
B	zinc oxide
magnesium and sulphur	**C**
calcium and chlorine	**D**
E	copper sulphide

20 Write out the word equation for the reaction between
each pair of elements forming the compound.

➡ *Pictures of atoms and molecules*

Scientists sometimes represent atoms as balls and we can use this model to represent reactions.

Burning sodium in chlorine

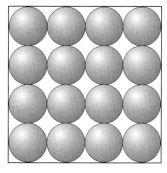

The element sodium is a solid.

All of the atoms are the same.

+

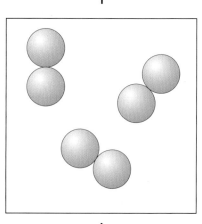

The element chlorine is a gas.

All of the atoms are the same and they are joined together in pairs to make molecules.

↓

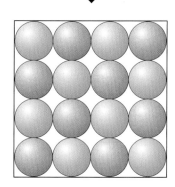

The compound sodium chloride is a solid.

A compound contains at least two different types of atom joined together.

Burning carbon in oxygen

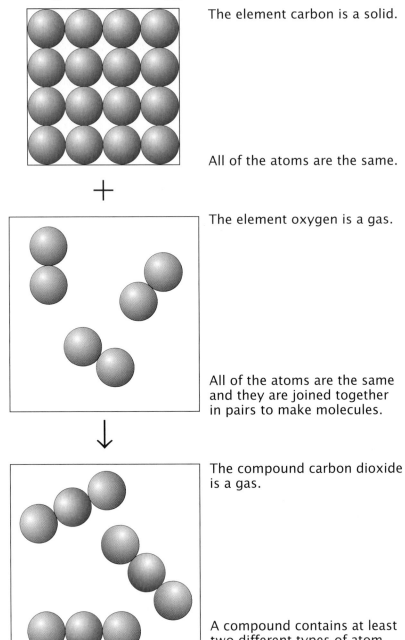

The element carbon is a solid.

All of the atoms are the same.

+

The element oxygen is a gas.

All of the atoms are the same and they are joined together in pairs to make molecules.

↓

The compound carbon dioxide is a gas.

A compound contains at least two different types of atom joined together.

Identifying elements and compounds

Particle or 'ball' diagrams showing pictures of elements and compounds can help to indicate whether the substance is a solid, a liquid or a gas.

21 A group of pupils tried to classify each of the particle drawings below. Read their comments and decide which you agree with and which you disagree with.

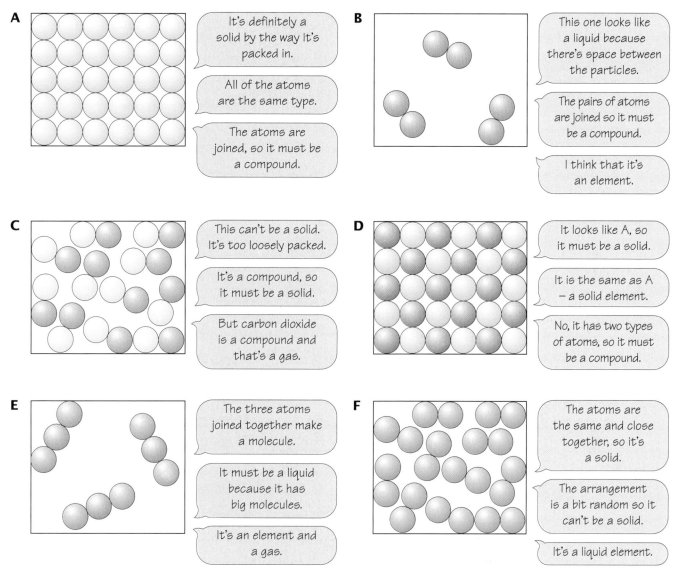

A

> It's definitely a solid by the way it's packed in.

> All of the atoms are the same type.

> The atoms are joined, so it must be a compound.

B

> This one looks like a liquid because there's space between the particles.

> The pairs of atoms are joined so it must be a compound.

> I think that it's an element.

C

> This can't be a solid. It's too loosely packed.

> It's a compound, so it must be a solid.

> But carbon dioxide is a compound and that's a gas.

D

> It looks like A, so it must be a solid.

> It is the same as A – a solid element.

> No, it has two types of atoms, so it must be a compound.

E

> The three atoms joined together make a molecule.

> It must be a liquid because it has big molecules.

> It's an element and a gas.

F

> The atoms are the same and close together, so it's a solid.

> The arrangement is a bit random so it can't be a solid.

> It's a liquid element.

22 Copy and complete this table and classify the pictures **A–F**.

Picture	Solid, liquid or gas?	Element or compound?	Reasons
A			
B			

Formulae of compounds

When two or more elements react together to form a compound, the **ratio** of the different atoms in the compound depends on the elements involved.

A chemical **formula** uses the symbols for the elements to show:

- which elements are present in the compound
- the ratio of the atoms of the different elements. For example, the carbon and oxygen atoms in carbon dioxide are in the ratio 1 : 2.

Name of compound	Formula	Number of atoms of each type in one molecule
sodium chloride	NaCl	Na Cl
carbon dioxide	CO_2	C O O
sodium sulphide	Na_2S	Na Na S

Note that if there are two or more atoms of an element in each molecule of the compound, this is shown in the formula by a small (subscript) number after the element.

23 Work out the missing entries **A–J** in the following table:

Name of compound	Formula	Number of atoms of each type in one molecule
potassium sulphide	K_2S	2 K 1 S
A	$MgCl_2$	**B**
C	**D**	1 Al 3 Cl
E	Fe_2O_3	**F**
G	**H**	2 Na 1 O
copper carbonate	$CuCO_3$	**I**
J	$ZnSO_4$	1 Zn 1 S 4 O

Time to think

1 For each of the following descriptions, decide whether it describes an element, a compound, or if it is not possible to tell.
   a) Made of one type of atom
   b) Made of two types of atoms joined together
   c) Made of two atoms of the same type joined together
   d) Exists as molecules
   e) Can be split into two new substances
   f) Made of atoms
   Check your answers with at least two other people. Which do you disagree about? How are you going to check who is correct?

2 Say whether each of the following is an element or a compound:
   b) iron
   b) copper oxide
   c) symbol Mg
   d) formula Cl_2
   e) formula NaCl
   f) symbol Co
   g) formula $CaCO_3$
   Again, check your answers with others.

3 Divide a page of your exercise book into four sections.

   ▪ In section 1, explain as clearly as you can the difference between metals and non-metals.
   ▪ In section 2, explain what the periodic table is.
   ▪ In section 3, explain the difference between elements and compounds.
   ▪ In section 4, explain why scientists use symbols and formulae to represent different chemical substances.

5 Sound

In this chapter you will learn:

→ that sound can travel through solids, liquids and gases, but not through a vacuum
→ that light travels much faster than sound
→ that sound is transferred by vibrating particles
→ what the frequency and amplitude of a sound are
→ how the ear works
→ that different people and different animals can hear different ranges of frequencies
→ that the loudness of sound is measured in decibels

You will also develop your skills in:

→ planning experiments using sound sensors
→ interpreting the patterns in data
→ describing sound qualities
→ framing a question about hearing that can be investigated
→ identifying and controlling variables
→ evaluating investigative work

→ → → WHAT DO YOU KNOW?

Key words
* vibrate
* pitch

You will already have learnt quite a lot about sound when you were younger. In pairs, look at the pictures then answer the questions.

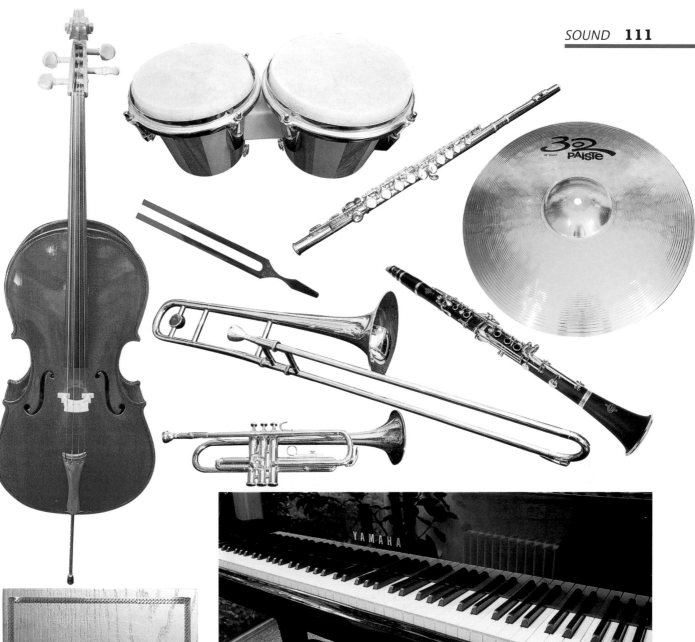

1 Can you name the sources of sound shown?

2 A sound is produced when an object is made to **vibrate**. You can do this in various ways such as banging, twanging and blowing. How is the sound produced in the musical instruments you have named?

3 When you change the **pitch** of a note, how does the sound change?

4 When you pluck a guitar string, how can you change the pitch of the note produced?

5 How do you produce a note from a tuning fork?

6 **a)** What variables could you use to classify musical instruments?
 b) Suggest the most useful way for a composer to classify them.
 c) How might an instrument maker classify them?
 d) How might the music teacher in school classify them?

How does sound travel?

Sound travels as a wave. A vibrating object creates sound by causing the surrounding material to move backwards and forwards. The surrounding material can be any substance, for example air or water or concrete. In fact the only place that sound cannot travel is a **vacuum**. Our ears detect the travelling **disturbances** and our brain interprets them as sound.

So, to hear a sound, first an object must vibrate (this could be the skin of a drum or the strings of a guitar). This sets the air vibrating near the drum skin or guitar string. These vibrations are transferred to nearby air particles and so the disturbance spreads out, rather like the ripples when a stone is thrown into a pond, and reaches our ears.

The bell jar experiment

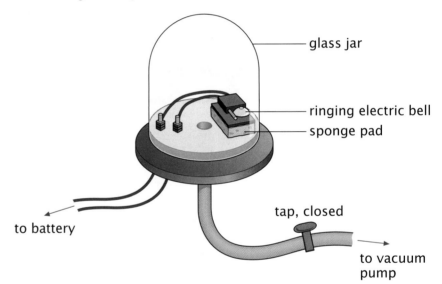

You may have seen this experiment. The bell is working inside the bell jar but no sound can be heard. Then the tap is opened and the sound of the bell can now be heard. Four pupils are discussing this experiment. This is what they say:

In your group, discuss the answers provided by the four pupils. What do you think?

1 Do you agree with all the pupils' statements? Are some more correct than others?
2 How would you explain what is happening here?

→ *Models of sound*

Key words
* amplitude
* frequency
* hertz

We have already referred to the particle model in Chapter 3. We can also use the model to explain how sound travels through air. Look at the series of pictures showing the air particles (greatly magnified). In addition to their normal motion, they are being disturbed by the vibration of the drum skin. The 1st picture shows the particles at the instant the drum is hit. In the 2nd picture, a very short time later, the air particle nearest to the drum (really a layer of air particles) has been set vibrating by the drum. In the 3rd picture the first air particle has moved further to the right and has transferred some energy to the next air particle.

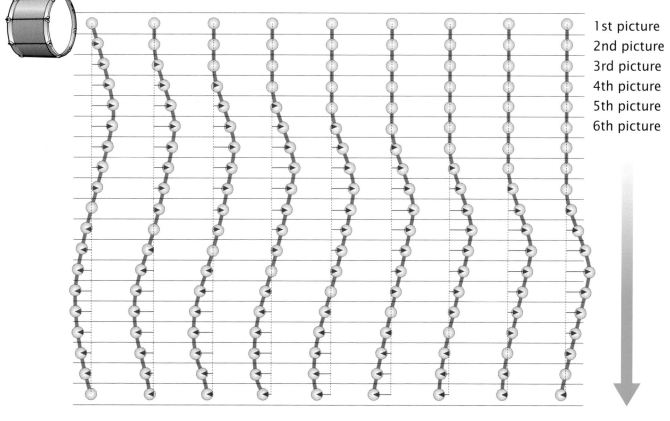

1st picture
2nd picture
3rd picture
4th picture
5th picture
6th picture

3 Explain what is happening in the 4th picture.
4 In which picture has the first particle moved its maximum distance?
5 In which picture has the first particle moved back to its original position? What happens to it next?
6 In which picture does the particle furthest from the drum start moving?

As the diagram on the previous page shows, the vibration of the drum skin has been transferred from left to right but the air particles are still roughly in the same place.

Because we cannot see air particles, a 'slinky' can be used to demonstrate the effect of sound travelling through air. Look at the series of drawings showing part of a slinky, which has been stretched along the bench.

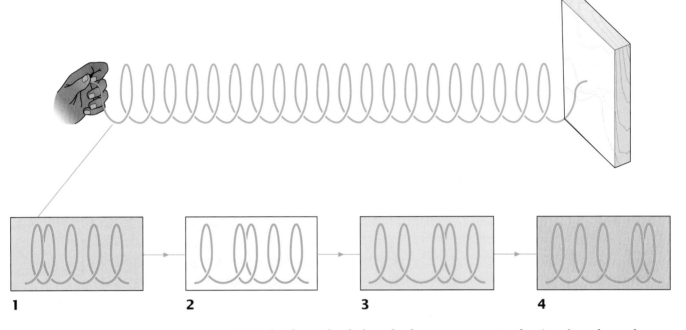

1   2   3   4

7 Which end of the slinky represents the 'ear' end, and which end represents the sound source?
8 In picture 1, what is happening to the first coil of the slinky? In which direction is it moving?
9 Picture 2 is slightly different from the previous one. How is it different? What has happened?
10 What has happened in picture 4?

This process continues all along the slinky, each individual coil displacing the next coil, and so the disturbance travels along the slinky. In terms of the energy transfer, the energy provided at one end of the slinky travels along the coils to the far end.

EXTENSION   11 Copy and complete the following table to show how the analogy of the slinky explains the way a drum sound reaches us.

Action	Slinky	Drum
Energy is transferred to the object.	The free end is pushed in and out.	The drum skin is hit with a stick.
Energy is transferred to particles that move.	The separate coils of the slinky move to and fro.	
Energy is transferred from one place to another.	This movement travels along the slinky as a wave to the other end.	
Energy is detected.	Person holding the other end feels the movement when it reaches the end.	

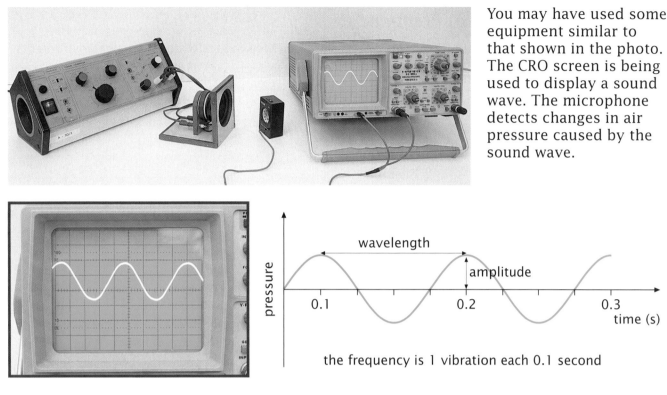

You may have used some equipment similar to that shown in the photo. The CRO screen is being used to display a sound wave. The microphone detects changes in air pressure caused by the sound wave.

wavelength

amplitude

pressure

0.1   0.2   0.3

time (s)

the frequency is 1 vibration each 0.1 second

12 What do you know about the variables **amplitude** and loudness, **frequency** and pitch?

13 Sketch how the picture on the screen changes when the sound gets louder.

We can explain this in terms of our particle model. For a loud note the air particles have been given greater energy and so they move back and forth over a greater distance, causing greater changes in pressure. The wave has greater amplitude.

14 Using the analogy of the slinky, what would you do to the slinky to demonstrate this?

15 a) Sketch how the picture on the screen changes when the frequency of the sound gets higher.

   b) Sketch how the picture on the screen changes when the frequency of the sound gets lower.

When the sound has a higher frequency, the air particles move back and forth more often.

16 What would you do to a slinky to demonstrate this?

We often use the word pitch when referring to a musical note. The higher the pitch, the higher the frequency of the note; the lower the pitch, the lower the frequency of the note.

We measure frequency in **hertz** (Hz). A frequency of 1 Hz is one vibration per second. The approximate frequency range of a violin is 200–3500 Hz, whereas a cello has an approximate frequency range of 63–630 Hz.

Information processing Frequencies

The table shows the frequency ranges of some musical instruments.

Sound source	Approximate frequency range
piccolo	630 Hz – 5 kHz
flute	250 Hz – 2.5 kHz
clarinet	200 Hz – 2 kHz
bassoon	55 Hz – 200 Hz
tenor saxophone	110 Hz – 630 Hz
trumpet	170 Hz – 1 kHz
tuba	45 Hz – 375 Hz
double bass	40 Hz – 200 Hz
organ	20 Hz – 7 kHz
piano	28 Hz – 4.1 kHz
xylophone	700 Hz – 3.5 kHz
violin	200 Hz – 3.5 kHz

1 kHz = 1000 Hz

1 Devise a way of representing this data graphically. For example, you could use a bar to represent the frequency range of the instrument.

2 Match the wave to one of the instruments pictured opposite:

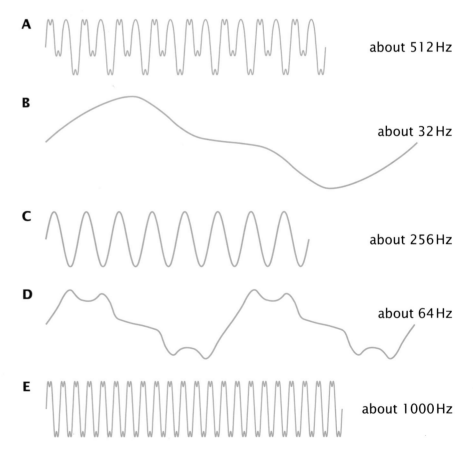

A about 512 Hz

B about 32 Hz

C about 256 Hz

D about 64 Hz

E about 1000 Hz

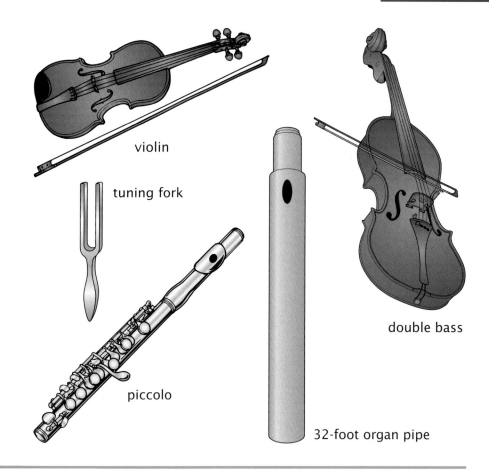

violin

tuning fork

piccolo

double bass

32-foot organ pipe

Musical instruments that produce sound by vibrating strings (stringed instruments) were first invented thousands of years ago. The Egyptians used a type of harp 5000 years ago.

Key word
* tines

Demonstrating vibrations

We can show that a source of sound is vibrating by a simple experiment with a tuning fork. The ends of a tuning fork are called the **tines**. If you hit the tines on a cork and touch them against a suspended ping-pong ball, the energy is transferred to the ball, which moves.

There are other ways of showing the vibration. If you have a strobe light whose frequency can be altered, you can try looking at the tines of the tuning fork under the strobe light and adjusting the frequency until the tines appear stationary. Alternatively, if you dip the tuning fork in water, it creates circular waves that spread across the surface.

If you gently touch the cone of a loudspeaker you will feel the vibration. Alternatively, place a few small polystyrene chips in the speaker cone and you will see them jump about when the speaker is switched on.

When a tuning fork is struck, the base is often placed on a 'soundboard'. In this case, the vibrating tuning fork, being connected to the soundboard, sets the soundboard vibrating. In turn, the soundboard is connected to the air.

17 Why is this done? How will it affect the sound heard?

18 If the tuning fork is placed on a rubber mat instead, how will this affect the loudness and the frequency (pitch)?

A tuning fork on a soundboard.

→ *Reflection of sound*

Sound can be reflected from surfaces. The diagram shows a simple experiment to demonstrate this. The sound is reflected in a similar way to light being reflected from a mirror.

19 a) What does this tell you about how the apparatus needs to be set up?
   b) If you change the angle that one tube makes with the reflecting surface, what must you do to the other?

Different surfaces reflect sound to a greater or lesser extent. You can demonstrate this by placing different materials in front of the reflecting surface. You could try foam rubber, thick curtain material, a metal sheet, a sheet of wood, or a polystyrene tile.

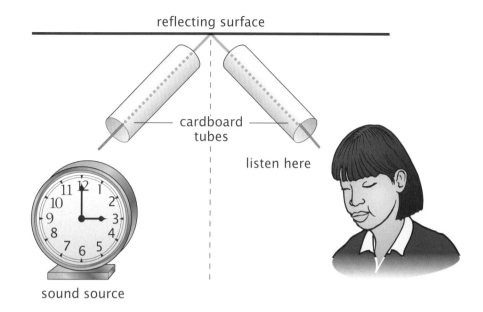

reflecting surface

cardboard tubes

listen here

sound source

→ *The speed of sound*

Key word
* echo

We know that sound travels much more slowly than light. If you watch a thunderstorm, you first see the flash of lightning and then hear the clap of thunder that follows it. Similarly, if you watch a firework rocket go off, you see the flash before you hear the bang.

The speed of light is very fast. Light travels at 300 000 km/s. Sound travels much more slowly. In air, sound travels at about 330 m/s. (The speed changes a little with the temperature.) Light travels nearly a million times faster than sound. You can use these facts to work out how far away a thunderstorm is. In 1 second, sound travels about 330 m. This means it takes sound about 3 seconds to travel 1000 m. The light from the lightning flash travels 1000 m in $\frac{1}{300000}$ s! So if you see the flash of lightning and then hear the thunder after 3 seconds, it is 1 km away. How far away is the storm if you have to wait 6 seconds?

EXTENSION 20 The new Hungerford Bridge across the Thames is just 1 km from Big Ben. If you stand on the bridge at exactly 6.00p.m. with a portable radio which plays the chimes of Big Ben, explain which you hear first, the chimes on the radio or the chimes directly from Big Ben. Why?

An **echo** occurs when a sound travels away from you, hits a barrier like a large building or a mountainside, and is reflected back. Sometimes you will notice this with a gunshot or a firework.

The echo travels twice as far as the distance between you and the barrier.

Sound travels at different speeds in different materials. This is because the particles that make up different materials are arranged differently. There are two main things that affect the speed of sound. One is the density of the substance; the other is how strong the forces are that hold the particles to one another.

In a solid, the particles are generally close together and closely connected to each other. The forces between the particles in a solid are greater than in a liquid, which are greater than in a gas. The result of this is that sound travels much faster through a solid than through a liquid or a gas.

At the top of the next page some speeds of sound in different materials are displayed as a bar chart.

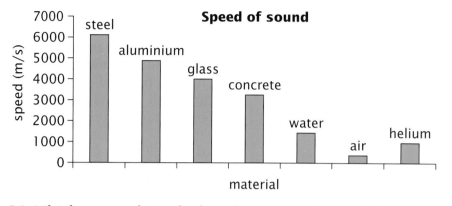

21 Which materials in the bar chart are solids, which are liquids and which are gases?

22 In which material does sound travel fastest? In which material does sound travel most slowly?

EXTENSION

23 In the bar chart, which is the densest material?

24 Can you think of a simple experiment which would show that sound travels through a liquid?

Time to think

- List all the words in the chapter so far that are new to you, and put them in alphabetical order. By each word, explain what it means.
- Write a summary of the work on sound so far, using as many words from your list as you can.

➡ *The ear and hearing*

Key words
* auditory canal
* eardrum
* ossicles
* hammer
* anvil
* stirrup
* cochlea
* auditory nerve

Our ear is an amazing device. It can hear a sound much fainter than a pin dropping, and yet also a noise as loud as an aircraft taking off without any damage. It can detect very low notes like the sound from a church organ pipe at 32 Hz, right up to a sound caused by a vibration of thousands of times a second. It can also pick out an individual conversation from a room full of people talking.

It is because we have two ears that we are able to locate the direction from which a sound comes. There is a simple way to test your ability to determine the direction of a sound. Cover your eyes and put a bunch of keys on the desk about a metre in front of you. Then ask someone to walk up and remove them. As soon as you hear them approaching you, point to the direction from which you hear them coming. How could you check whether it makes a difference if you use only one ear?

The ear is made up of three parts – the outer ear, the middle ear and the inner ear. The outer ear, the part outside your head, acts as a collector of sound waves. This sound travels down the **auditory canal** and reaches the **eardrum**. This is a piece of skin stretched tightly across the end of the ear canal. It is made to vibrate by the sound waves hitting it. Three small bones called the **ossicles** are attached to the eardrum. Their names are the **hammer**, the **anvil** and the **stirrup**. They pass on the vibrations through the middle ear to the inner ear. The main part of the inner ear, called the **cochlea**, is coiled like a snail shell. It contains a liquid. The vibrations are transferred to this liquid. This movement of the liquid triggers many hair-like nerve cells. These sensory cells pass on the information along the **auditory nerve** to the brain. The brain then interprets this sound.

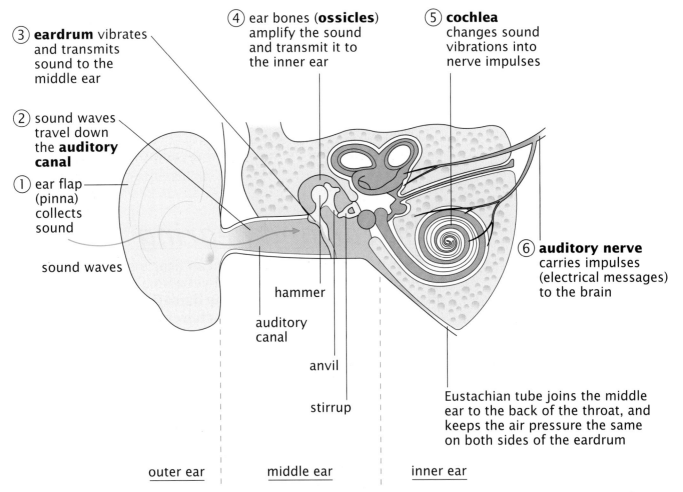

③ **eardrum** vibrates and transmits sound to the middle ear

② sound waves travel down the **auditory canal**

① ear flap (pinna) collects sound

sound waves

④ ear bones (**ossicles**) amplify the sound and transmit it to the inner ear

⑤ **cochlea** changes sound vibrations into nerve impulses

⑥ **auditory nerve** carries impulses (electrical messages) to the brain

hammer

auditory canal

anvil

stirrup

Eustachian tube joins the middle ear to the back of the throat, and keeps the air pressure the same on both sides of the eardrum

outer ear | middle ear | inner ear

25 Look at the drawing above and then make a table with three columns to show the three parts of the ear. In each column list the main components that make up this part of the ear. Part of the table is shown below.

Outer ear	Middle ear	Inner ear
ear flap (pinna)	hammer	cochlea

26 Where is the eardrum found?
27 What does the Eustachian tube do?
28 Some people think of the outer ear as a funnel. Why is this?
29 What happens to the eardrum when sound hits it?
30 Why do you think scientists chose the names hammer, anvil and stirrup for the ear ossicles?
31 What does the cochlea contain?
32 How does information get from the ear to the brain?
33 What role does the brain play in hearing?

The frequency range of our hearing is from approximately 20 Hz to 15–20 kHz, depending on our age. While an adult may hear sounds up to about 16 000 Hz, children can hear higher frequencies up to perhaps 23 000 Hz, and a dog can hear as high as 45 000 Hz.

Sometimes young children are unable to hear the full frequency range. This can be due to a condition called 'glue ear'. There is a sticky substance that is lodged in the ear. This limits the higher frequencies that can be heard. The condition can be treated by having 'grommets' put in, which allow the substance to escape.

You may have used some apparatus similar to the equipment shown in the photo for producing sounds of varying frequency. The frequency generator is connected to the loudspeaker and as the dial is turned, the frequency of the sound produced increases. You can also connect a CRO so that it displays the waveform of the sound given out.

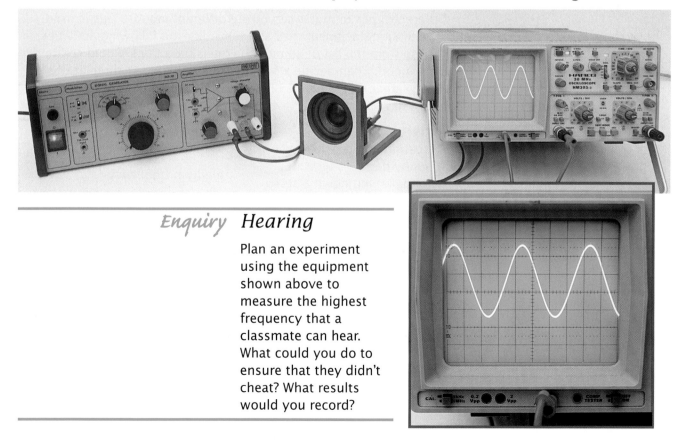

Enquiry Hearing

Plan an experiment using the equipment shown above to measure the highest frequency that a classmate can hear. What could you do to ensure that they didn't cheat? What results would you record?

Information processing Animals' hearing

The table shows the hearing ranges of different animals.

Animal	Approximate frequency range (Hz)
human	40–16 000
dog	67–45 000
cat	45–64 000
cow	23–35 000
sheep	100–30 000
rabbit	360–42 000
mouse	1000–91 000
gerbil	100–60 000
guinea pig	54–50 000
hedgehog	250–45 000

Animal	Approximate frequency range (Hz)
bat	2000–110 000
beluga whale	1000–123 000
elephant	16–12 000
porpoise	75–150 000
goldfish	20–3000
tuna fish	50–1100
bull frog	100–3000
chicken	125–2000
canary	250–8000
owl	200–12 000

Look at the results above and decide how you can present the data in a suitable graph or chart. Can you show the animals that can hear the highest frequencies and also those that can hear the lowest frequencies? You may wish to represent the range of frequencies that different animals can hear, or the highest, lowest or mean frequency. You may wish to separate the data for birds and fish from the mammals.

Creative thinking Mood music

Different types of music can create different moods. This is used in television documentaries and films. For the following activities, choose from the list of sounds the one(s) you think would create the right mood. Then decide which instruments (two or three at the most, rather than a whole orchestra) you would choose to play the music for each activity.

Activity

A floating in a lake on a warm sunny day

B tobogganing down a steep snowy slope

C shopping in a large shopping centre on Christmas eve

D climbing a tree

E watching a parachute float to the ground

Sound list

high frequency

medium frequency

low frequency

high amplitude

medium amplitude

low amplitude

EXTENSION Either using musical instruments or other objects that you can make vibrate, create a piece of music for one of the activities above. Play it to the others in your group and see if they can decide which activity it goes with and explain why the music gave them clues about it.

Word play Match up each of these terms with one of the descriptions below. The beginnings of the words should give you some clues.

binaural hearing   ultrasound   infrasound

A sounds above the normal range of hearing
B hearing with both ears
C sounds below the normal range of hearing

EXTENSION
One of the words can also be used to mean 'recording or transmitting through two channels to give an impression of depth'. Which word do you think this is? Why?

➡ *Ultrasonics*

Key words
* ultrasonic
* echolocation
* sonar

We cannot hear **ultrasonic** waves but we can make use of them in various ways. They are used to produce ultrasonic imaging, for example. This is sometimes called an ultrasound scan. It is used in hospitals to look at a foetus in a mother's womb. Ultrasonic imaging is used in preference to X-ray imaging as X-rays could harm an unborn baby. Ultrasound scans are also used to check blood flow in arteries and veins.

Another use of ultrasonic waves in medicine is as a surgical tool. Sometimes people develop gallstones and kidney stones. These are very painful, and one technique of treating them is to focus pulses of an ultrasound beam on them, which breaks them up into very small pieces.

Ultrasonics is also employed as a cleaning method. The high frequency vibrations shake the dirt off metal surfaces.

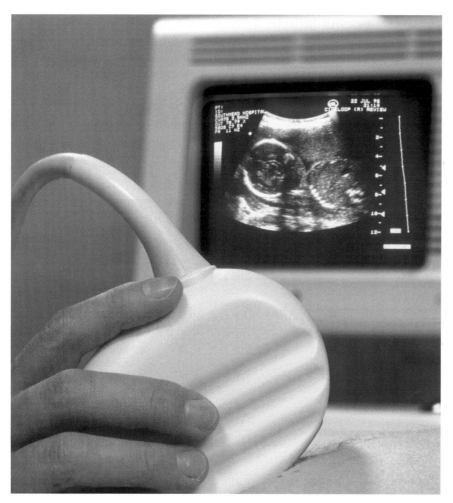

An ultrasound scan of a foetus.

Some animals such as bats and dolphins use ultrasonic waves in a specialised technique called **echolocation** that allows them to pinpoint objects and other animals, even in the dark.

The 'flying fox' is in fact a type of bat. Bats are the only mammals that can fly.

Bats are flying mammals that are found in many places around the world. Bats can see very well, probably better than we can at dusk, but even with good eyesight they are unable to see their insect prey in complete darkness. To solve this problem, many species of bat (but not all) use echolocation. There are two general types of echolocation system. The tiny pipistrelle bat, for example, uses a frequency range from 40 to 80 kHz. The lesser horseshoe bat, on the other hand, sends out an almost constant frequency of 110 kHz. The bat's echolocation is a very sensitive system. The bat emits a 'chirp' in the air in front of it. If the sound wave hits a flying insect, the bat then detects the wave reflected from it. The bat is able to determine the type of insect and its direction, and can use the echolocation system to avoid other obstacles that are in its flight path.

The pipistrelle bat feeds on insects which it finds by echolocation.

Bats are not the only mammals that use echolocation. The dolphin produces a high-pitched 'click' at 150 kHz. Each 'click' lasts for about 0.2 milliseconds (this is 0.000 2 seconds), so in 1 second the dolphin can make 5000 of these sounds! Using this method dolphins can locate objects and shoals of fish. There are different reflections from skin, bone and rocks, so they are able to construct an ultrasonic image of an object. How the dolphin's echolocation system works is still not entirely clear and is an area of ongoing research.

The dolphin's echolocation system has been copied in the sonar navigation system.

The word **sonar** comes from the phrase 'sound navigation and ranging'. It uses the reflection of high frequency sound waves (ultrasonic waves) to measure the depth of the sea. It is used in ships to locate obstacles or to map the sea floor. A sonar unit consists of an ultrasonic transmitter and a receiver. The ultrasonic beam will penetrate through hundreds of metres of water and will bounce off a solid object such as a submarine. The receiver detects the reflected beam.

➡ ## *Sound levels and noise*

Key word
✳ decibel

Scientists have carried out many experiments on the loudness of sound. The faintest sound that a human can hear is called the 'threshold of hearing'. The loudest sound that the ear can safely hear without suffering any damage is about a billion times louder. Scientists have agreed on a scale for sound level. Because the range is so enormous, the scale is based on multiples of 10. It is called the **decibel** scale. On this scale the threshold of hearing is 0 decibels (abbreviated to 0 dB). If we hear a sound of loudness 60 dB and it increases to 70 dB it will seem twice as loud. A change of 10 dB means either a doubling or a halving of the loudness we can hear.

The table shows the average sound level in decibels of different noises.

Source	Sound level (dB)
faintest sound heard	0
rustling of leaves	10
whisper	20
normal conversation	60
busy street traffic	70
factory	80
rock concert	100
pneumatic drill at 5 m	110
jet taking off	120

When we refer to 'noise', however, we usually mean unwanted sound. Too much noise is called noise pollution. This can affect people working in certain environments, for example musicians, someone using a pneumatic drill, machine operators in factories or tractor drivers. There are ways of reducing the noise and also of protecting workers from exposure to noise. Machines may be mounted on rubber mats to absorb the noise they produce. Near airports, houses have double glazing with an air gap of several centimetres; soil banks may be built to deflect the noise. Other materials such as cork wall coverings and thick curtains are also effective. Pneumatic drill operators and other workers wear ear protectors to ensure that the sound levels are not damaging. It is possible that over-exposure to sound levels over 80 dB can permanently damage your hearing.

Information processing ## Noise levels

1 The picture shows the information provided by a French firm on sound levels. Look at the information and refer to the table above. Produce your own scale for measuring sound levels.

L'échelle des bruits

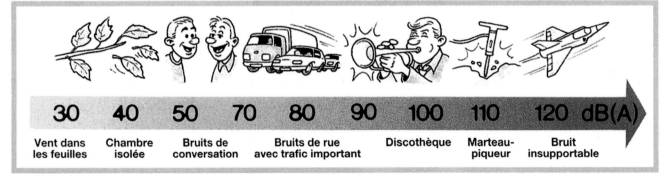

30	40	50	70	80	90	100	110	120 dB(A)
Vent dans les feuilles	Chambre isolée	Bruits de conversation	Bruits de rue avec trafic important		Discothèque		Marteau-piqueur	Bruit insupportable

2 The following results were obtained using a noise level meter. It was taking measurements at different distances from a pneumatic drill.

Noise level (dB)	Distance (m)
110	5
98	10
80	20
62	30
52	40

a) Plot a graph to show these results. What pattern do you notice?
b) Use your graph to estimate the noise level 25 m from the drill.
c) Estimate what the noise level would be 50 m away.

Enquiry ## Investigating sound

Below is a list of things you could investigate.

- What affects how the pitch of a vibrating string or elastic band changes?
- Use a sound sensor to investigate the sound insulation of different materials.
- Measure the noise level of a variety of sounds.
- Carry out a survey of noise pollution.
- Are two ears better than one in detecting the direction sound is coming from?
- Does the size of the outer ear affect hearing sensitivity?
- Does hearing range decrease steadily with age?

Decide what you are going to investigate and plan your work, including consideration of variables, collection of suitable data and evaluation of results. Ask your teacher to check your plan.

Time to think

1 Think of a revision question for each of the words below. Test a partner to see if they know the right answers to some of your questions. Then try some of your partner's questions. Make a note of all the questions and answers that you find difficult. Go back to check the parts of this chapter where these words were introduced.

- frequency
- hertz
- echo
- loudness
- ultrasonic
- sonar
- amplitude
- decibel
- ossicles
- vibrate

2 Divide a page of your exercise book into four sections. In each section describe an experiment on sound and explain what the experiment shows.

3 Name as many parts of the ear as you can, and by each part's name write its function (job).

4 How do bats use sound waves differently from humans?

6 Respiration

In this chapter you will learn:

→ **how cells are supplied with the materials needed for respiration**
→ **how cells in animals and plants release energy**
→ **that the process of respiration is similar in all cells**
→ **that cells can respire aerobically and anaerobically**
→ **that scientific ideas about how materials circulate in the human body have developed over time**

You will also develop your skills in:

→ **making and presenting observations**
→ **using sampling as a means of controlling experiments**
→ **explaining predictions**
→ **evaluating**
→ **making inferences and assumptions based on limited evidence**
→ **creative writing**

→ → → ## WHAT DO YOU KNOW?

In Chapter 1 (Food and digestion) you found out that the body needs food to provide energy and materials for growth, for repair and for production of body heat.

1 In your group, make a flow diagram that summarises how and where food is digested. This outline diagram of the digestive system will help to remind you.

Now think back to the work you did about cells in Year 7, and answer question 2.

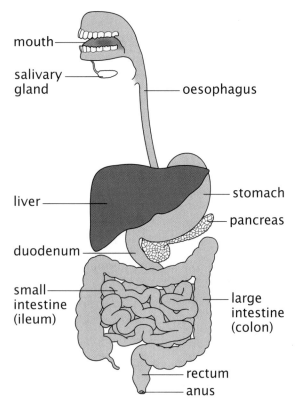

mouth
salivary gland
oesophagus
liver
stomach
pancreas
duodenum
small intestine (ileum)
large intestine (colon)
rectum
anus

2 a) What are cells?

  b) Write down what you think 'respiration' is.

  c) What is the most important chemical reaction that happens in all plant and animal cells? (The title of this chapter is a clue!)

  d) Why do living things need energy?

Make a note of your answers. You will need to look at these again when you get to the end of this chapter.

Cells: the body's powerhouse

Key words
* membrane
* selective
* permeable
* cytoplasm
* metabolic
* mitochondria

The cell **membrane** is one of the most important parts of a cell. It holds the contents of the cell together and stops unwanted chemicals entering from outside the cell. It allows water, oxygen and food materials, including sugar, into the cell. It allows waste, including carbon dioxide, out. The membrane is **selective** in what it allows to pass in and out of the cell. It is called a selectively **permeable** membrane.

The **cytoplasm** of the cell is a jelly made from proteins dissolved in water. Most of the chemical reactions of the cell take place here. Chemical reactions involved in releasing energy are called **metabolic** reactions.

Small round and oval shapes can be seen in the cell cytoplasm with an electron microscope. These are **mitochondria**. A single one is called a mitochondrion. These mitochondria are the parts of the cell that release energy from sugar molecules. The number of mitochondria in a cell can give you a clue about what that cell does. The more mitochondria, the more energy released in the cell. So active cells have more mitochondria.

1 **a)** In which of these types of cell would you expect to find the most mitochondria?
  * a cell that is part of a leg muscle
  * a cell that is part of the skin

  b) Why do you think that?

2 Check that you know the parts of a cell and what they do. Draw a large annotated diagram of a cell to explain what you know.

Information processing

How big?

The photo shows a mitochondrion as seen with an electron microscope. The actual size of a mitochondrion is about 2 micrometres long. By how much has the one in the photograph been magnified?

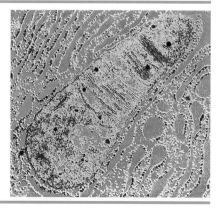

1 centimetre is 0.01 m
1 millimetre is 0.001 m
1 micrometre is 0.000 0001 m

Sugar: the body's power supply

Key word
* glucose

How does a sugar molecule get from a piece of toast you eat to a muscle in your leg where it is used to help you run up stairs?

3 Here is a list of parts of the body. Not all of the parts listed are on the molecule's journey, but some parts listed may be passed through more than once.
- heart
- oesophagus
- blood vessels
- lungs
- stomach
- muscle
- liver
- kidneys
- intestines

Discuss in your group the route the molecule takes from your mouth to a muscle in your right leg. Assume the molecule takes the most direct path possible.

Different types of sugar

There are many kinds of sugar in the food we eat, but all of them can be broken down to the simplest type which is called **glucose**.

4 Find out the names of these sugars:
   a) the sugar people put in their tea
   b) the sugar in milk
   c) the sugars in jam
   d) the sugars in cola (non-diet!).
5 a) Which type of food is digested down to simple sugar? (Look back at Chapter 1 if you can't remember.)
   b) What does this type of food provide for the body?

The label shows what a 'sports' drink contains, and what the manufacturers claim it can do for you.

In tests against water, athletes using isotonic Dyno Sport drinks are proven to improve their sporting performance by 33%*. Why? Sport scientists have proved that depletion of carbohydrate energy stores and fluid impairs performance. Dyno Sport is isotonic – it is specially formulated to be in balance with your body's own fluid. It quickly delivers a boost of carbohydrate energy to the working muscles and supplies fluid fast, which together maximise performance and endurance. Drink Dyno Sport before, during and after sport or excercise.   *Journal of Sports Sciences 1995,13,283 – 290

LEMON FLAVOUR ISOTONIC DRINK WITH ADDED ENERGY – RELEASING B VITAMINS

INGREDIENTS: Water, Carbohydrate Blend (Glucose Syrup, Maltodextrin), Citric Acid, Acidity Regulator (Sodium Citrate), Preservatives (Potassium Sorbate, Sodium Benzoate), Sweetners (Aspartame, Acesulfame K), Antioxidant (Ascorbic Acid), Flavouring, Stabilizer (Gum Acacia), Vitamins (Niacin, Pantothenic Acid, B6, B2, B12), Colour (Beta Carotene), Contains a source of Phenylalanine

NUTRITION INFORMATION (Typical values per 100ml): Energy 118kj (28kcal), Protein – Trace, Carbohydrate 6.4g, Fat – Nil, Riboflavin (Vit B2) – 0.05mg (3.4% RDA), Niacin – 0.61mg (3.4% RDA), Vit B6 – 0.07mg (3.4% RDA), Vit B12 – 0.03µg (3.4% RDA), Pantothenic Acid – 0.20mg (3.4% RDA). Each 500ml bottle provides 17% RDA of the vitamins listed. Typical Mineral Values per 100ml: Sodium 50mg, Potassium 9.9mg, Calcium 2.0mg, Magnesium 0.6mg. Refrigerate once opened and consume within 4 days. Best served chilled. Dyno Sport is a registered trademark.   500ml

LEMON FLAVOUR ENERGY DRINK

L301233/10

6 Discuss these questions in your group:
   a) Do you know what each of the Dyno Sport drink's ingredients provides for the body?
   b) Do you think this drink will do what the labelling claims?
   c) In your opinion, are these drinks 'healthy'? Give reasons for your answer.

→ *Releasing energy*

Key words
* aerobic
* ATP
* anaerobic
* lactic acid

The tin can explosion shows that sugar contains energy.

7 Draw the diagram in your exercise book and add labels to indicate the chemical reaction that takes place and the types of energy released. (HINT – Blowing provides oxygen from the air.)

This dramatic demonstration shows that it is possible to release the energy in sugar. A similar (but more controlled) chemical reaction occurs in the cells of our bodies. This is what we call **aerobic** respiration. Some energy is released as heat to maintain our body temperature. The rest of the energy must be stored and carried to parts of the body where it is required for growth and to help make new materials. The cells contain a special molecule that 'captures' the energy from glucose. This molecule is called **ATP** (this stands for a very long chemical name that you do not have to remember, adenosine triphosphate). This 'energy molecule' carries the energy to where it is needed.

8 What do you think the word 'aerobic' means?
9 Why is ATP a 'special' molecule?

Aerobic respiration

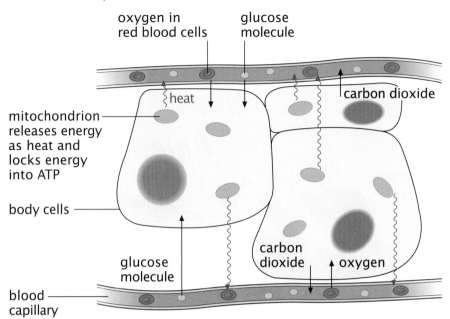

Aerobic respiration is the normal form of respiration. It requires oxygen and releases the most energy from glucose. 1 gram of glucose produces 15.6 kilojoules of energy. When our cells respire in this way we have to breathe oxygen in and breathe carbon dioxide out. We also have to excrete (get rid of) the extra water created, in our urine.

Anaerobic respiration

Anaerobic respiration happens when there is less oxygen available. It also releases energy from glucose but not as much: 1 gram of glucose will produce about 0.65 kilojoules of energy. When yeast respires anaerobically it produces carbon dioxide and alcohol. When our cells respire anaerobically they produce **lactic acid**. Too much lactic acid poisons our muscles (we get cramp).

10 What do you think the word 'anaerobic' means?
11 Why might our cells switch from aerobic to anaerobic respiration during a race?
12 Why might we get muscle cramp during a race?

Modelling aerobic respiration

You can think of an analogy to respiration if you imagine a city. Constant production of energy is necessary to keep the city alive. Energy arrives stored in fuel (such as coal, gas, or nuclear fuel rods). It is converted, in a power station, into a more useable form – electricity – that is then distributed to where it is needed throughout the city.

Like cities, cells are active and energetic. They too need a constant supply of energy and they get it in the same way: by converting fuel.

Creative thinking *City analogy*

Using the analogy of a city for aerobic respiration in a cell, copy and complete this table.

	City	Cell
Fuel supply	coal, gas, nuclear fuel rods	
Transport	roads, rail	
Energy conversion site	power station	
Usable energy form	electricity	
Transport	wires	
Uses	heat, light, power	

13 Which of these statements best represents the chemical process of respiration?

  A Glucose and sugar give energy, carbon dioxide and water.

  B Oxygen and glucose give energy, carbon dioxide and water.

  C Carbon dioxide, water and glucose give oxygen and energy.

  D Sugar and oxygen give glucose, carbon dioxide and water.

  E Energy and carbon dioxide give oxygen, sugar and water.

Check your answer with others. When you are sure you have the correct answer, write it as a word equation in your exercise book. (Look back at pages 103–104 if you have forgotten how to write a word equation.)

Inference

Key words
* inference
* hypothesising

Inference is part of scientific thinking. This happens when we base an idea on a few facts we know or observations we make. We are inferring something when we try to describe a pattern or broader picture on the basis of this limited information. Information is always limited because it is not practical for us to have total knowledge about everything. If everything were known, there would be no need for inference.

Since science does not claim to know everything, inference is behind all science. It is important to note, also, that inference underlies most thinking, even the unscientific type. Scientific inference is, however, not like using 'common sense'. What distinguishes scientific inference is that the process is made explicit (described clearly) and it follows certain rules.

Inference in science involves at least four main ways of thinking:

1 **hypothesising** (proposing a logical explanation for facts that can be tested through investigation)
2 sampling
3 designing
4 interpreting.

We may use some or all of these thought processes when we are asked to make an inference based on an investigation. We may also use inference to help us design a good scientific investigation.

Reasoning   ## Alive or not?

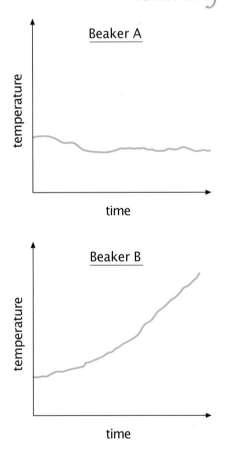

Look at these drawings of two lots of seeds. Beaker **A** contains boiled seeds of wheat and beaker **B** contains seeds of wheat that have been soaked for a few days in water.
  The graphs on the left show the temperatures in each beaker over 5 hours.

1 Why do you think the seeds in beaker **B** show a rise in temperature?

2 Think of a likely explanation for the slight warmth in beaker **A** at the start of the investigation.

3 How would you improve this investigation?

4 What inference can you make about what the seeds are doing in each beaker?

EXTENSION   5 Alice's hypothesis was that there would be no change in temperature in beaker **A** because the seeds die when boiled and so cannot respire. Do the results support or disprove Alice's hypothesis?

6 Jane's hypothesis was that respiration would occur in beaker **B** until all of its food supply was used up, and so there would be an increase and then a decrease in the temperature in beaker **B**. Do the results support or disprove Jane's hypothesis?

Rates of respiration

Key words
* indicators
* litmus
* limewater
* universal indicator
* rate
* bicarbonate indicator solution

14 a) Can you remember from your Year 7 work which of the **indicators** listed below change with acids and alkalis?
b) Which of them change to indicate carbon dioxide?
c) What changes would you observe in each case?
  * **litmus**
  * **limewater**
  * **universal indicator**

This diagram shows how respiration **rate** can be investigated in small animals. As they respire, they produce carbon dioxide. Carbon dioxide dissolves in water to make a weak acid. **Bicarbonate indicator solution** is another indicator which detects changes in acidity. It is purple when no carbon dioxide is present, red with a very little carbon dioxide and yellow with a lot of carbon dioxide.

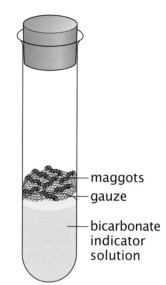

— maggots
— gauze
— bicarbonate indicator solution

15 The bicarbonate indicator solution was red when it was put into the tube, then it turned yellow after 5 minutes.
a) Why was it red, and not purple, to start with?
b) Why did it turn yellow?

Enquiry ## Investigation 1

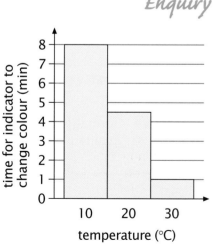

Peter noticed that if he put his fishing maggots into the fridge, they did not turn into flies as quickly as they did if he left them out in his shed. He hypothesised that the cold slowed down their development. He assumed that there would be a correlation between their rate of respiration and their development. He also hypothesised that they would be more active when they were warm and this would increase their rate of respiration.

He designed an experiment to test his hypotheses. Here is a graph of his results using the set-up shown above.

1 Which is the input variable and which the outcome?

2 Write a title for Peter's experiment that explains what he is investigating.

3 What inferences is he testing?

4 Write a plan that Peter might have used to set up his investigation so that it gave him the data shown in his graph.

5 What would he need to control in his investigation to make it a fair test?

6 What happens to the time for the indicator to change as the temperature increases?

EXTENSION **7** Does the graph support both of Peter's hypotheses? What other evidence do you think he should look for to support either of his hypotheses?

8 Some people might criticise this investigation because Peter took only three readings. How could Peter repeat the investigation in a more reliable way?

Enquiry ## Investigation 2

Peter decided to investigate the respiration rates of other living things to see how they compared with maggots. He used a wood louse, some maggots, a small mushroom, a large chunk of apple and a control tube.

1 How do you think he set up this new investigation?

2 How many times do you think he needed to repeat his investigation of each living thing, so that he could assume his data were reliable?

3 Why should he average his results and how would he do this?

4 How would he set up a control tube?

5 In which tube do you think the indicator changed colour first? Why?

EXTENSION **6** How could he judge when the living things had all produced a similar amount of carbon dioxide?

7 a) Which living thing do you think had the most respiring cells? Why?
  b) How would having more respiring cells affect respiration rate?

8 How could Peter adapt the investigation to investigate respiration in cress seedlings?

9 Make a table that he could use to record his results and calculate averages. Recommend what he should do with his results next.

Enquiry ## Investigation 3

Key words
* qualitative
* quantitative

1 Design an investigation to show that a human breathes out more carbon dioxide than he or she breathes in.

2 Would this give **qualitative** or **quantitative** information? (Quantitative information uses measurements; qualitative information is descriptive.)

Enquiry ## Investigation 4

Key words
* inhaled
* exhaled

1 Think of a way of showing that we breathe out water vapour. Describe your idea using drawings and notes.

2 Does this give qualitative or quantitative information?

3 How could you show that air breathed out is warmer than air breathed in?

4 Make a table summarising the differences between **inhaled** and **exhaled** air. Which of these differences can be demonstrated practically and which come from information that you have read about or heard?

Time to think

Here is a list of some of the main ideas you have been learning about in this chapter so far:

- anaerobic respiration
- aerobic respiration
- making inferences
- hypothesising
- setting up a control
- how cells release energy
- qualitative and quantitative data
- reliability.

Arrange these in three lists: a red list for 'I'm not sure what this means', an amber list for 'I know quite a bit about this, but I'm not sure about some things', and a green list for 'I know all about this'. Compare your lists with a partner's lists. If any of your red or amber items are in your partner's green list, get him or her to help you understand them. Do the same if you know about some things he or she is not sure about.

What will you do if you both have the same things in your red lists?

How do we get oxygen into our bodies?

Most cells respire aerobically and so need oxygen for respiration:

glucose + oxygen → carbon dioxide + water

energy

Talk in your group about how you think oxygen gets from the air around you to your leg muscle cells for respiration. Make some 'think bubbles' on a large sheet of paper and write each of your ideas in one of the bubbles.

I think that I breathe in using . . .

I think my lungs are . . .

Blood helps because . . .

Key words
* lungs
* alveoli
* capillaries
* diffusion
* trachea
* bronchus

The lungs

It is the **lungs** that get oxygen into the body and carbon dioxide out of it. Their function is to pass the air we inhale close to our blood supply, so that oxygen can pass into the blood. Also, carbon dioxide and water can pass out of the blood into the air that we exhale. The lungs are adapted to do this by having special structures called **alveoli**. These are like tiny bags of air. Each lung is made up of millions of alveoli. Each single air sac, or alveolus, is surrounded by a network of tiny, thin blood vessels called **capillaries**.

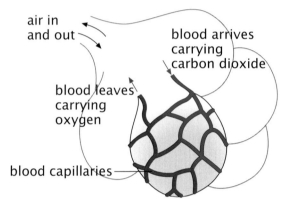

air in and out
blood arrives carrying carbon dioxide
blood leaves carrying oxygen
blood capillaries

Gas exchange in an alveolus.

Substances pass between the air in the alveolus to and from the blood by a process called **diffusion**.

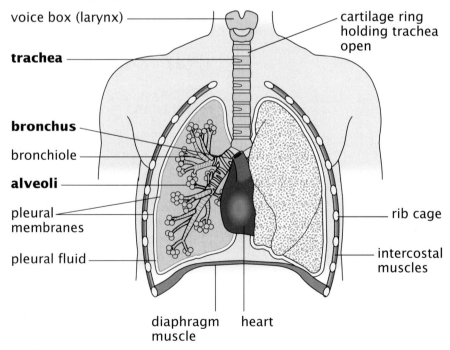

voice box (larynx)
cartilage ring holding trachea open
trachea
bronchus
bronchiole
alveoli
pleural membranes
pleural fluid
rib cage
intercostal muscles
diaphragm muscle
heart

The lung system.

16 Many diseases have names that end in 'itis'.
   a) Which part of the lung system is infected if someone has 'tracheitis'?
   b) Where is the infection if someone has 'bronchitis'?

DID YOU KNOW?

If all the alveoli in one person's lungs were smoothed and spread out they would cover an area about 70 metres square.

Breathing

The amount of air we can hold in our lungs is called the lung capacity.

- Time how long you can comfortably hold your breath in before you have to exhale.
- How long can you keep exhaling before you have to draw in another breath?

The composition of inhaled and exhaled air

	Inhaled	Exhaled
nitrogen	78%	78%
oxygen	21%	18%
carbon dioxide	0.004%	3%
other gases	1%	1%

17 Make two pie charts to compare the composition of inhaled and exhaled air.

Enquiry *Planning a survey*

1 a) Plan and carry out a survey of other people's ability to hold their breath.

   b) Think of a hypothesis for why some people can hold their breath longer than others. What questions will you need to ask the participants in your survey to see if your hypothesis is a likely explanation?

2 a) Design a simple piece of equipment to measure how hard some one can 'puff'. Think about hygiene and safety.

   b) What might reduce someone's ability to blow air out of their lungs efficiently?

Assessing a patient's lung capacity.

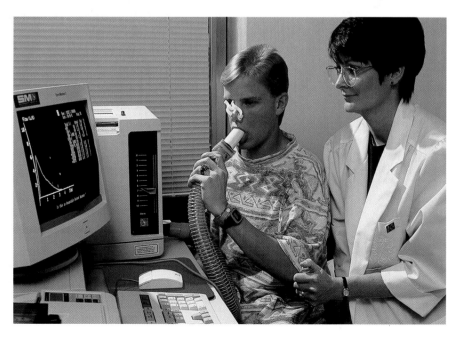

Not getting enough oxygen

Key words
* symptoms
* compressed
* rupture
* embolism
* decompression

HOLIDAY HEALTH for MOUNTAINEERS

Lack of oxygen at high altitudes (over 2500 m) affects most people to some extent. The affect may be mild or severe and occurs because less oxygen reaches the muscles and the brain at high altitude. This makes the heart and lungs compensate by working harder.

Mild **symptoms** include headache, lethargy, dizziness, difficulty sleeping and loss of appetite. Severe symptoms include breathlessness, a dry, irritating cough (which may progress to the production of pink, frothy sputum), severe headache, lack of coordination and balance, confusion, irrational behaviour, vomiting, drowsiness and unconsciousness.

Treat mild symptoms by resting at the same altitude until recovery, usually a day or two. Paracetamol or aspirin can be taken for headaches. You can avoid acute altitude sickness by ascending slowly – have frequent rest days, and spend two to three nights at each rise of 1000 metres. If you reach a high altitude by trekking, acclimatisation takes place gradually and you are less likely to be affected. Drink extra fluids. The mountain air is dry and cold, and moisture is lost as you breathe. You may not notice the evaporation of sweat and could get dehydrated. Eat light, high-carbohydrate meals for more energy. Avoid alcohol as it may increase the risk of dehydration.

Mountaineers aiming to reach very high altitudes need to be equipped with oxygen cylinders.

JOIN UP WITH DIVERSE DIVERS

If you want a sport that puts you under a lot of pressure, try underwater diving. You can even feel some of the effects of pressure in a swimming pool. Down just a few feet under water, your ears begin to hurt. That's caused by pressure on your eardrums. Where does that pressure come from? It's the weight of all the water – and air – above you.

Pressure influences how divers use air. At 10 metres, for example, the increased pressure means your lungs hold twice as much air as they do at the surface – and you'll breathe all the air in your tank twice as fast. The deeper you dive, the more quickly you use up the air in your tank. When you breathe **compressed** air from an oxygen tank underwater, its pressure is regulated so that the air spaces in your body are at the same pressure as the surrounding water. But if you breathe compressed air under

water and then ascend, holding your breath, as the pressure around you decreases your lungs expand. Air sacs in your lungs could **rupture**, causing an air **embolism**, which means that bubbles of air enter your bloodstream and block circulation to your brain.

Come and learn to dive properly with us and avoid getting 'the bends,' or **decompression** sickness. The longer you stay down and the deeper you go, the more nitrogen

dissolves into your body tissues. If you ascend too rapidly, the dissolved nitrogen comes out of solution too quickly and forms bubbles in your tissues. You could experience severe pain (particularly in joints), dizziness, blindness, paralysis and convulsions. You must ascend slowly and, under certain circumstances, take 'decompression stops' on the way up. This allows the dissolved nitrogen to come out of the body safely.

18 Read the two extracts about mountaineering and diving.
   a) What does 'ascending' mean?
   b) What similarities are there between 'the bends' and altitude sickness?
   c) How does ascending slowly help in both cases?
   d) Why do divers and high altitude mountaineers use oxygen cylinders?

DID YOU KNOW? Your lungs are so elastic that when you are resting you need to make no effort for your lungs to spring back and squeeze out the air.

Enquiry ## Designing an investigation

When cells are working hard they need more energy. This means more glucose and more oxygen are required.

How would you investigate the effect of increasing exercise on the rate of breathing? Think about the input and outcome variables, how to make the investigation a 'fair test' and safe, and how to record the results.

The heart

Key words
* aorta
* vena cava
* pulmonary artery
* pulmonary vein
* atrium
* ventricle

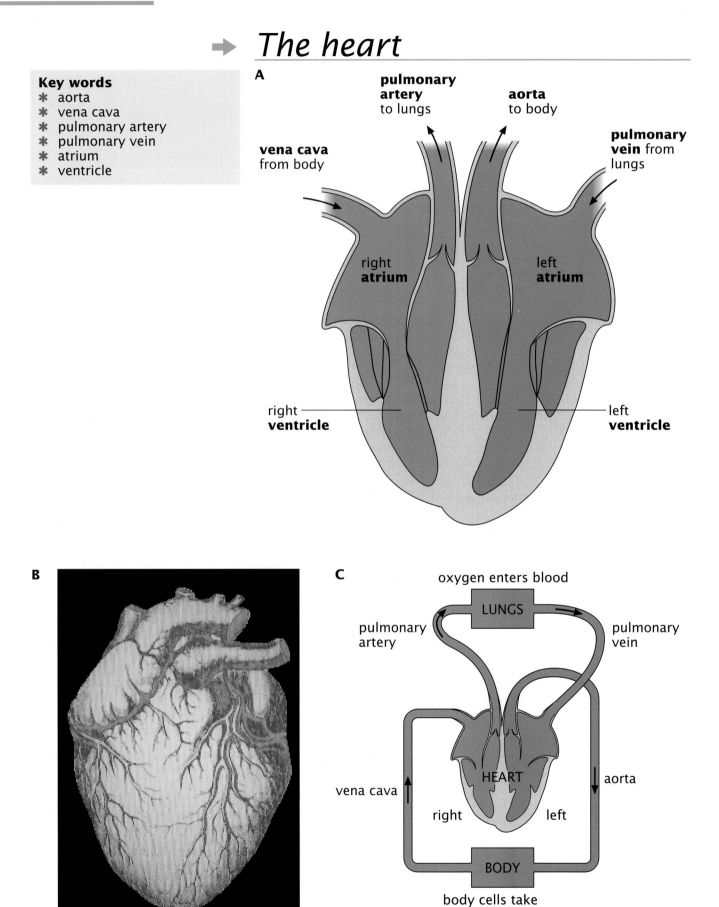

A

pulmonary artery to lungs

aorta to body

vena cava from body

pulmonary vein from lungs

right **atrium**

left **atrium**

right **ventricle**

left **ventricle**

B

C

oxygen enters blood

LUNGS

pulmonary artery

pulmonary vein

vena cava

HEART

aorta

right

left

BODY

body cells take oxygen from blood

D

E

The illustrations **A–E** show five different ways of representing the heart. Look at each and discuss these questions with a partner:

19 **Observation questions**
  a) Describe exactly what you see in each picture.
  b) What is each showing?
  c) Are some pictures more detailed than others?
  d) How 'real' is each? How do you know?

20 **Knowledge checking**
  Summarise what you know about each picture. Say what you conclude from what you see.

21 **Interpretation questions**
  a) What do each of the pictures tell you about the biological function of the heart?
  b) Are any of them more helpful than others? Why?
  c) Do any of the pictures indicate other, non-biological, functions of the heart?
  d) Why do you think these pictures have been chosen?

DID YOU KNOW?

- A human heart weighs between 250 g and 400 g.
- About 25 litres of blood flows through it in 1 minute.
- It beats at 65 beats per minute on average.
- Over a 70-year lifespan it will beat about 2 391 480 000 times.
- It has a fuel consumption of 26 cm^3 of oxygen at cruising speed and 150 cm^3 at high speed.

Information processing ## Via the heart and back

Imagine you are a blood cell leaving the lungs, carrying oxygen. You want to transport this oxygen to the body as quickly as possible. Make yourself a simple route map showing your journey to the heart, out to the rest of the body and back to the lungs for more oxygen, via the heart.

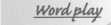 *Word play*

In your group think of as many different sayings as you can which include the word 'heart'. Here are some examples to get you started:

'Have a heart!'
'Home is where the heart is.'

Why do you think we have so many 'hearty' sayings?

Creative thinking **Valentine card**

My heart is like a singing bird
Whose nest is in a watered shoot;
My heart is like an apple-tree
Whose boughs are bent with
        thickset fruit;
My heart is like a rainbow shell
That paddles in a halcyon sea;
My heart is gladder than all these
Because my love is come to me.

Christina Rossetti (A Birthday)

Design a Valentine card that one biologist might send to another biologist. You could write a poem, too.

Electrocardiograms

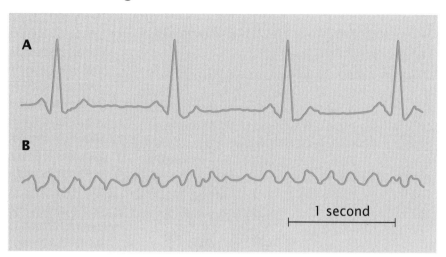

An **electrocardiogram** or ECG shows the way someone's heart is beating. **Electrodes** are attached to the person's skin, near the heart, so that the electrical signals made by the heart's natural 'pacemaker' can be picked up and amplified. The pacemaker is a small patch of special muscle in the heart wall that 'triggers' the whole heart muscle to contract.

22 a) ECG **A** shows a healthy heart with large regular contractions. What do you infer from ECG **B**?
   b) What might patient **B** be suffering from?

Heart attacks

If the heart does not get a steady, regular supply of oxygen it cannot function effectively. It will beat irregularly and may stop all together. This is a heart attack or **cardiac arrest**.

The heart gets its sugar and oxygen from a special set of blood vessels that pass through the heart muscle. (The cells of the heart cannot use the blood from the atria and ventricles.)

A reduction in the blood supply to the heart could cause a heart attack. Blocking or narrowing of the arteries reduces blood flow. This can occur if someone has too much fatty stuff in their bloodstream. This fatty substance is **cholesterol**. People who smoke, eat too many fatty foods or do very little exercise are likely to have high cholesterol levels, possibly leading to blocked blood vessels.

23 Write a few sentences to explain the link between cholesterol and heart attacks.
24 Make a warning poster to put up in the teachers' staff room, warning them of the danger to their hearts of unhealthy living.

EXTENSION

Development of ideas about the heart and circulation

A doctor called Claudius Galen (c.131–201), living in Greece, was one of the first people to record his observations on dissecting the hearts of many different animals. He was puzzled about how blood circulated through the two sides of the heart. He hypothesised that the heart's central dividing wall of muscle (the septum) might have tiny holes or pores in it, which allowed blood to seep from one side of the heart to the other.

In the fifteenth century, the Italian artist and scientist Leonardo da Vinci (1452–1519) drew some very accurate pictures of the heart and its valve system, based on his dissections of corpses. He used his drawings to design a hydraulic pump.

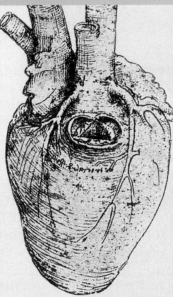

One of Leonardo da Vinci's drawings of the human heart.

Up until his time, dissecting human bodies had not usually been allowed, as it was considered to be disrespectful. Andreas Vesalius (1514–1564) continued this new practice of dissection and explained the general structure of the heart, veins and arteries. He also tried to find holes by poking hairy bristles into the septum. He failed to find any.

Only with William Harvey's work (1578–1657) did it become clear how the two sides of the heart act like pumps and how the blood circulates between the lungs, the heart and around the body. Harvey's theories were not believed by the other doctors of his day, who still thought that Galen's ideas were correct and that there were tiny holes in the central wall.

Ibn-Al-Nafis was a thirteenth-century Muslim physician. He was the first to describe the way the blood circulates between the heart and the lungs (the pulmonary circulation), several hundred years before William Harvey's description. This was an important landmark in the understanding of the heart. In finding that the wall between the right and the left ventricle of the heart is solid and without pores, he disputed Galen's view that the blood passes directly from the right to the left side of the heart. Ibn-Al-Nafis correctly inferred that blood must pass from the right ventricle to the left ventricle through the lungs. The significance of his inferences remained unknown by physicians in western countries. It was only in the twentieth century that his work was brought to light.

Ibn-Al-Nafis (1213–1288) demonstrating his theory of blood circulation.

In 1896 Professor Rehn carried out the first successful heart surgery in Frankfurt, when he stitched up a hole in the heart of a wounded patient. From then on heart surgery became an important, specialist branch of medicine, and new and better techniques for repairing damaged hearts have been developed ever since.

In 1967 Professor Christian Barnard transplanted a beating heart from a brain-dead patient into a 54-year-old man. The patient only lived for 18 days after the operation because his body rejected the new heart. From 1983, the use of cyclosporin, a powerful drug that suppresses the body's immune system, improved the success rate of heart transplants. People now live for many years after a heart transplant.

Heart drugs

Key word
✳ pharmacologist

Blood clotting in the blood vessels of the heart is another cause of heart attacks. Aspirin is effective in preventing blood clots forming. It contains salicylic acid. Knowledge of the pain-relieving properties of salicylic acid goes back more than 2000 years. The Greek physician Hippocrates (c.430BC) knew that juice from the bark of willow trees, which contains the acid, could be used to treat pain. Up until the Middle Ages, herbalists still boiled willow bark for this reason.

In 1828 a Munich **pharmacologist**, Johann Büchner, boiled willow bark into a yellow substance he called 'salacin'. A year later, in France, the substance was converted to crystal form, and in Italy salacin was refined to form salicylic acid. Acetylsalicylic acid (ASA) was finally produced in Strasbourg in 1853 and was named 'Aspirin'. This synthetic product was offered at a tenth of the price of naturally produced salicylic acid, but it tasted awful and often had what was described as an 'aggressive effect' on the mucous membranes. A low dosage form for heart treatment was created.

Aspirin is still not suitable for everyone, even those with heart disease. Between 2% and 6% of the population may get upset stomachs from aspirin.

Another major drug that has increased the chances of people surviving with heart conditions is extracted from the common foxglove, *Digitalis purpurea*. In the eighteenth century, William Withering noted that some folk remedies for 'dropsy' used ground-up foxglove leaves in very small quantities. This helped the puffiness and swellings of dropsy to go. He realised that a weak heart could cause 'dropsy', and he started using foxglove extract to help his patients with heart conditions. However, the drug could cause death in too high a dose, and it took another 200 years before the safe production of digitalis medicine became established.

'Beta-blockers' are a whole range of modern drugs that slow down the heart beat and so reduce blood pressure. They are prescribed after a heart attack to prevent further attacks.

1 In your group, discuss how ideas about the heart and blood circulation have developed as scientific methods have improved.

2 Use the three headings below to summarise how you think theories have changed. Put the names of the scientists in order, from the most ancient to the most recent.

Scientist	Inferences	Evidence for making inferences

Research ▷ Use the internet to find out more about scientific discoveries to do with the heart. You could:

- find out what the Chinese knew in the second century;
- learn more about Leonardo de Vinci's scientific methods;
- find out who Servetus was and what his connection was with Ibn-Al-Nafis.

How the heart beats

① **Relax and refill**
The muscles in the walls of the heart relax. Blood seeps in under low pressure from the veins, which come from the whole body and the lungs.

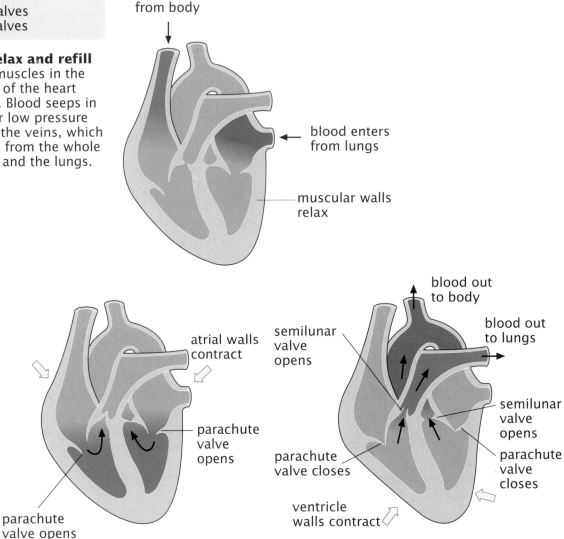

blood enters from body

blood enters from lungs

muscular walls relax

atrial walls contract

parachute valve opens

parachute valve opens

blood out to body

blood out to lungs

semilunar valve opens

semilunar valve opens

parachute valve closes

parachute valve closes

ventricle walls contract

② **Atria contract**
The thin walls of the upper chambers of the heart, the atria, squeeze the blood through the **parachute valves** into the lower chambers, called the ventricles. The 'pacemaker' in the right atrium wall starts the squeezing of the muscles.

③ **Ventricles contract**
The muscle contraction jumps down to the bottom point of the ventricle walls and spreads upwards through the ventricles. Blood is forced into the arteries through the **semilunar valves** under high pressure. The arteries lead to the whole body and the lungs. The parachute valves then snap shut. You can hear this as the loud part of a heartbeat if you put your ear on someone's chest.

25 Look back at the diagrams of the heart and lung blood supply on page 144. Name the blood vessels, the parts of the heart and the valves that the blood travels through, from picking up oxygen in the lungs to reaching body cells, then back, full of carbon dioxide, to the lungs again to collect more oxygen. When you are sure you have the order correct, draw a flow diagram.

The effect of exercise

A Heart rate:
   140 beats/minute

Breathing rate:
   100 litres/minute

B Heart rate:
   60 beats/minute

Breathing rate:
   10 litres/minute

C Heart rate:
   170 beats/minute

Breathing rate:
   1490 litres/minute

26 Above are three photos of an athlete in action. Put them in the right order. What information did you use to do this task?

27 a) Why are the heart and breathing rates very different in each picture?
   b) Why are the heart and breathing rates not the same before and after the race is over?

EXTENSION 28 a) An athlete at the Olympic games said when she had finished a sprint, 'I felt as if I was swimming in a sea of lactic acid and I just had to get out'. What do you think she meant?
   b) Would someone participating in the curling event have felt the same way? Give a reason for your answer.

EXTENSION Hole in the heart

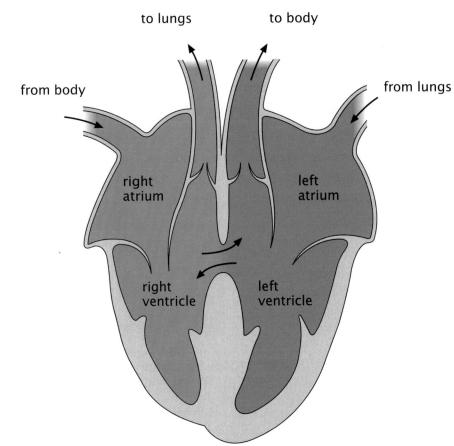

About 6 in every 1000 babies are born with heart problems. The most common is a 'hole in the heart' where the wall dividing the left and right sides of the heart is not fully formed and blood can leak straight through from one side to the other. This is shown in the diagram (where the size of the hole is exaggerated). Sometimes the hole is so small that it may be years before it is detected. A larger hole can be serious and needs surgery.

29 Write a short pamphlet for parents explaining what a 'hole in the heart' is. Think about what symptoms the baby may have. Explain why the baby might look 'blue'. You could do some research on the internet.

Time to think

1 Copy and complete this summary:

Respiration is the release of energy from _____.
It takes place in animal and plant _____, within organelles called _____.
Oxygen and glucose for respiration are transported to cells by _____.
Aerobic respiration requires glucose and _____.
Anaerobic respiration requires glucose.
Aerobic respiration releases energy, _____ _____ and _____.
Anaerobic respiration releases energy, _____ _____ and _____ _____, which gives you muscle cramps if a lot is produced.
Aerobic respiration gives (more/less) energy than anaerobic respiration per molecule of glucose.

Check back to the notes you made at the start of this chapter. Have your ideas about what respiration means changed?

2 Copy this drawing of a heart. Working with a partner, label your drawing as fully as you can.

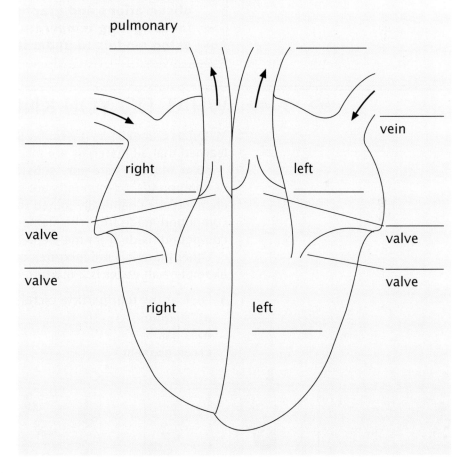

pulmonary

_____ _____

vein

_____ _____

right   left

_____   _____

_____   _____
valve   valve

_____   _____
valve   valve

right   left

_____   _____

7 Compounds and mixtures

In this chapter you will learn:

→ that combining atoms together in different ways makes new compounds
→ how to tell the difference between an element, a compound and a mixture
→ how to tell the difference between the formation of new compounds by a chemical reaction and the formation of a mixture

You will also develop your skills in:

→ deciding how many measurements are needed for reliable results
→ presenting data as graphs
→ interpreting and drawing conclusions from observations and graphs
→ investigating temperature changes as liquids cool
→ using models to understand compounds and mixtures

→ → → WHAT DO YOU KNOW?

Materials can exist as gases, liquids or solids. In Chapter 4 you learned that all materials are made from just 92 elements.

Some materials are pure substances which may be either elements or compounds. Compounds are substances in which two or more elements are chemically joined together. Carbon dioxide is a compound made from the elements carbon and oxygen. Water is a compound made from the elements hydrogen and oxygen.

Other materials are mixtures of two or more substances. For example, salt water is a mixture of salt and water.

1 Look at the four particle pictures below. Which one represents:
  a) a liquid
  b) a gas
  c) an element
  d) a three-element compound
  e) a solid compound
  f) a liquid compound?

A

B

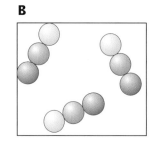

C

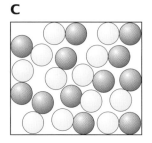

D

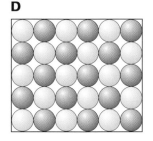

2 Make a list of as many elements as you can think of. Check with others in your group.

3 Name five compounds and state the elements found in each compound.

➡ # *Compounds and their elements*

Sodium chloride

When hot sodium is placed in chlorine, it burns with a yellow flame to form a white solid.

sodium + chlorine → sodium chloride

There has been a chemical change and the new substance, the compound sodium chloride, looks and behaves very differently from the elements.

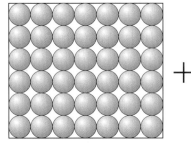 + 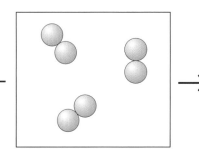 →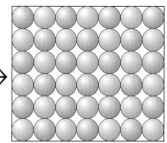

The element sodium. A very reactive metal which can explode in water.

The element chlorine. A very reactive, poisonous gas which is quite soluble in water.

The compound sodium chloride (common salt). Not very reactive. A white solid, used in our food to improve the flavour.

In Book 1 we looked at the idea of **ratio** when learning about microscope lenses and also dissolving. For example, a solution of 5 g of sugar in 20 cm^3 of water has a ratio of sugar to water of 5 : 20, which is the same as 1 : 4.

1 a) How many sodium particles and chlorine particles are there in the particle picture of sodium chloride?
b) What is the simplest ratio of sodium : chlorine?

This ratio is always the same for sodium chloride, no matter how much you have, wherever it is found and however it is made. When the ratio of one variable to another is always the same we say that one variable is **proportional** to the other. This is why the formula for sodium chloride is NaCl. For every sodium particle there is one chlorine particle in sodium chloride.

Water

When the colourless gas hydrogen is mixed in a test tube with the colourless gas oxygen and then lit, a small explosion occurs and water vapour is formed.

hydrogen + oxygen → water

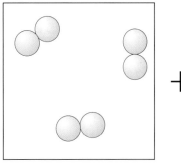 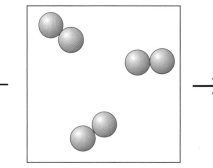 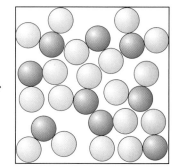

The element hydrogen. A very reactive gas which forms an explosive mixture with air.

The element oxygen. A very reactive gas which causes fierce fires.

The compound water. Not very reactive. All living things need water to survive.

2 **a)** How many hydrogen atoms and oxygen atoms are there in the particle picture of water?
 b) What is the simplest ratio of hydrogen : oxygen in water?
 c) The formula for hydrogen is H_2 and for oxygen is O_2. What do you think the formula for water is?

We can use particle pictures of water vapour to work out the ratio of hydrogen : oxygen in different numbers of water molecules:

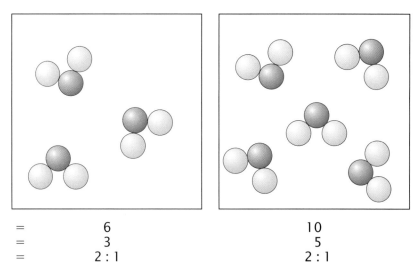

Total number of hydrogen atoms	=	6	10
Total number of oxygen atoms	=	3	5
Ratio of hydrogen : oxygen	=	2 : 1	2 : 1

The ratio of hydrogen : oxygen is always the same for water. The number of hydrogen particles is proportional to the number of oxygen particles. The formula for water is H_2O.

Compounds and mixtures

If hydrogen and oxygen gases are mixed together and not ignited, they do not combine. Any ratio of hydrogen : oxygen can be obtained:

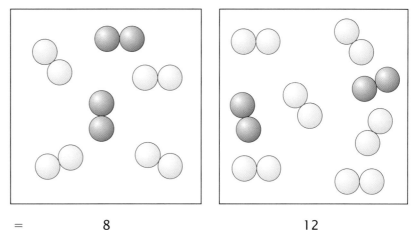

Total number of hydrogen atoms	=	8	12
Total number of oxygen atoms	=	4	4
Ratio of hydrogen : oxygen	=	2 : 1	3 : 1

- In a compound, the ratio of the different types of atoms is always the same – it is proportional.
- In a mixture, the ratio of the different types of atoms can have any value – it is not proportional.

Properties of compounds and mixtures

Look at the descriptions of hydrogen, oxygen and water on page 156. There is a difference between the properties of water and the properties of a mixture of hydrogen and oxygen.

3 Would it be possible to separate hydrogen and oxygen from:
  a) a mixture of hydrogen and oxygen
  b) water?
4 What happens if a burning match is placed in a test tube of:
  a) a mixture of hydrogen and oxygen
  b) water vapour?

Do compounds react?

So far in this chapter, we have looked at chemical reactions between two elements, but in your earlier work there have been lots of examples of compounds reacting together. For example, limestone (calcium carbonate) reacts with an acid. You can tell that a reaction is happening because bubbles of a gas are formed.

5 There are many different types of observations that can tell you that a reaction is happening. Can you think of some?

Limestone reacting with acid.

→ *How do reactions happen?*

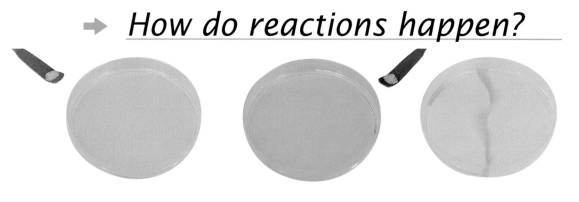

A spatula end of white lead nitrate powder is placed in the water at one side.

A spatula end of white potassium iodide powder is placed in the water at the other side.

After a short time, a band of yellow powder appears.

The above photographs show a chemical reaction in which lead nitrate has reacted with potassium iodide to form a yellow substance (lead iodide).

Use the particle theory to try to answer the following questions.

6 Which two elements are present in the compound lead iodide?

7 Where has the lead come from and where has the iodine come from to make the lead iodide?

8 How did the lead and the iodine get into the middle of the dish?

9 What must happen for lead iodide to form?

Time to think   Here are some concepts and words connected with materials:

non-metals	elements
magnesium	compounds
chemical reaction	MgO
formulae	oxygen
molecules	symbols
sea water	air
metals	atoms
magnesium oxide	pure substances
mixtures	

Work in a group, make a concept map for materials, using all of the concepts and words listed above. Follow these steps 1–4:

1 Pick out the main ideas.

2 Sort the remaining words into groups belonging to the main ideas.

3 Draw the concept map, linking the words with arrows.

4 Write in a link on each arrow.

An example of how to start the concept map is shown opposite.

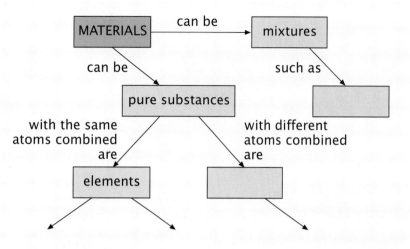

Explain your concept map to another group. Listen carefully to how they have constructed their concept map and try to ask them some questions about it.

⇒ *Elements, compounds and mixtures*

Elements	Compounds	Mixtures
sulphur	sodium chloride	granite
bromine	pure water	milk

- Elements contain only one type of atom.
- Compounds contain two or more types of atom joined together in a fixed ratio.
- Mixtures contain two or more substances mixed together.

A **B** **C** **D**

E

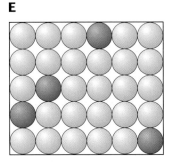

10 Which drawing **A–E** shows:
  a) a pure element
  b) a pure compound
  c) a mixture of an element and a compound
  d) a mixture of two elements
  e) a mixture of two compounds?
11 One of the drawings represents bromine.
  a) Which drawing represents bromine?
  b) What state (solid, liquid or gas) is the bromine in the drawing?
  c) How many atoms are there in each bromine molecule?

EXTENSION 12 Which drawing could be:
  a) steel (iron with a small amount of carbon)
  b) sodium chloride (NaCl)
  c) a mixture of hydrogen chloride (HCl) and carbon monoxide (CO)?

➡ *Air*

Key word
✳ atmosphere

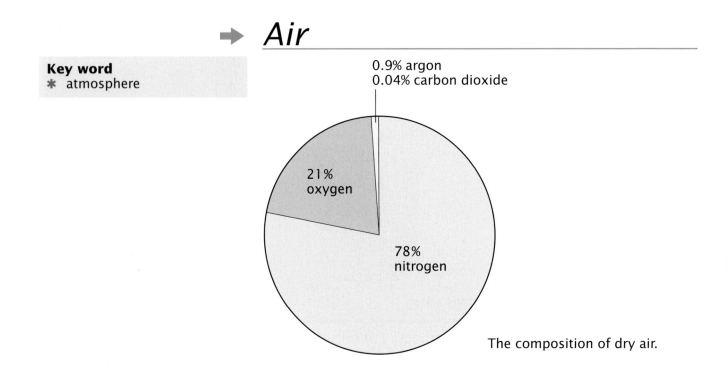

0.9% argon
0.04% carbon dioxide

21% oxygen

78% nitrogen

The composition of dry air.

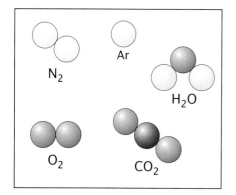

A particle picture of air.

13 a) Name three substances in air that are elements.
  b) Name one substance in air that is a compound.
  c) Name one substance in air that exists as separate atoms.
  d) Name the two elements and one compound that exist in air as molecules.

Air is one of the most important mixtures on Earth for all living things. The mixture of gases surrounding any planet is called its **atmosphere**. When the Earth was first formed about 4.5 billion years ago, the atmosphere was very different. The gases came from volcanoes and contained carbon dioxide, sulphur dioxide, nitrogen and water vapour. About 3 billion years ago, the first water plants evolved. Plants use the carbon dioxide in the air to make their food and when they do this they produce oxygen. This caused the amount of oxygen in the atmosphere to increase by a small amount. This provided enough oxygen for simple sea creatures like jellyfish or plankton to survive. Eventually land plants evolved and, by the time that the first land-living creatures had evolved, about 0.4 billion years ago, the atmosphere contained 15% oxygen. Today the atmosphere has about 20% oxygen.

14 a) Which part of the air is most important for living things?
  b) What do living things use this part of the air for?
  c) Plants also need carbon dioxide. Why?
  d) How has the atmosphere changed over the last 4.5 billion years?

This painting by Joseph Wright shows a travelling scientist in the eighteenth century demonstrating the effect on a bird of removing its air.

The components of air
All of the different gases in air have their uses.

Nitrogen
Liquid nitrogen is very cold and it is used for freezing food rapidly and for storing human tissues. Nitrogen gas is fairly unreactive, so it is sealed inside food packages to stop the food from 'going off' (see page 201).

Oxygen
Oxygen is used for patients with breathing difficulties. It is also used in steel making and in oxyacetylene welding.

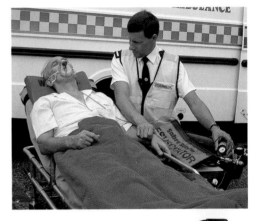

Carbon dioxide
The gas is used to supply the bubbles in fizzy drinks. It is also used to put out fires. Solid carbon dioxide is very cold and is sometimes used by ice cream sellers on beaches to stop the ice creams melting.

Argon
This gas is very unreactive and is used inside light bulbs because it does not react with the white-hot metal filament.

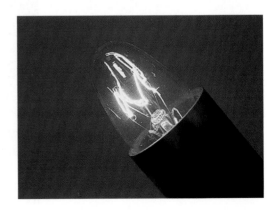

Key words
* boiling point
* fractional distillation

Separating air

Since air is a mixture of several gases, they must be separated before they can be used. In the Book 1 topic *Solutions* you saw that there are different ways of separating mixtures.

15 What method is used to separate:
   a) the coloured dyes in a green ink
   b) pure water from sea water
   c) salt from rock salt?
16 Which method would you use to separate the different substances in air?

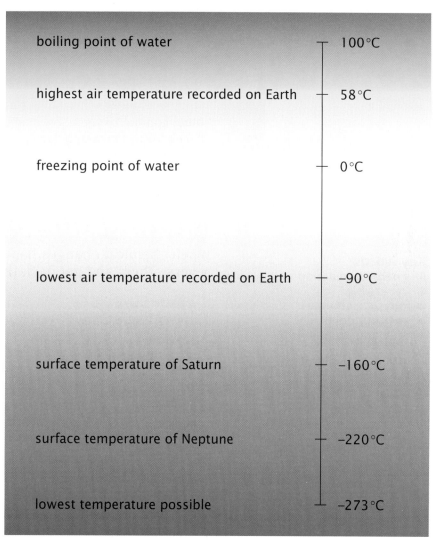

boiling point of water	100 °C
highest air temperature recorded on Earth	58 °C
freezing point of water	0 °C
lowest air temperature recorded on Earth	−90 °C
surface temperature of Saturn	−160 °C
surface temperature of Neptune	−220 °C
lowest temperature possible	−273 °C

In an air distillation plant, air is first cooled down until it forms a liquid at about −200 °C. It is then carefully warmed up. When the **boiling point** of one of the substances is reached, the particles stop behaving as they do in a liquid and become a gas. Each gas has a different boiling point. Water vapour and carbon dioxide are removed at the start of the process. Then each remaining gas can be separated in turn. This process is called **fractional distillation**.

An air distillation plant.

The boiling points of the constituent gases are:

Substance	argon	helium	nitrogen	oxygen
Boiling point (°C)	−186	−269	−196	−183

EXTENSION

17 a) The process starts at −200 °C. Which substance is still a gas at the start of the process, because it has such a low boiling point?
  b) Which substance distils first (at the lowest temperature)?
  c) Which two substances are difficult to separate because their boiling points are so close together?

DID YOU KNOW?

Scientists did not realise until the late eighteenth century that air was a mixture of gases. The French scientist Antoine Lavoisier discovered oxygen and named it after the Greek word '*oxus*' which means acid producer. He incorrectly thought that all acids must contain oxygen. The name of the gas argon comes from the Greek '*argos*' meaning 'lazy', because it would not react with any other substances.

➡ *Melting and boiling*

When chemical changes happen, it is very difficult to reverse them and get back the starting materials.

Key words
* chemical reaction
* reversible
* physical changes
* melting point
* freezing point

For example, making toast is a **chemical reaction** between the substances in the bread and the oxygen in the air. You cannot get a slice of bread back from a slice of toast. Similarly, methane (natural gas) burns in oxygen in a Bunsen burner to form carbon dioxide and water, but you cannot take the carbon dioxide and water and reform methane and oxygen. Chemical reactions are not easily **reversible**.

However, **physical changes** are reversible. Ice can be heated until it melts to form water. The water can then be cooled until it freezes to reform ice. The **melting point** of ice and the **freezing point** of water are the same, 0 °C.

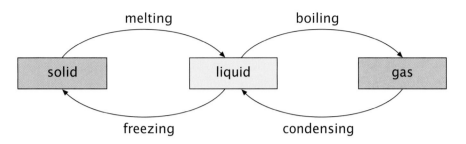

Almost all substances can exist as a solid, liquid or gas, depending on the temperature. Living on Earth, we always think of the metal lead as a solid. On the planet Venus it would normally be a liquid because the surface temperature of the planet is roughly 470 °C and the melting point of lead is 328 °C.

Melting and boiling points of some common substances

Substance	Melting point (°C)	Boiling point (°C)
aluminium	660	2467
ammonia	−80	−33
chlorine	−101	−35
helium	−272	−269
hydrogen	−259	−253
iron	1535	2750
lead	328	1740
methane	−182	−164
nitrogen	−210	−196
silicon dioxide (sand)	1610	2230
sodium chloride	801	1413
sulphur	119	445
water	0	100

Reasoning *Solid, liquid or gas?*

Room temperature is about 20 °C.

1 Which of the substances in the table above would be solids at room temperature? What do you notice about the melting points of these solids?

2 Which of the substances in the table would be gases at room temperature? What do you notice about the boiling points of these substances?

3 Use the data in the table to explain why water is a liquid at room temperature.

Reasoning *Different planets*

Approximate surface temperatures of some planets in the Solar System

Planet	Approximate surface temperature (°C)
Mercury	170
Venus	470
Earth	15
Mars	−60
Jupiter	−140
Neptune	−220

Use the data in this table and the table on page 165 to answer the following questions about the states of the substances on different planets. In each case, write a sentence to explain your reasoning.

1 On which planet would sulphur be:
   a) a liquid   **b)** a gas?

2 On which planets would ammonia be:
   a) a solid   **b)** a liquid   **c)** a gas?

3 Why is Earth the only planet with liquid water?

EXTENSION   **4** Which two substances could be in the atmosphere of Neptune?

➡ *Boiling pure substances and mixtures*

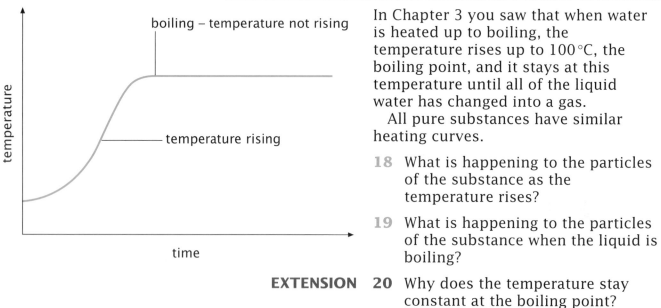

boiling – temperature not rising

temperature rising

temperature

time

In Chapter 3 you saw that when water is heated up to boiling, the temperature rises up to 100 °C, the boiling point, and it stays at this temperature until all of the liquid water has changed into a gas.

All pure substances have similar heating curves.

18 What is happening to the particles of the substance as the temperature rises?

19 What is happening to the particles of the substance when the liquid is boiling?

EXTENSION   **20** Why does the temperature stay constant at the boiling point?

Do mixtures show a similar heating curve?

A group of pupils decided to investigate this question using common salt and water as the mixture. They first had a quick discussion about salty water:

1 If Ben is right, what does salt do to the boiling point of water? Does it make it higher or lower?

2 If Ellie is right, what does salt do to the boiling point of water? Does it make it higher or lower?

Ben and Sophie decided to carry out an investigation:

- They took 100 cm³ of water in a measuring cylinder and poured it into a beaker.
- They weighed out 10.0 g of common salt and dissolved it in the water.
- They then heated the solution and measured the temperature every minute.

3 What is the input variable and what is the outcome variable?

This is their results table:

Time (min)	0	1	2	3	4	5	6	7	8	9	10
Temperature (°C)	20	33	54	75	92	100	102	103	104	104	105

Processing
4 Draw a graph of these results. Remember that the input variable goes on the horizontal axis.

Interpretation
5 What does the graph show?

Conclusion

6 Do mixtures show a similar pattern to pure liquids when they are heated?

Ellie and Tom decided to carry out an investigation as follows:

- They measured out 100 cm³ of water from a measuring cylinder into each of three beakers.
- They then weighed out different amounts of salt for each beaker.
- They heated up the solutions until they boiled and measured the boiling point.

This is their results table:

Mass of salt dissolved in the water (g)	10	20	30
Boiling point (°C)	102	103	106

Interpretation

7 Is there a pattern to these results? What is the pattern?

Conclusion

8 Do mixtures show a similar pattern to pure liquids when they are heated?

Evaluation

9 Was the method used by Ellie and Tom a fair test? Explain your answer.

10 How could you improve Ellie and Tom's method to give more reliable values for the temperatures?

11 How could you improve Ellie and Tom's method so that they could plot a line graph of their results?

Testing for purity

- Pure substances have fixed boiling points.
- Mixtures do not have fixed boiling points. This is because they can contain different amounts of a number of substances.

These facts can be used as a test for the purity of a substance. For example, pure water will boil at a fixed temperature (100 °C) until it has fully evaporated. Salt water will boil at a temperature above 100 °C and the boiling point will continue to rise as the water evaporates.

Similarly, the freezing/melting point of a pure substance is fixed. Pure water forms ice at 0 °C but sea water has to drop several degrees below this before it starts to freeze. This can also be used as a test for purity. The liquid under test is cooled in a container which is surrounded by a cooling mixture of ice, water and salt. The temperature of the liquid is measured regularly and a cooling curve is plotted.

Enquiry ## Which liquid is pure?

Working in a group, discuss how you would solve the following problem.

You are given about $10\,cm^3$ of each of two liquids labelled **X** and **Y**. One is a pure liquid and the other is a mixture of this liquid and another substance dissolved in it. Make a plan to find out which one is the pure substance and to measure its freezing point.

You should note down:

- what equipment you will need
- each step in your method
- how often you will take a reading
- an outline of your results tables.

EXTENSION Sketch an outline of the graph that you would expect for the pure substance. Label the axes of your graph and give the graph a title.

Time to think

1 Make a list of 20 materials.
   a) Use a red colour to indicate which materials are elements.
   b) Use a blue colour to indicate which materials are compounds.
   c) Use a green colour to indicate which materials are mixtures.
   d) Which of your materials are solids? What does this tell you about their melting points?
   e) Do any of your materials have boiling points below room temperature? How do you know?

2 Invent a game that will help people to remember whether materials are:
   - pure or mixtures
   - elements or compounds
   - gases, liquids or solids.
   Try out each others' games and evaluate them.

8 *Light*

In this chapter you will learn:

→ that light travels in a straight line at a fixed speed in a particular material
→ that non-luminous objects are seen because light scattered from them enters the eye
→ how light is reflected at flat surfaces
→ how light is refracted at the boundary between two different materials
→ that white light can be split to give a range of colours
→ about the effect of colour filters on white light, and how coloured objects appear in white light and in other coloured lights
→ how the eye works

You will also develop your skills in:

→ choosing the scales for axes and graphs
→ plotting non-linear graphs
→ interpreting the patterns in data
→ using ratios
→ choosing an appropriate range of data to be collected in experiments
→ planning experiments using dataloggers

→ → → WHAT DO YOU KNOW?

The drawing shows a room without windows; there is a ceiling light and a clock on the mantle shelf. Copy the drawing. Draw in lines with arrows to show how the person sees the time on the clock. Explain what the lines represent and write a sentence of explanation.

1 Which of the following are sources of light?

Moon	mirror
Mars	candle flame
Sun	laser
fluorescent tube	tungsten lamp
glow-worm	TV set

2 Discuss the following topics with a partner to see how much you know already:
- how shadows are formed
- how mirrors work
- how lenses work.

DID YOU KNOW?

Light travels at about 300 thousand kilometres every second in air. This means that the light from the Sun takes about $8\frac{1}{2}$ minutes to reach the Earth.

→ *Light travels in straight lines*

Key word
* ray

We know that light travels in straight lines. But how can we show this? You may have seen the demonstration shown in the photo (left), with a laser and a box containing smoke. The path of the light through the smoke can be seen. The smoke particles scatter some of the light and this then allows you to see where the beam of light is travelling. At a disco or open-air concert, smoke generators are often used to show the laser beams.

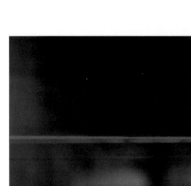

DID YOU KNOW?

The word laser comes from:

Light **A**mplification by **S**timulated **E**mission of **R**adiation

We call a very narrow beam of light a **ray**. The ray travels in a straight line from the light source.

1 A shadow is formed when an object blocks rays of light. You can use the length of a shadow to calculate the height of an object. Look at the picture below. The stick is 1 m high, and it has a shadow that measures 1.5 m long. The shadow of the flagpole is 30 m long. Can you work out how tall the flagpole is?

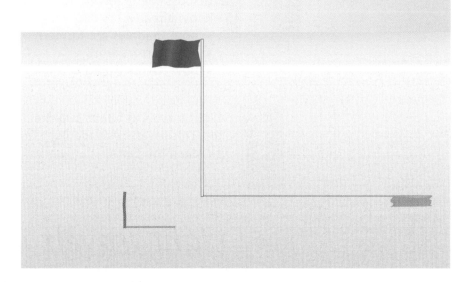

The pinhole camera

At one time the construction of a pinhole camera was a popular activity in science lessons. In fact, you may have made one yourself. The earliest mention of this type of device was by the Chinese **philosopher** Mo-Ti in the fifth century BC. He recorded the creation of an **inverted** image formed by light passing through a small hole into a darkened room. He called this darkened room a 'collecting place' or the 'locked treasure room'. In Europe it was called a 'camera obscura', from the Latin for dark chamber (*camera* is Latin for chamber or room, *obscura* is Latin for dark). Aristotle (384–322BC) also understood how the camera obscura worked.

The tenth century Arabian scholar Alhazen of Basra had a portable tent room for solar observation and gave a full account of the **principle** of the camera obscura. In 1490, Leonardo da Vinci gave two clear descriptions of the camera obscura in his notebooks. Many of the first camera obscuras were large rooms like that illustrated by the Dutch scientist Reinerus Gemma-Frisius in 1544 for use in observing a solar eclipse.

Experiments with lenses and mirrors led to further developments of the camera obscura. In the sixteenth century an Italian, Giovanni Battista Porta, created a portable camera obscura as an aid for drawing. There is a story that he also made a huge 'camera' in which he seated his guests, having arranged for a group of actors to perform outside so that the visitors could observe the images on the wall. But the sight of upside down performing images was too much for the visitors; they panicked and fled, and Battista was later brought to court on a charge of sorcery!

The engraving (left) shows a camera obscura used by the Jesuit scientist Athanasius Kircher (1602–1680). Camera obscuras were used mainly by scientists, artists or as playthings of the rich until the eighteenth century, when they then became a more popular attraction, increasingly appearing on seafronts.

Once photography had been invented, light sensitive papers and chemicals allowed images seen in portable camera obscuras (or pinhole cameras) to be fixed permanently.

Pinhole photography depends on the principle that light travels in straight lines. A dark room is all that is required to view the effect. When a small hole lets light rays enter a darkened room, an upside-down image of the world outside is seen on the opposite wall. A small box version of this 'walk-in' pinhole camera can be constructed which behaves in the same way.

1 Look at the diagram showing a simple pinhole camera. It shows an (inverted) image of a distant tree. If the length of the camera is 15 cm and the height of the image is 6 cm, how tall is the tree if it is 30 m from the pinhole in the camera?

2 If the person holding the camera moved it 10 m further away from the tree, would the image look bigger or smaller than before? How much will its size have changed?

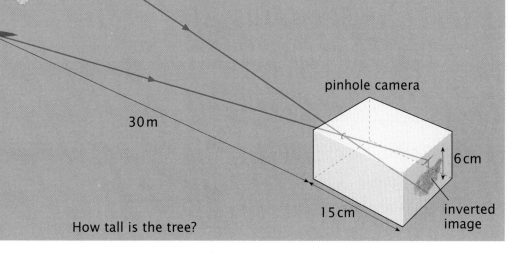

30 m

pinhole camera

6 cm

15 cm

inverted image

How tall is the tree?

The transmission of light

Key words
* transparent
* translucent
* transmit
* opaque

Both **transparent** and **translucent** materials allow light to pass through them. They **transmit** light. Transparent materials let light through and do not form a shadow. Examples are clear glass and Perspex. Translucent materials allow light through, but you cannot see details through them. Examples are frosted glass, such as you might see in a bathroom window, and tissue paper. A translucent object can form a shadow, but it will not be very dark or sharp.

Opaque materials do not transmit light. They form sharp, dark shadows.

DID YOU KNOW?

A light year is the distance that light would travel in one year. Some galaxies are so far away that the light we see started its journey towards the Earth millions of years ago.

Information processing Investigating light

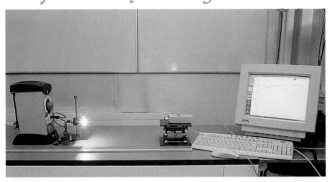

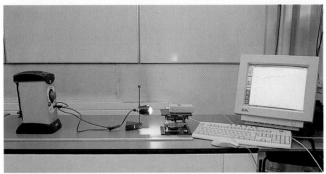

The photo shows the equipment used by some pupils to investigate how the brightness of a lamp changes as you move further away from it. Their results are shown in the table. The light sensor was placed at different distances, and at each distance a reading was taken of the light level.

Distance of sensor from lamp (cm)	Relative light level
20	27
30	13
40	8
50	6
60	5
70	4
80	3.3
90	2.3
100	2.0

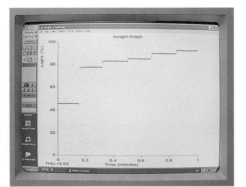

1 Plot a graph of the results in the table. You can either plot it by hand or use a spreadsheet.

2 What are the variables in this investigation?

3 Was this a fair test? Why?

4 Write a sentence to explain how the light level changes with the distance from the lamp.

You can use a light sensor like this to perform a variety of investigations. Here are a few suggestions:

- Which of a range of light sources is the brightest?
- How much light passes through different sorts of sunglasses?
- How much light is transmitted through different translucent materials such as polythene, frosted glass, greaseproof paper?

5 Choose one of these investigations and write a brief outline of your method. Construct the results table that you might use.

➡ *The reflection of light*

Key words
* reflected
* plane

When a ray of light is bounced away from a shiny surface we say that it has been **reflected**.

An object can only be seen if light from it enters our eyes. So, to see this page, for example, light from the Sun or a lamp is reflected off the surface of the page and into your eyes. Because the surface is not perfectly smooth, the rays of light are reflected in many different directions. If a surface is very smooth, such as a piece of polished metal or a mirror, the light is reflected in a definite direction.

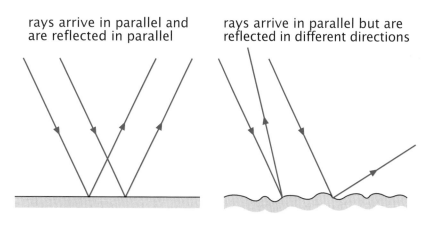

rays arrive in parallel and are reflected in parallel

rays arrive in parallel but are reflected in different directions

Reflection from a smooth surface. Reflection from a rough surface.

You may have used a ray box to show how light travels. An example of one in use is shown in the picture overleaf. The slit in the box lets through a narrow ray of light from the bulb. The light ray shows up on the sheet of paper that the equipment is sitting on. As you already know, the light travels in a straight line. The light ray hits the **plane** (flat) mirror and is reflected from it.

Because the plane mirror has a flat, smooth surface, it reflects light well. When a ray of light hits it at an angle, you can see that it bounces off at the same angle.

Light bounces off a smooth reflecting surface like balls bouncing off a smooth wall or snooker balls hitting the table cushion. A smooth wall reflects the balls regularly, but they would be randomly scattered by a rough wall. Think of throwing a ball against a rough rock face. It would not be possible to predict the direction in which it would bounce off.

There are a number of simulations available on the internet where you can investigate the effect of shining a ray of light at a plane mirror and observe how it is reflected.

The law of reflection

Key words
* normal
* incident
* angle of incidence

To show where a ray of light will go when it is reflected by a plane mirror, a line called the **normal** is drawn at right angles (90°) to the mirror. The ray shining onto the mirror is called the **incident** ray, and the ray that bounces off the mirror is called the reflected ray. The two angles that scientists measure are not the angles between the rays and the mirror but the angles between the rays and the normal to the mirror. The two angles each side of the normal are called the **angle of incidence** and the angle of reflection, and they are equal. This is called the law of reflection:

angle of incidence = angle of reflection

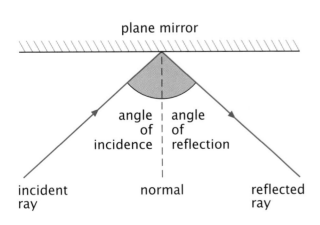

Where is the image?

The drawing shows how to locate the image of a whiteboard marker pen using a second marker pen. When the part of pen 2 above the mirror appears exactly in line with the part of pen 1 seen in the mirror, wherever the eye is located, then pen 2 is at the position of the image of pen 1.

Illusions

Key word
✳ illusion

We can use mirrors to create an **illusion**. Often the mirrors are placed at angles. The use of two mirrors at 45° to the incident light is illustrated by the simple periscope.

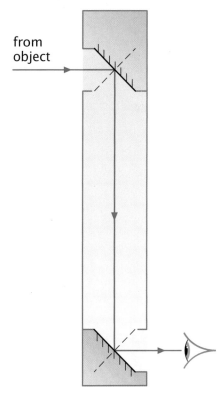

A simple periscope.

'Pepper's Ghost' is one illusion you can set up. The candle looks as if it is alight in the water, but the flame seen in the water is not real. The flame is an image set up by the reflecting glass. In the theatre, ghosts can be made to appear on stage using a similar method.

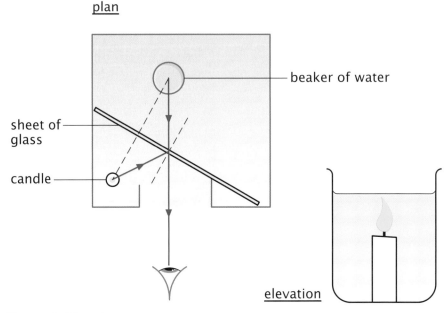

'Pepper's Ghost'.

Other illusions make use of an arrangement of several mirrors. The next diagram shows the arrangement for the old illusion of 'looking through a brick'.

2 Can you explain how this illusion works?

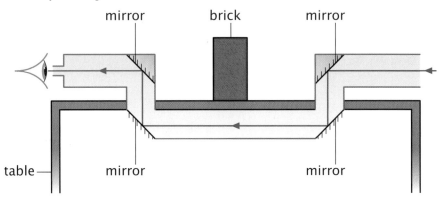

'Looking through a brick'.

→ *The refraction of light*

Key words
* refracted
* refraction
* total internal reflection

Light will pass through transparent materials such as glass and water. But light may be bent as it travels across the boundary between two materials, for example from air to glass. We say that the light is **refracted**. **Refraction** is the name given to the change in direction of light as it passes from one transparent material to another.

The diagram shows a ray of light passing through a glass block. The reason that the light is bent or refracted as it leaves the block is because it travels more slowly in the glass than in the air. Look at the direction in which the light bends when it travels from the glass into the air. The dotted line is the normal. As you can see, when the light travels from glass to air it bends away from the normal.

Note that the light is not refracted as it enters the semi-circular block because it is incident along a radius, that is, along the normal of the curved surface.

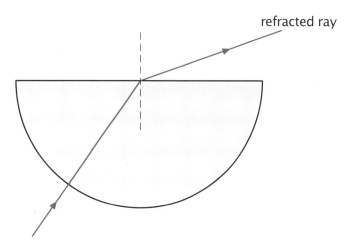

refracted ray

Measuring refraction

You may have plotted the path of light rays through rectangular and semi-circular glass blocks. The results obtained by a group of pupils are shown in the table.

Use these results to draw the paths taken by the rays through a semi-circular glass block. The rays of light enter the block along a radius. This means that they do not bend on entering the glass block, only on leaving it.

Angle in glass	Angle in air
10°	15°
20°	31°
30°	49°
40°	75°

If you look carefully at the photos on the previous page, you may see that as well as the light that is refracted out of the glass, there is also some light reflected back. In some situations all of the light is reflected, and this is clearly shown in the diagram below. This is called **total internal reflection**.

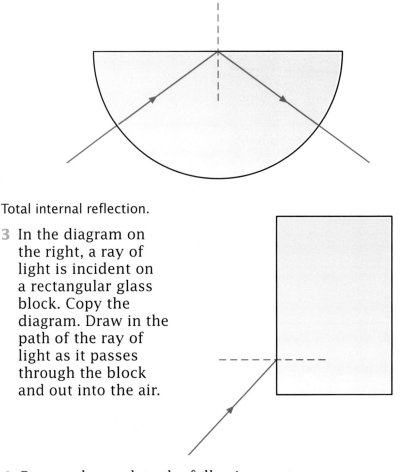

Total internal reflection.

3 In the diagram on the right, a ray of light is incident on a rectangular glass block. Copy the diagram. Draw in the path of the ray of light as it passes through the block and out into the air.

4 Copy and complete the following sentence:
As the light ray hits the surface of the glass block, some light is _____ but the rest passes into the glass block and is bent _____ the normal drawn in the block. At the far side of the glass block, the light travels from the glass into the air and it is bent _____ the normal drawn in the air.

The second normal was not drawn on the diagram, but you should have included it on your completed diagram. If you had drawn this accurately using real results, you would notice that the ray of light emerging from the glass block is travelling in the same direction as the ray of light entering the glass block. It is, however, displaced sideways. It is parallel to the ray entering the block.

Objects can appear bent when partially immersed in water. This is because of the refraction of light. The photo shows the appearance of a pencil in water, and the diagram shows what is happening to the light.

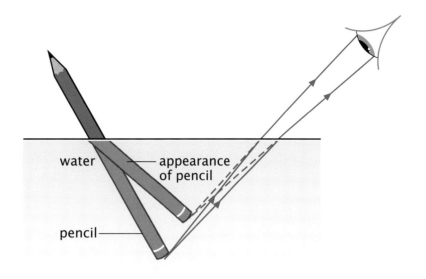

You can use this idea to perform the trick of 'the appearing coin'. A coin is placed at the bottom of a sink or bowl. You step back until the coin is just out of view. When someone fills the sink with water (carefully, without moving the coin), the coin becomes visible.

5 The drawing shows what is happening. Can you explain it?

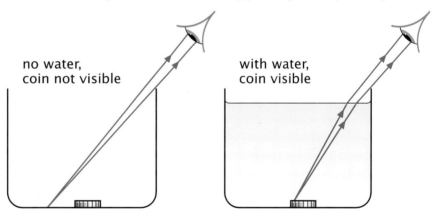

<u>*Time to think*</u>

In this chapter so far, you have looked at:

- the pinhole camera and camera obscura
- the reflection of light
- illusions using mirrors
- the refraction of light.

Get into a group of four and each choose one of the above topics for a 3-minute presentation. Take it in turns to give your presentation to the other members of your group. After each one, the rest of the group 'traffic light' the performance:

Green means a clear explanation has been given with all the correct scientific terms.
Amber means a reasonable explanation has been given, but some terms have been missed out or used incorrectly.
Red means the explanation was not clear.

Make sure the reasons for red or amber scores are explained. If you score amber or red, use the advice given to you to write an improved draft of your presentation. If you score green, then select a second topic to prepare for presentation.

Understanding light

Science is an ever-growing and continually challenged set of ideas. One of the first scientists that we know who worked on light was Ibn-Al-Haitham or Alhazen. He was born in 965 in Basra, Persia (now Iraq) and was educated in Basra and Baghdad. He then spent most of his life in Spain, and there conducted research in optics, mathematics, physics, medicine and the development of scientific methods. He carried out experiments on the propagation of light and colours, optical illusions and reflections. He examined the refraction of light rays through transparent media (air, water) and discovered the laws of refraction.

Ibn-Al-Haitham (Alhazen) (c. 965–1040).

Sir Isaac Newton's contributions to science in the seventeenth century were enormous. It had been known for many years that white light passing through a glass prism emerges as light of many colours. But Newton was the first person to investigate it scientifically.

Isaac Newton (1642–1727).

'Nature and Nature's laws lay hid in sight;
God said, "Let Newton be", and all was light.'
Alexander Pope (1688–1744).

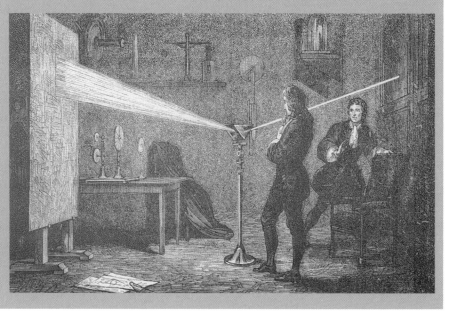

Dispersion

The splitting of white light into colours is called **dispersion**. An ordinary triangular prism can separate white light into colours. The range of colours is called a **spectrum**. Each colour making up the white light is bent, or refracted, by a different amount; those towards the violet end of the spectrum are bent the most and those towards the red end of the spectrum are bent the least.

Historically, we say that the spectrum has seven colours:

red, orange, yellow, green, blue, indigo, violet

However, many people find indigo difficult to see.

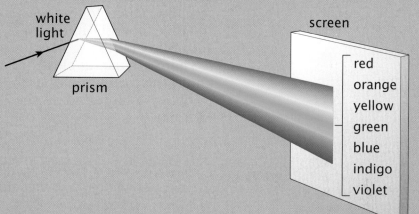

Newton performed a further experiment. Having passed the white light through the prism and split it into the colours, he then passed the separate colours through a second prism and recombined them to produce white light. This was an important experiment.

1 Why is light refracted when it travels from one medium to another?
2 What is an optical illusion?
3 Why does a prism split white light into coloured light?
4 Some people thought that the prism was responsible for putting the colours into the white light. How did Newton's experiment show that this was not the case?

Word play

Mnemosyne was the Greek goddess of memory and mother of the nine Muses. The Greek word 'mnemon' means mindful. This is the origin of the word mnemonic.

Here is an example of a mnemonic. The first letter of each word gives you the first letter of the planets, in order: Mercury, Venus, Earth, Mars, Jupiter, Saturn, Uranus, Neptune, Pluto.

My **V**ery **E**ducated **M**other **J**ust **S**erved **U**s **N**ine **P**izzas

Mnemonics are a useful aid to memory. Here is one to help you remember the colours of the spectrum: red, orange, yellow, green, blue, indigo, violet.

Richard **O**f **Y**ork **G**ave **B**attle **I**n **V**ain

Do you know any others?

Rainbows

Rainbows are formed when rays of light from the Sun are refracted in raindrops. To see a rainbow, the Sun needs to be behind you and the arc of the rainbow will then be in front of you. Sometimes more than one rainbow can be seen. The photo shows a primary rainbow and you can also see a faint secondary rainbow. The colours are in the reverse order in the secondary rainbow.

There are useful clips about the formation of a rainbow to be found on the internet.

 Here are some of the key words of this chapter in a word spiral. Can you find them and then think up some good clues?

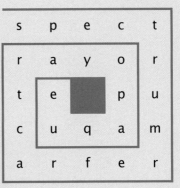

EXTENSION
Make up your own word spiral using other key words from this chapter.

Colours and colour mixing

Key words
* absorbs
* primary colours
* secondary colours
* receptors
* cones

An object looks the colour it does because it reflects (or, if it is transparent, transmits) the colour we see and it **absorbs** all the other colours. A red shirt looks red because it reflects red light and absorbs the rest. If you shine yellow light (which contains green and red light) onto a green jumper, the jumper absorbs the red light and reflects the green light, and so it appears green.

We need to be clear about the difference between mixing coloured paints and mixing coloured lights.

- The three **primary colours** of light are red, blue and green. These colours cannot be made by mixing any other colours of light together.
- The primary colours are combined in equal amounts to form the **secondary colours**. The secondary colours are yellow, magenta and cyan. Magenta is a sort of purple; cyan is a sort of turquoise.

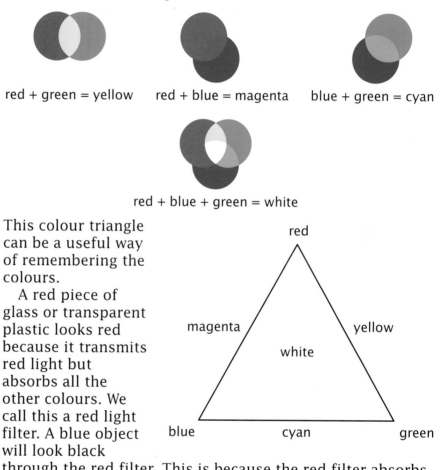

red + green = yellow   red + blue = magenta   blue + green = cyan

red + blue + green = white

This colour triangle can be a useful way of remembering the colours.

A red piece of glass or transparent plastic looks red because it transmits red light but absorbs all the other colours. We call this a red light filter. A blue object will look black through the red filter. This is because the red filter absorbs the blue light coming from the object. A green object would also look black, while a white object would appear red. A yellow filter allows both red and green light through.

6 What are the three primary colours of light?
7 What colour would a red object appear through a blue filter? Why?
8 If you had a cyan filter, which primary light colour would it absorb? Which two colours would it allow through?

EXTENSION 9 a) If a red object was viewed through a cyan filter, what colour would it appear? Why?
      b) What colour would a blue object appear? Why?
      c) What colour would a white object appear? Why?

The human eye has light sensitive cells or **receptors**, called **cones**. There are three types of cone. Each cone is sensitive to a different part of the spectrum of white light: the three primary colours red, green and blue. The brain interprets other colours by combinations of stimulations to each of these three colour receptors.

→ *Optical illusions and the eye*

Eyes are the receptors for light but it is the brain that 'sees'. Sometimes our brains can see things in different ways; these are optical illusions. Look at the pictures below – can your brain see each one in more than one way?

'Liar'.

Find 'the hidden tiger'.

Old woman or young girl?
Hint – The old woman's
nose is the young girl's chin.

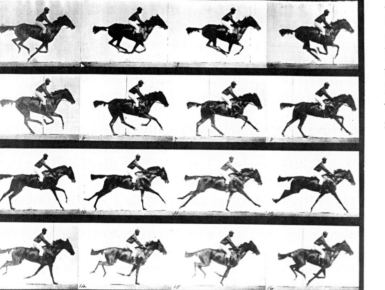

Another type of optical illusion
depends on the delay between
successive images being processed
by our eyes and brain. We use this
when we watch a film. There are
25 frames shown every second but
we are unable to see them as
separate pictures.

Some of the earliest moving images made use of this. Here
is an example that you can easily make yourself. It shows a
cage with a bird apparently inside it. The drawings are
made on two circles of card which are then glued together
and twirled round and round on twisted threads.

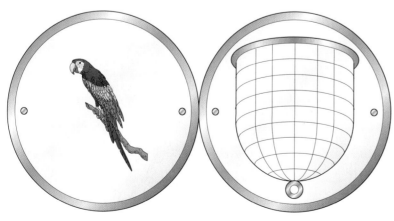

To send information from the eyes to the brain, electrical impulses travel along the **optic nerve**. The position near the back of each eye where the optic nerve leaves is called the 'blind spot'. This is because there are no receptors here to detect light. We are normally not aware of this because our brain automatically fills in the missing bits. However, we can fool our brain and show its existence with the following experiment. Below there is a dot and cross. Close your left eye. Look at the spot with your right eye, holding the book at arm's length. Slowly bring the book nearer to you. At some point the cross will disappear. The image of the cross is at your blind spot. Then as you continue to bring the book nearer the cross will reappear.

●   +

EXTENSION

Key words
* cornea
* retina
* iris
* pupil

The eye

Our eyes are almost spherical. When we see an object it is because light from the object has entered our eyes. First the light passes through the **cornea**, which is transparent. Then it passes through the lens, and finally it falls on the back of the eye or **retina**. The retina contains thousands of light sensitive cells. Nerves lead from each of these cells to the optic nerve, which then travels to the brain.

The **iris** is the distinctive coloured ring at the front of the eye, with a hole in the middle. It controls the amount of light entering the eye. It is a bluish or brownish colour in most people. The hole in the middle of the iris is called the **pupil**. The muscles of the iris change the pupil's size. In bright light the pupil is very small to limit the light entering the eye. In a dark room the iris contracts (shrinks). This means that the pupil becomes larger, letting in more light.

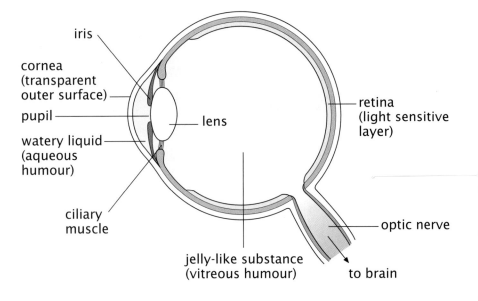

Most of the eye is filled with a clear jelly-like substance. Just as in a pinhole camera, the image on the retina (the back of the eye) is upside down. Our brain interprets the image so that we see things the right way up.

Time to think

Think about the ideas you have read about and the activities you have done in this chapter.

- What has been the most interesting part of the chapter for you? Why?
- Can you list any new ideas or facts that you have learned in this chapter? Show other people in your group your list and check theirs. Have they learned the same new things as you?
- Which part of the work in this chapter did you find most difficult? Work with a friend to try and sort out any problems or misunderstandings you have. If you still have any problems, check with your teacher.

9 Microbes and disease

In this chapter you will learn:

➜ that most micro-organisms have the same characteristics as other living things
➜ that viruses are living because they reproduce
➜ how micro-organisms can make useful products
➜ how some micro-organisms can cause diseases and illness
➜ how the human body can defend itself from infections caused by micro-organisms
➜ what immunisation is and how vaccines work
➜ how some common diseases are transmitted

You will also develop your skills in:

➜ carrying out practical investigations safely and hygienically
➜ collecting sufficient and reliable data
➜ identifying and controlling variables
➜ designing investigations
➜ explaining results and observations, using hypotheses
➜ creative writing

➡ ➡ ➡ WHAT DO YOU KNOW?

Key word
* micro-organism
* microbe

Look at the photos. Each shows a **micro-organism**, or something a micro-organism (or **microbe**) has created. Some photos show helpful things and some show harmful things. Make a two-column table listing helpful and harmful effects of microbes. The first entries have been completed as an example.

Helpful	Harmful
Bread made with yeast	Mould growing on bread

fungus

fungus

fungus

bacteria

fungus and bacteria

fungus

bacteria and fungus

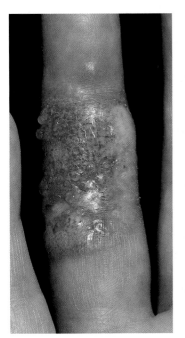

virus

virus

virus

Word play

Discuss in your group what you think each of these words means:

- germs
- bacteria
- microbes
- micro-organisms
- bugs

Imagine you are writing a 'Dreaded diseases dictionary'. What entries would you make for each of these words? You might like to illustrate your definitions and perhaps write a sentence showing the word in use.

What are micro-organisms?

Scientists group living things into five **kingdoms**:
* animals
* plants
* **fungi**
* **protista**
* **bacteria**

Micro-organisms are found in all five of these kingdoms. Most micro-organisms exist as single cells or unspecialised groups of cells. Protista are one-celled organisms. Micro-organisms are usually difficult to see without the aid of some form of technology, such as a magnifying glass or microscope.

Bacteria are among the most numerous organisms on Earth. They are found in almost every environment and are both helpful and harmful to humans. Bacteria can be classified into three groups determined by their shape. Some are shaped like spheres, some like rods and some like spirals. Most are 0.5 to 1.5 micrometres in size.

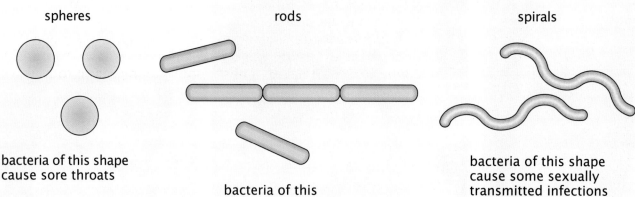

spheres

bacteria of this shape cause sore throats

rods

bacteria of this shape cause typhoid

spirals

bacteria of this shape cause some sexually transmitted infections e.g. syphilis

The three groups of bacteria.

Bacteria and protista are types of micro-organisms. They are living things, so they show all the characteristics of life.

1 Do you remember the seven characteristics of life?

In the past, scientists thought that **viruses** were non-living because they do not have a cell structure. The only sign of life they show is the ability to reproduce. However, they are now classified as micro-organisms.

2 **a)** Do viruses feed?
 b) Which characteristic(s) of life do viruses show?
3 Where do you think fungi get their food? Look again at the photos on pages 190 and 191 if you need help.

→ *Useful micro-organisms*

Bacteria help create silage. This is a rich fermented grass product that is made by farmers to feed their animals through winter. You will see huge black plastic rolls of silage in fields.

Silage bales provide winter feed.

Antibiotics are substances produced by micro-organisms that kill other types of disease-causing bacteria or prevent them from multiplying. Penicillin-based antibiotics are produced by penicillin fungus. Some antibiotics come from bacteria. Antibiotics can cause **allergic** reactions in some people. These people cannot use antibiotics to treat infections.

High quality vinegar is made when bacteria turn wine into ethanoic acid. Butter, yoghurt and cheeses are made when bacteria make milk go sour, turning milk sugar (lactose) to lactic acid.

Yeast, a fungus, is used to make bread, beer and wine.

Bacteria and fungi can be used to create new protein-rich foods for vegetarians. These foods can be made to look and taste like meats.

INGREDIENTS
Mycoprotein*(88%), rehydrated egg white (free range), roasted barley malt extract.

*Mushroom protein.
 Not a GMO.

Bacteria are used to treat sewage so that solid waste is converted to harmless sludge and a smelly gas called methane.

Insulin, a drug that helps people suffering from diabetes to control their blood sugar levels, has recently been produced using bacteria.

Sewage treatment works rely on micro-organisms.

4 Why is yeast an important micro-organism in the food industry?

5 What is mycoprotein used for?

6 How are bacteria important in sewage treatment?

Reasoning ## Yeast – an amazing fungus

Here are five slices of bread, each from a different loaf baked in the research and development laboratories of Harvest Time Loaves Ltd. Beside each is a checklist of ingredients that were used to make each loaf, a note of the temperature at which each was proved (left to rise), and a taster's comments. The same amount of flour was used for each loaf.

		sugar	yeast	temperature for proving
A *nice texture*		✓	✓	*25°C*
B *not as nice as first slice*		✓	✓	*5°C*
C *denser texture*		✗	✓	*25°C*
D *dense, unrisen*		✓	✗	*5°C*
E *dense, unrisen*		✓	✓	*100°C*

1 Which loaf would you recommend for mass production? Why?

2 Why is yeast important in bread making?

3 What are the input variables in this investigation?

4 What are the outcome variables?

5 Is this a good investigation for the company to use to change its recipe for bread?

6 How could you provide the company with more reliable information? Make a short report for the company, saying what other investigations you think they should carry out to improve their bread-making process.

Damaging micro-organisms

Some micro-organisms cause diseases. We sometimes call these '**germs**'. Diseases make us ill. The signs of **infection** may include a headache, a sore throat, a rash, swollen glands, or fever (high temperature). These are all called **symptoms**.

What causes disease?

In the middle of the nineteenth century, the French scientist Louis Pasteur discovered that there are micro-organisms in the air and that they are responsible for making food go bad. He suggested that they might also cause disease. Previously many people had thought that diseases were punishments from God or that they were caused by bad smells.

A German doctor called Robert Koch (1843–1910) subsequently showed that cholera and tuberculosis are caused by types of bacteria. He took blood samples from patients with these diseases and grew them on agar jelly. He then injected some of the growing bacterium into mice and they caught the same diseases.

Robert Koch.

Micro-organisms that cause diseases are called **pathogens**, from the Greek word meaning 'to create suffering'.

7 How could a doctor on the telephone diagnose that the person has a throat infection?

8 What is the scientific word for germs?

DID YOU KNOW?

In 1977 scientists tested Martian soil for germs but found none. Germs have been found on the Moon, and Moon dust contains chemicals that kill germs.

Key words
* amoeba
* pseudopodia
* dysentery
* chlorophyll
* parasites
* retroviruses
* prion

Meet the pathogens

Amoeba

The **amoeba** is a one-celled organism (of the kingdom protista) that changes shape as it moves about. It is propelled by **pseudopodia**, temporary 'feet' that form from bulges in the cell membrane. It causes amoebic **dysentery**, a gastro-intestinal disease, and other illnesses. In parts of the world with poor quality water supplies, amoebic dysentery kills many people.

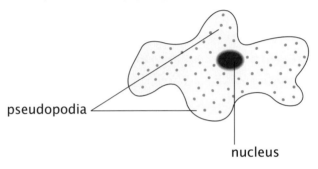

pseudopodia

nucleus

Amoeba (actual size about 1 mm).

Bacteria

Bacteria are a group of organisms that can live all around us in the air, in the soil and in water, as well as inside other organisms. They cause diseases such as strep throat, scarlet fever, typhoid, bubonic plague, tetanus, and other serious illnesses. Look at the names of lozenges sold to help ease sore throats. Their names are often based around the word 'streptococcus', the name of the bacterium that causes sore throats. Bacteria may form clumps or colonies. Although cellular, they have no nucleus. They have a strand of DNA. Bacteria reproduce by dividing. Some bacteria may be older than your great-grandfather!

Fungi

Fungi are organisms that are plant-like but contain no **chlorophyll**. They may live as single cells (for example yeasts) or as multi-cellular organisms (for example mushrooms). There are at least 40 species of fungi that cause disease in humans, including athlete's foot, ringworm and thrush.

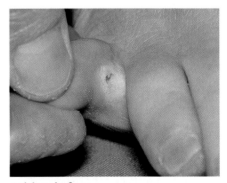

Athlete's foot.

Parasites

These include a wide range of pathogens that cause such diseases as malaria, schistosomiasis and scabies. **Parasites** are single-celled or multicellular organisms which have complicated life cycles – they must live part of their lives in another organism. Malaria parasites spend part of their life cycle in mosquitoes. They enter into humans when the mosquito takes a blood meal. Trypanosoma parasites in the tsetse fly similarly pass into human blood after a bite from the fly, and cause 'sleeping sickness'.

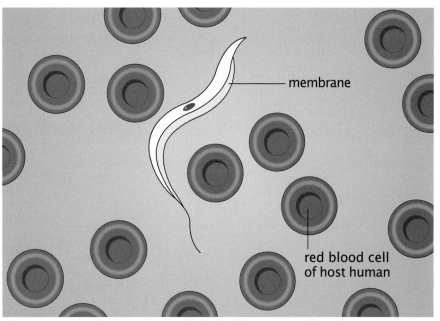

membrane

red blood cell of host human

The trypanosoma parasite moves by flapping its membrane.

Viruses

Viruses are smaller than bacteria. They are between 20 and 250 billionths of a metre in length. Scientists classify viruses as micro-organisms because, like other organisms:

- they reproduce in some fashion
- their genetic material undergoes changes (mutations)
- they direct the production of large molecules.

To reproduce, viruses stick to the cell of a 'host' organism and inject their genetic material (DNA or RNA) into it. Once inside, the virus's genetic material takes control, making the host cell produce more copies of the virus. Often, so many new viruses are made that the host cell bursts and releases several hundred individual viruses.

Most viruses are short strings of DNA. **Retroviruses**, including herpes and HIV, are made of RNA, a genetic material similar to DNA.

Proteins

The only infectious protein known about today is the **prion**. This is the smallest known pathogen. Scientists think that when its shape is altered, this normal protein can 'infect' other proteins, causing them to change shape as well. Prions may be the cause of diseases in many animals. The familiar disease of this type is BSE (bovine spongiform encephalytis – 'mad cow disease').

this type of virus causes sore throats

this type of virus causes tobacco mosaic disease

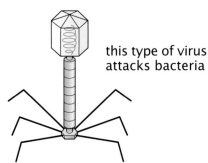

this type of virus attacks bacteria

Viruses can only be seen with an electron microscope. Their average width is 100 nm.

DID YOU KNOW?

Up to 10 000 bacteria or 10 million viruses could be stretched across your thumbnail in a chain.

Information processing *Some nasty diseases*

Read this table then answer the questions following it.

Disease	Micro-organism causing it	Transmission method	Symptoms	How long it lasts	Tissues affected
chicken pox	virus	breathed in, contact	itchy spots	few days	blood, skin
common cold	virus	breathed in, contact	runny nose and eyes, sneezing	few days	mucous membranes of respiratory tract
German measles (rubella)	virus	breathed in, contact	red rash, swollen glands	2 weeks; can be fatal to babies	skin, respiratory organs, foetus in womb
influenza (flu)	virus	breathed in, contact	high temperature, aching body, headache, cold-like symptoms	1–2 weeks	mucous membranes of respiratory tract, gut, nervous system
measles	virus	breathed in, contact	rash, swollen glands, sore eyes, sneezing in the early stages, white spots inside the mouth	2 weeks	skin, respiratory organs
mumps	virus	breathed in, contact	swollen glands	3–4 days	salivary glands
polio	virus	from infected food and water	paralysis, muscles waste away	paralysis may last for rest of life	gut, spinal cord
smallpox	virus	breathed in, contact	spots which form scabs, often scars left, raging fever	1–2 weeks, but often fatal	skin, the lining of the mouth and throat (mucous membranes)
AIDS	virus	contact with infected body fluids, e.g. blood	all infections caught easily	for rest of life, often leads to death from pneumonia	whole immune system
tuberculosis	bacteria	from infected milk (unpasteurised), breathed in	racking cough, fever, aching bones	damaged lungs for rest of life	lung and bone tissue destroyed
diphtheria	bacteria	breathed in	severe fever; can lead to heart failure	few weeks, but effects can last for rest of life; can be fatal	throat, blood, heart, nerves
diarrhoea	bacteria	unwashed hands, from contaminated food and water	temperature, vomiting, stomach cramps	few days to a week	digestive system

Disease	Micro-organism causing it	Transmission method	Symptoms	How long it lasts	Tissues affected
whooping cough	bacteria	breathed in	painful, racking cough	few weeks to several months; can be fatal to babies and young children	bronchioles
amoebic dysentery	protista	dirty drinking water, contact with faeces	severe diarrhoea, blood loss in faeces	few days to a few weeks; can be fatal if it leads to excessive dehydration, particularly in young and old people	large intestine
sleeping sickness	protista	bites from the tsetse fly	drowsiness, failure to eat	can last a lifetime and often leads to death	bloodstream, brain and spinal cord
malaria	protista	bites from mosquito	high fevers	can come and go during rest of life	blood, liver
athlete's foot	fungus	contact with surfaces carrying the fungus spores	itchy and flaking skin	can come and go usually for week at a time	foot, particularly between the toes
ringworm	fungus	contact with surfaces carrying the fungus spores	itchy skin rashes	few weeks	skin, scalp

1 Which do you think are the three most dangerous diseases to catch?

2 What made you make these decisions?

3 Ask other people in your group if they agree with your choices. If they do not, why not?

4 Which of these diseases have you had? Design a way of gathering and presenting information about which diseases people in your class have had.

5 How do you think you 'catch' a cold?

6 Talk in your group about the various ways you think diseases spread, and make some notes. You may need do some library research.

When a disease spreads very fast to a lot of people it is called an **epidemic**.

7 Can you think of any recent epidemics in the world? You could read some newspapers or look up 'epidemics within last six months' on the news pages of the internet.

DID YOU KNOW?

When someone sneezes, thousands of droplets of water containing germs shoot out in a huge cloud at speeds of up to 70 miles per hour.

EXTENSION

Viruses

Martinus Beijerinck was the first scientist to discover a virus in the late 1800s. He was a Dutch botanist. He found out that juice extracted from the leaves of diseased tobacco plants could re-infect healthy tobacco plants, even though he had filtered out the bacteria. He checked that the juice had no bacteria in it by showing that no colonies grew when he put the juice onto culture plates. He inferred (see page 135) that the disease agent was smaller than a bacterium, and he called it a 'filterable virus'. The word virus is based on the Latin word for poison.

Forty years later, in 1935, Wendell Stanley succeeded in isolating crystals from infected tobacco plant leaves. These crystals were proteins. As crystals they did not cause disease but when they were dissolved in water they could infect healthy plants. This was a puzzle. Crystals are not thought to be living. Stanley thought that viruses must be both living and non-living – halfway between the states. In 1937, Sir Fredrick Bawden showed that 'virus crystals' were in fact nucleic acids, DNA and RNA, found in the cells of all living things.

1 Why do you think Stanley thought the virus crystals were non-living?

2 Whereabouts in the cell is DNA normally found?

3 How did scientists infer that it was not bacteria that caused disease in tobacco plants?

4 How would you show that Stanley's 'filterable virus' was living and able to infect tobacco plants, and not just a liquid poison that would weaken and disappear? (HINT – living things must be capable of reproduction.)

Time to think Divide a piece of paper into four sections. In each section put one of these headings: *Bacteria, Viruses, Fungi, Parasites*. Look through the chapter so far and decide on four important facts to go under each heading.

Compare your summary with those of three other people.

How infectious diseases spread

From person to person.

Through the air.

In water.

From animals.

In soil.

9 Can you think of any **infectious** illness you or your friends might have caught in any of these ways?

Reasoning ## TB transmission by badgers

Read this extract from a website about TB **transmission**.

BROCKEYE BADGER PRESS

!News from the world of badgers and badger protection!

The aim of this page is to keep you up to date with developments in the fields of badger research and badger protection.

Tuberculosis (TB) is a **contagious** disease which farmers believe is transmitted by badgers.

The Government-backed Badger Cull
Report filed: March 14th, 1999

For many years farmers have claimed that badgers transmit tuberculosis (TB) to their cattle. In 1999, the Government started funding a major research programme to discover if badgers are increasing the likelihood of cattle catching TB. The research team have designed an investigation to collect data. They are carrying out three 'treatments' in several randomly selected areas of the country. These are known as 'triplets'.

The 'triplet' treatments are:

Proactive culling – all badgers living in a randomly selected area will be culled (killed).

Reactive culling – only badgers in an area in contact with livestock on farms that have already been infected with TB will be killed.

No cull – the badgers are left undisturbed.

The North Devon triplet was one of two triplets chosen for the launch of the badger culling experiment. The other triplet is on the borders of Gloucestershire and Herefordshire, and it is anticipated that culling will commence there.

1 Why is it dangerous for cows to catch TB?

2 What is TB caused by?

3 Why do you think the treatments are known as 'triplets'?

4 Why is there a 'No cull' treatment?

5 Do you think each treatment area must be the same size or can they be any size? Explain your answer.

EXTENSION The Government-appointed research team started its work in February 1998. Their job was to advise Government Ministers on the design and analysis of the randomised trial to test the effectiveness of badger **culling** as a means of controlling bovine (cattle) TB. Here is what the research team wrote in their report to DEFRA (the Department for Environment, Food and Rural Affairs):

Report to DEFRA

Having reviewed the existing research evidence, we consider that the following key scientific questions must be addressed.

A Source of infection:
i. Is the badger the main source of TB for infection of cattle?
ii. Do other wildlife species contribute to cattle infection either directly or by forming a source of infection for badgers?
iii. How significant is cattle-to-cattle transmission as a source of infection?

B Risk of infection:
i. Do different farming systems or farm management practices increase or reduce the risk of transmitting infection to cattle?
ii. What factors influence the amount of infection of TB in local badger populations, for example:
   • population density
   • social group structure
   • climatic conditions?

---

6 Do you think the culling 'triplet' treatments are likely to answer the research team's first question?

7 How might the scientists investigate their second and third questions?

8 How do you suggest they find out about the factors that influence the amount of infection of TB in badger populations? (You might find Chapter 12 helpful.)

There is a lot of concern about killing badgers. Many conservation groups are organising protests and petitions.

9 Discuss in your group whether you think the Government was right to commission this investigation, which involves killing badgers. Do you think they could get the same information in other ways, without killing badgers? Do you think the investigation they suggested looks well designed?

➡ # *Protecting food*

Fresh food does not stay fresh for long with micro-organisms around. Different methods of treating food to protect it from 'going off' are shown below.

Cold treatment – fridges and freezers.

Drying – **dehydration**.

Heat treatment – canning, sterilising.

Chemical treatment – pickling, sugaring, smoking, salting.

Irradiation – treated with radioactivity.

10 Look at all the treatments in the pictures. What do you think are the necessary factors for microbes to live and multiply?

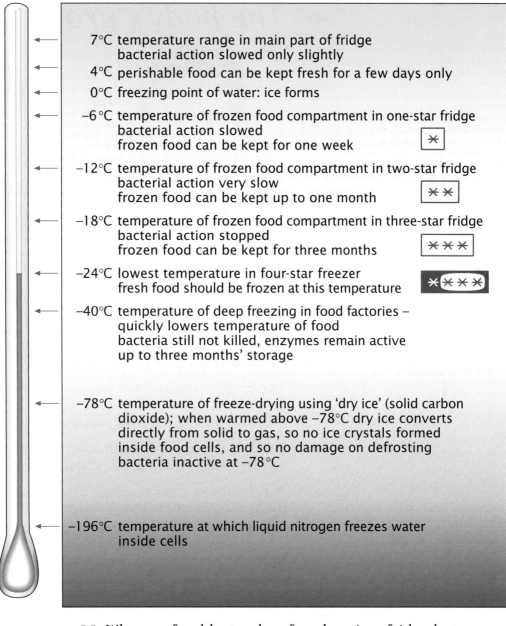

7°C temperature range in main part of fridge
bacterial action slowed only slightly

4°C perishable food can be kept fresh for a few days only

0°C freezing point of water: ice forms

−6°C temperature of frozen food compartment in one-star fridge
bacterial action slowed
frozen food can be kept for one week

−12°C temperature of frozen food compartment in two-star fridge
bacterial action very slow
frozen food can be kept up to one month

−18°C temperature of frozen food compartment in three-star fridge
bacterial action stopped
frozen food can be kept for three months

−24°C lowest temperature in four-star freezer
fresh food should be frozen at this temperature

−40°C temperature of deep freezing in food factories –
quickly lowers temperature of food
bacteria still not killed, enzymes remain active
up to three months' storage

−78°C temperature of freeze-drying using 'dry ice' (solid carbon
dioxide); when warmed above −78°C dry ice converts
directly from solid to gas, so no ice crystals formed
inside food cells, and so no damage on defrosting
bacteria inactive at −78°C

−196°C temperature at which liquid nitrogen freezes water
inside cells

11 Why can food last only a few days in a fridge but several months in a freezer?

12 Why is freeze-dried food mostly undamaged when defrosted?

Research
- Visit the cold treatment area of a supermarket. How does the supermarket make sure the foods are kept cool? How do they monitor the temperatures? You may need to ask staff some questions.
- How do you think most of our foods have been treated – cooled, canned, dehydrated, or irradiated?
- Your Food Technology teacher can help you find out more about food **preservation**. You could also find out about public health inspectors and what they do to make sure the food we eat is as hygienic as possible.

The body's protection

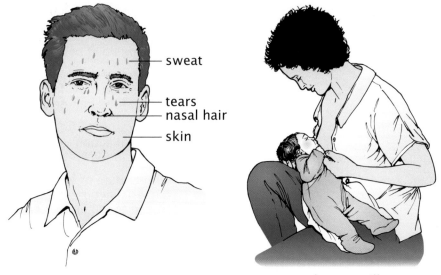

sweat

tears
nasal hair

skin

breast milk

All of these protect us from infection.

The body defends itself against viruses, bacteria and other foreign material that tries to enter it. The skin is the first defence that an invading micro-organism reaches.

13 How do you think micro-organisms get through the skin? How does the body try to prevent this?

If a pathogen does manage to get through the skin, blood rushes to the area of infection causing the skin to look red and swollen. It may also get hot. Pathogens can die if they get too hot. If the infection is severe, the white blood cells send a message to the brain, which responds by increasing the rate at which body cells release energy. The skin may turn pale, because the blood stays deep in the body so it does not lose heat to the air. This is what we call 'running a temperature' or 'having a fever'.

Your nostrils and mouth are open to the air, so this is another way micro-organisms can get into the body.

14 How do the nose, mouth and gut try to stop pathogens entering?
15 Why do you think it is unhealthy to pick your nose or pick at scabs?
16 Imagine you have a big sister (you might already have one!). What advice would you give her if she developed a large spot on her face?

The lymph system

The body's main defence involves the **lymph system**, which is a series of fine tubes of fluid running around the body connecting lymph 'nodes'. These are mainly grouped in your groin, your armpits and behind your ears.

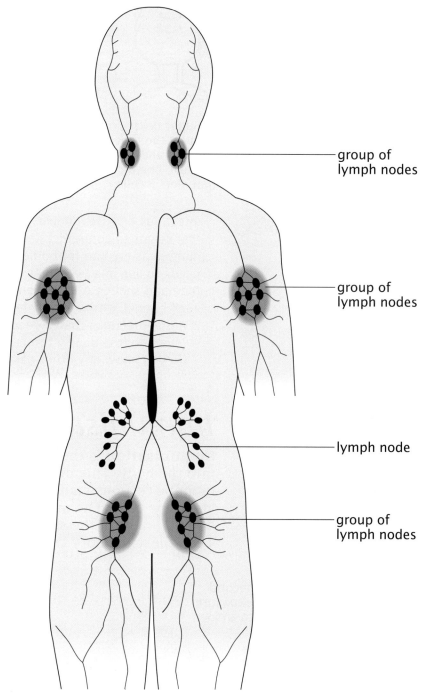

group of lymph nodes

group of lymph nodes

lymph node

group of lymph nodes

The lymph system.

The lymph nodes store two kinds of white blood cells – T cells and B cells – ready to fight infection.

Bone marrow makes B cells.

Thymus gland makes three kinds of T cells.

B cells identify chemicals (**antigens**) produced by the germs and make **antibodies** – chemicals that neutralise the poisonous antigens

T helper cells identify the types of germ and produce chemicals that alert B cells

T killer cells search out and destroy germs

T suppressor cells stop other T and B cells attacking germs too fiercely and damaging body tissues

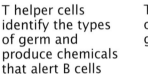 *Word play* Infectious disease involves a paradox. A 'paradox' is something that seems to contradict itself. Here the paradox is that pathogens are bad for bodies, causing illnesses, but a pathogen needs to live in a body that is healthy enough to provide it with food and shelter. A pathogen that kills its host would make itself extinct, because an infected host who is walking around is more infectious than a dead body. So pathogens tend to evolve into less deadly forms.

Do you know any other paradoxes?

Immunisation

Key words
* immunisation
* vaccines

Immunisation is the deliberate introduction of an antigen into the body. This provokes an immune response. An immune response is the production of antibodies with 'memory' cells. The memory cells remain in the blood circulation until the same antigen tries to invade again. Then these memory cells remind the body how to make the antibodies to attack the invader. This time the antibody is produced much more quickly and so kills the pathogens before they make the person ill.

Vaccines stimulate this immune response. They can be taken orally (as drops in water, for example) or be injected.

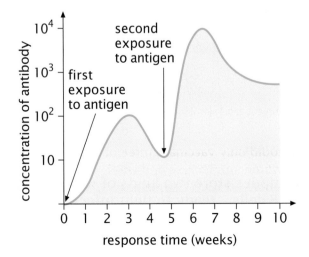

17 Look at the graph. Explain what is happening to the concentration of antibody in the bloodstream during the response time shown.

Vaccines used to be made using horse blood serum. Serum is the blood fluid without any blood cells in it. Nowadays vaccines are produced using hens' egg protein, human serum or by genetic engineering.

18 Why do you think we have changed the way we make vaccines?

New vaccines are difficult and expensive to produce. It takes about 12 years to develop a new one and can cost between £50 million and £100 million to test it. Governments have to decide if the benefits are worth these high costs. They need to consider:

- the cost of immunising everyone
- the chances of side effects from the vaccine
- the percentage of the population likely to suffer from the particular disease.

Reasoning ## Who to vaccinate?

Decision making about such important issues is not easy. Here are some questions for you to debate in your group:

1 If you had only a limited amount of flu vaccine in your town, who would you vaccinate and why?

2 Hepatitis B is the ninth most common cause of death in the world, even more infectious than the AIDS (HIV) virus. It is responsible for about 80% of liver cancers. At least 5% of the world's population are believed to be carriers of the virus. There is a vaccine to help reduce the likelihood of infection.

The table summarises the percentage of patients in different groups who are also infected with hepatitis B:

drug abusers	24%
male homosexuals	8%
people with bleeding disorders	less than 1%
people in close contact with hepatitis B carriers	10%
transfusion patients	1%
people with tattoos	2%
mentally handicapped people	less than 1%
healthcare staff	3%
people who have had surgery, dentistry or injections	3%
people who have travelled abroad	8%

a) If you could only vaccinate three of these groups of people, which would you choose and why?

b) How would you warn people about the risks of hepatitis B?

Research | Carry out a survey to find out how many people in your year group have been vaccinated. Do they know why they were vaccinated and what they have been vaccinated against?
How will you present your data?

Time to think | There are thousands of harmful micro-organisms around. If you were asked to tell some primary school pupils about how they could reduce their chances of catching diseases, what would you tell them?

Look back over the work you have done in this chapter so far. Discuss the ideas in a group and together design a clear and easy-to-read booklet to educate 8-year-olds about disease prevention.

Cholera

Key word
* pandemic

In 1831 the first known outbreak of cholera in Britain occurred. It had started in the Ganges valley of India in 1826 and was carried by men in armies as they fought across Europe. This transmission of a disease across several countries, with large numbers of people being infected, is called a **pandemic**. There have been pandemics of cholera that reached Britain in 1831–32, 1848–49, 1853–54, and 1866. Cholera died out in Europe in 1923, the last pandemic being in 1912.

In the 1854 pandemic that swept across Europe, the source of the trouble in London was a water pump in Broad Street in the Soho area. It was eventually found that sewage was leaking into it. Within 10 days, 500 people had died. People had previously thought the cause of cholera was 'bad vapours' in the air. It was Dr John Snow who found out that cholera outbreaks were linked to drinking dirty water. He kept a list of deaths from cholera in the Soho area and recorded them on a map.

How the water pump in Broad Street had become infected was not clear, but Dr Snow had the handle taken off the pump and the outbreak stopped. Cholera had killed about 0.5% of the population of the area.

Between 1800 and 1850 the population of London had rapidly increased and 1858 was known as the year of the 'Great Stink', when the River Thames smelled so bad that the Houses of Parliament had to close. Huge open sewer pipes carried human waste into the river.

A cartoon from an 1850s edition of *Punch*.

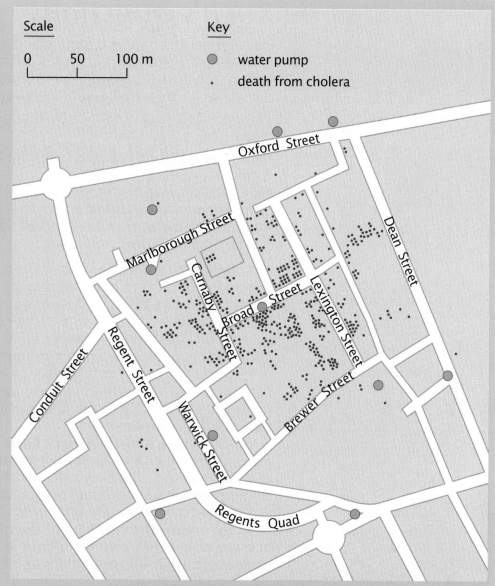

Dr Snow's map of cholera deaths in 1854 may have looked something like this.

By the early 1900s sewage treatment plants had been built and drains had been closed. Today it is illegal to pollute rivers and waterways with human sewage.

1 How was the spread of cholera eventually stopped?
2 Why did Dr Snow's map help people to understand what was causing the cholera outbreaks?
3 What indicates that cholera is a water-borne disease?

DID YOU KNOW?

The average household produces about 300 litres of sewage a day and uses about 2 miles of toilet paper a year!

EXTENSION ➡

Koch's questions

Key words
* inoculated
* infectivity

Identifying what causes a particular disease can be tricky. The German microbiologist Robert Koch (see page 195) said that only after a positive answer to four questions could we say that agent 'X' causes disease 'Y'. Here are his four questions:

- Is the agent (the infective organism) present in every case of the disease?
- Can the agent be isolated from the host and grown in a laboratory dish?
- Can the disease be reproduced when a pure culture of the agent is **inoculated** into a healthy susceptible host?
- Can the same agent be recovered again from the experimentally infected host?

Although Koch's questions have been very helpful in the development of vaccinations, they have some limitations. Some agents (including prions and viruses) do not grow in a laboratory dish, but only in a living cell.

Ethically, 'healthy susceptible host' testing cannot be done with people. It is necessary to use lab animals or livestock. Testing the **infectivity** of a possible human pathogen in other animals always raises a question: if the pathogen doesn't infect the lab animal, does that mean it cannot infect humans?

In performing tests to satisfy Koch's requirements, careful scientists always use un-inoculated control animals as a comparison. The only difference between the 'experimental animals' and the 'control animals' is the inoculation, or deliberate infection. Controls need to be used to remove the chance that the experimental animals became sick for unrelated reasons, such as their genetic makeup or other experimental conditions.

19 Make your own notes in your exercise book on Koch's method for identifying the causes of a particular disease.

Information processing ## Diphtheria

Here is a graph showing the death rate from diphtheria over 100 years.

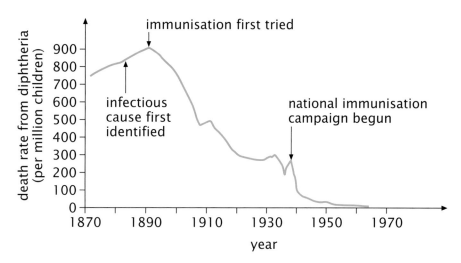

1 What are the three variables in the graph?

2 There is correlation between two of the variables. Which are they and what does the correlation indicate?

3 When was the national immunisation programme introduced? Why do you think it was introduced then?

➡ # *Diseases of animals*

Foot and mouth disease

Look at these maps of Britain showing how foot and mouth disease spread in 2001.

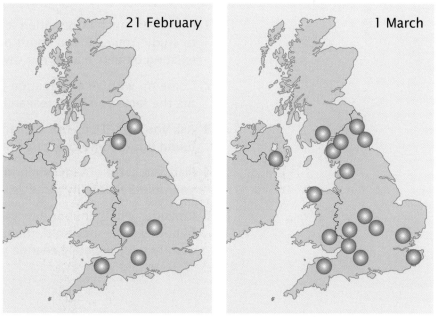

20 Why do you think foot and mouth disease spread so rapidly?

Key word
* quarantine

Rabies

Rabies is a disease caused by a virus. All mammals can catch it. It attacks the nervous system and usually kills the victim. Pet animals can catch it from wild animals if they are bitten. Because Britain is an island, rabies has not yet been a problem here. Pets entering the country are usually required to go into **quarantine** for 6 months. This is now changing because there are inoculations that can be given to pets to prevent them transmitting rabies. You can now get a 'pet passport'.

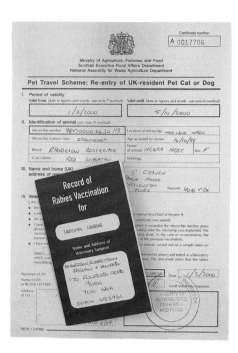

21 What kind of organism causes rabies?

22 Why is rabies rarely a problem in Britain?

23 Can people catch rabies? How do you know?

Enquiry ## Creating and testing a hypothesis

A hypothesis is a testable explanation that fits the facts known or evidence gained. Scientists use hypotheses to help them design experiments and investigations, and to plan relevant observations.
When you are making a hypothesis, this is what you should do:

1 Gather as much information as you can about a subject you want to study. You can read about other people's findings, analyse existing data or make your own observations.

2 Come up with an explanation (yours or one you have found) that fits the facts you have researched.

3 Ask yourself, 'Does this explanation fit all the information I have found out or can I come up with a better explanation?'

4 Plan and carry out investigations or observations that will test your explanation (hypothesis).

5 Consider whether your new pieces of evidence support your hypothesis or not. If not, then think again. You may need to modify or completely change your hypothesis.

EXTENSION

Look at the cartoon story. In your group, discuss these questions:

a) What is your hypothesis about the type of disease and how Tom has caught it? How much of your hypothesis is supported by evidence in this story and how much of it relies on your knowledge or research?

b) How could you investigate the explanation you have given?

c) What do you think should happen to pets that catch this disease?

d) Would a pet goldfish catch this disease?

e) How would you check if wild animals in the area had the disease?

f) What would you do to ensure that no one else caught these diseases?

Word play   Add at least two more important words each to your group's 'Dreaded diseases dictionary' that you started at the beginning of this topic.

Growing micro-organisms to study them

Like all living things, micro-organisms need food to get their energy. If they are pathogens then their food comes from us – our bodies are their meat and drink. If we want to study bacteria and fungi we can grow them on a special kind of jelly called 'agar' in small plastic dishes. Given some warmth, they will multiply very rapidly. Bacteria, for example, can double in number in 20 minutes.

Enquiry ## Investigating the effectiveness of antiseptics

Karl carried out some experiments to find out which antiseptic mouthwash was the best.

1 What do you think he means by 'best'? List the criteria you would use to judge one mouthwash against another.

Here is his description of what he did:

- First I made up four dishes with food jelly in (agar). These dishes are specially designed to grow bacteria on.
- Then I poured 5 cm³ of a solution full of bacteria into each dish and put the lids on the dishes. I was very careful with hygiene and washed my hands very thoroughly after doing this.
- I swirled the bacteria solution round in the dish until it covered the whole surface of the agar.
- I made four identical circles of filter paper and dipped one circle into each of four different mouthwash solutions:
    A Marvelmouth mouthwash
    B Slurper mouthwash
    C Baccikill mouthwash
    D Oralclean mouthwash
- I put circles **A**, **B**, **C** and **D** into a dish each and put on their lids. I left all the dishes in a warm dry place for a few days. The bacteria grew and multiplied into a cloudy coloured layer over the jelly.
- Here are my results. Where the jelly is clear is where the bacteria have not grown. This is in a ring of clear jelly around each of the filter papers.

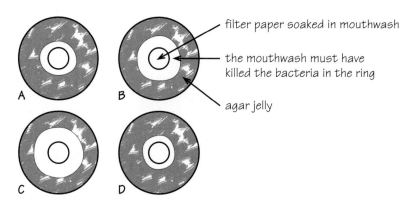

filter paper soaked in mouthwash

the mouthwash must have killed the bacteria in the ring

agar jelly

Look at Karl's description of his investigation and his drawings.

2 How do you think he tried to make his investigation a 'fair test'?

3 What should he do next to record the results of his investigation?

4 Make a record of his results. Will you record them as a table, make a graph or present them in a different way? Talk in your group about how best to record the results.

5 Do you think he has found out which is the best mouthwash?

6 His teacher says that she does not think he can assume that the mouthwashes are killing the bacteria. Why do you think she tells him to think again and improve his investigation? What advice would you give him to improve it?

7 What is an antiseptic?

EXTENSION **8** Toothpaste, mouthwash, kitchen surface cleaners, anti-perspirant deodorants and baby-bottle sterilising fluids all contain antiseptic chemicals. Select one of these antiseptic solutions and design an investigation to see how much of it you would need to kill bacteria as quickly as possible. You will need to make comparisons between different strengths of solutions.

How would you be certain that you had enough data to make reliable inferences?

Research ▶ What other antiseptics can you find around your home or at school? List them and write down the ingredients that each contains.

 DID YOU KNOW? Honey is a good antiseptic. The high sugar content dehydrates microbes. Hospitals sometimes use honey-soaked dressings to prevent large wounds getting infected.

➡ *Medicines*

Some medicines help fight diseases by preventing bacteria in your body from growing. Antibiotics are an example. They work only against bacteria. Doctors will only prescribe an antibiotic if they think your immune system cannot cope with the bacterial infection quickly.

24 Find out why doctors always advise patients to finish a course of antibiotics.

25 Has anyone in your group taken antibiotics recently? If so, what for? How many did they have to take and for how long?

Some medicines do not fight the disease but help to control the pain or symptoms. Aspirin and paracetamol work in this way.

Homeopathic medicines try to help the body's own defence system fight the disease.

Antiseptics attack pathogens that try to enter your body, for example if you cut yourself. They are not to be swallowed.

Creative thinking ## Poster design

Look back at the nasty diseases on pages 198–199. Which ones can be cured by antibiotics?

Some people expect to be given antibiotics when they visit the doctor with an infection of any sort. Design a poster for your doctor's surgery which makes clear why you should not be given antibiotics for any minor infection, and why it is important to finish the full course of antibiotic drugs if they are prescribed to you.

EXTENSION

An antibiotic may be classified as 'narrow-spectrum' or 'broad-spectrum', depending on the range of bacterial types that it affects. Narrow-spectrum antibiotics are active against specific bacterial types. Broad-spectrum antibiotics are active against all bacterial types and are particularly useful when the infecting agent (bacteria) is unknown. The problem with broad-spectrum antibiotics is that they kill all bacteria in your body. There are some bacteria that help the body stay healthy, particularly in your gut and in the vagina. If these are affected by a broad spectrum antibiotic prescribed for an unknown infection, for example a septic finger, then the patient's finger may get better but there may be side effects such as a stomach upset or a vaginal infection.

From: Dr Care
To: Doctorline
Date:
Subject: Antibiotic resistance

Dear Doctorline
How can I reduce the threat of antibiotic resistance in my patients?

From: Doctorline
To: Dr Care
Date:
Subject: Re: Antibiotic resistance

Dear Dr Care
If possible, choose narrow-spectrum rather than broad-spectrum antibiotics. In other words, use the most specific or targeted antibiotics possible. Save the newer, broad-spectrum drugs for infections that resist the older drugs.

Doctorline help – your professional on-line help service

1 Explain why the emailed response from 'Doctorline' shown on the opposite page is good advice to give Dr Care.

Here are some questions that someone might ask, if their doctor prescribes an antibiotic:
- Why do I need an antibiotic?
- What is this particular antibiotic supposed to do?
- Is this drug likely to cause any side effects?
- Is there anything I can do to prevent these side effects?
- Should I take the drug at a specific time? With or without food?

The patient should also tell the doctor about any previous reactions to drugs, special diets, allergies or other health problems.

2 Use the suggested questions above and also the advice given to Dr Care to produce a health information leaflet for teenagers. You could use your IT skills to make a 'mock up' of the leaflet, adding in suitable graphics.

Time to think

Work with at least two other people to create 20 questions to use in a class quiz about the work in this chapter. Write each question clearly on a card and put the answer on the back. Make sure you learn the answers to your questions!

Collect up all the sets of 20 questions created by the whole class. Divide the class into teams. Your teacher will be the quiz master. See which team wins the most cards.

Make a note of any questions that you cannot answer. Later, find the answer to these questions from this chapter.

10 *The rock cycle*

In this chapter you will learn:

➡ **about the three main kinds of rocks – sedimentary, metamorphic and igneous**
➡ **that rocks change over time**
➡ **about the rock cycle**
➡ **about volcanoes and how they erupt**

You will also develop your skills in:

➡ **information processing**
➡ **constructing graphs**
➡ **making predictions**
➡ **using evidence to explain ideas**

➡ ➡ ➡ WHAT DO YOU KNOW?

In Chapter 2 you learned about sedimentary rocks. How much do you remember from that chapter? Read the story below and answer the questions that follow.

ROCK AND ROLL *Part 1*

Imagine that you are a rock the size of a football. Your home is on a sunny hillside and you can see down into a deep valley with a river far below. Sometimes it is very hot there. Can you feel the sunlight warming you? What will happen to you when you get sunburnt?

During the winter you get worried too, about the ice that freezes in the crack on the top of you. This crack grows bigger each year because the ice pushes hard on the sides of the crack.

One spring it is very wet, with more rain than you can ever remember. The rain pours in little streams rushing down the hillside. You feel the water flowing over you and into the soft mud below. Suddenly you feel a rumbling and the Earth begins to shake. You look uphill and a large wall of mud rushes down and sweeps you up. You begin to roll down, down, down into the valley. Ouch! You hit another rock and you split along the crack. Now you are two halves rolling down the hill. Splash! You land in the river.

For days and days the fast flowing, strong waters push you. Rolling and bumping along you are getting all broken up into gravel and sand. Finally the river flows into the sea and takes you with it. Your many pieces settle onto a large, flat area, along with millions of other pieces of sand, gravel, silt and quite a few shells with bodies inside. Some pieces settle on top of you and you are getting squashed. More and more weight presses down. Your pieces get pushed and stuck together with other pieces. You are now hardening and becoming a sedimentary rock.

1 Explain how the crack in the rock gets bigger every year. What is this process called?

2 Explain the descriptions of what is happening to the rock. Use these words to help you:

weathering   erosion   transport   deposition   burial

3 What happens to the rock pieces as they get carried along by the river?

EXTENSION   As well as sediment, rivers bring many chemicals to the sea in solution. These chemicals were dissolved from the weathered rocks by rainwater. Just like the sediment, all these chemicals stay in the sea, which is why the sea tastes salty.

4 Imagine you are a salt crystal inside a rock. Describe how you end up in the sea.

5 Put these sentences in the correct order to show how sedimentary rocks are formed:
- The lower layers become more squashed and they harden.
- Pieces of rock fragments become more and more weathered until, eventually, they become grains of sediment.
- As one layer builds on another, the lower ones get squashed.
- The sediments are deposited in layers in shallow seas and lakes over millions of years.
- The grains are transported, for example by water and wind, and eventually deposited.
- The lower layers were deposited first, and newer layers on top.

DID YOU KNOW?

The first geologist on the Moon was Harrison Schmitt, who was part of the Apollo 17 mission. From the rock samples he collected, scientists have been able to learn many things about the Moon.

➡ *Sedimentary rocks*

Key words
* fossils
* geological time period

How can you spot a sedimentary rock?

- Sedimentary rocks will often have layers through them.
- They will often contain **fossils**, which are fragments or impressions of animals or plants preserved within the rock.
- Grains of the rock may be scraped off easily and sometimes the rocks crumble.

How do you tell how old the rock is? One way to tell the 'age' of a rock – the **geologic time period** that it belongs to – is to look at any fossils the rock may contain. If any of the fossils are unique to one of the geologic time periods, then we know the rock was formed during that particular time period. Another way is to use the 'What's on top?' rule.

1 When you find layers of rocks in a cliff or hillside, are younger rocks on top of or underneath older rocks?

The 'What's on top?' rule works in most cases, although sometimes layers of rocks have moved so much that the rule cannot be used.

The oldest rock that has ever been found is more than 3.9 billion years old. The Earth itself is at least 4.6 billion years old, but rocks from the beginning of the Earth's history have changed so much from their original form that they have become new kinds of rock. By studying how rocks form and change, scientists have built a solid understanding of the Earth we live on and its long history.

Some common sedimentary rocks

Sandstone is one of the most common sedimentary rocks. It is made from sand grains eroded from older rocks, cemented together and then hardened into new rock.

Uluru, also known as Ayers Rock, in Australia, the world's largest monolith (single rock), is made of sandstone. This rock has special spiritual meaning for the Australian Aboriginal people.

Key words
* sandstone
* limestone
* calcite
* crystalline
* permeable

Uluru (Ayers Rock, Australia).

Another common sedimentary rock is **limestone**. Most types of limestone are made from the mineral **calcite** (calcium carbonate). Many sea creatures take in dissolved calcium carbonate to make their skeletons or hard shells. Limestone is then formed from the remains of shells that have settled on the seabed. Types of limestone that contain only calcite are white. But most limestones contain other minerals, for example iron oxide (rust), and the remains of living things. These cause the rocks to vary in colour, especially when they are exposed to weathering elements such as air and water.

2 Geologists use many clues to identify rocks. How could an acid help them to identify a limestone rock?
3 What colour would you expect limestone to be if it contained iron oxide?

Most limestones are layered and contain fossils of shellfish and other animals that lived in shallow seas. The texture of limestone ranges from coarsely **crystalline**, in which you can see the large crystals quite easily, to very fine-grained. The crystals in the fine-grained material, which is usually mixed

DID YOU KNOW? Chalk is a variety of limestone that is composed mainly of calcium carbonate fragments from microscopic plants.

with clay, are visible only with the help of a microscope. Many limestones are **permeable** rocks. This means that they will let water pass through them. Other sedimentary rocks, such as mudstone and clay, are impermeable.

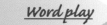

Word play What do you think 'impermeable' means?

Information processing **Roman baths**

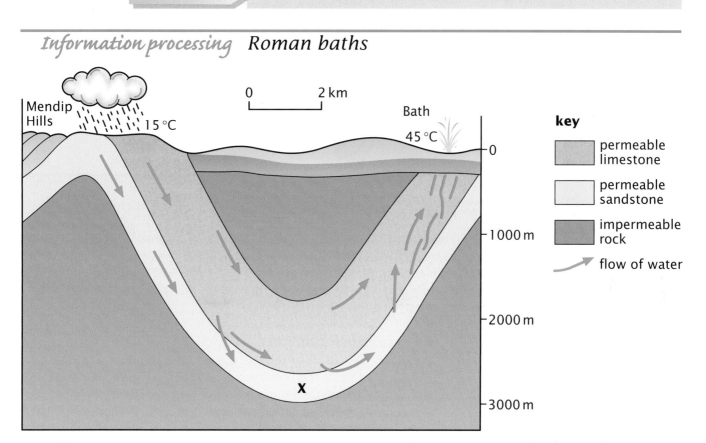

Look carefully at the drawing of the rock layers beneath the Mendip Hills and the city of Bath.

1 What is the temperature of the rainwater as it soaks into the Mendip Hills?

2 How much warmer is the water when it reaches the baths at Bath?

3 Why doesn't the water get to the surface before it reaches the Roman baths?

EXTENSION 4 Can you think of two reasons why the water flows from the Mendips to the Roman baths?

5 Predict what the temperature of the water will be at **X**. Give as many reasons as you can.

The Roman baths in Bath.

6 Water reaches Bath faster via the sandstone than it does via the limestone layer. Here are three different explanations. Which one do you agree with? Make sure you discuss this in your group before you decide.

It's because the pressure is greater in the sandstone layer than in the limestone.

The temperature is higher in the sandstone so it's pushed through quicker.

Maybe it's to do with the permeability – how easily the water can squeeze through the rock.

Geology

Key word
* terminology

James Hutton.

The founder of modern geology is generally agreed to be James Hutton (1726–1797), a Scottish medical man and farmer. Hutton was very interested in the history of the Earth and in the processes that change the Earth's surface.

Before Hutton's time most geologists believed the Earth was only a few thousand years old. They believed that the Earth's physical features were the result of terrible events.

Hutton's studies of the rock formations of his native Scotland helped him to formulate his most famous work, 'Theory of the Earth'. He made many observations about rock formations and how they were affected by erosion. His **terminology** and rock formation theories became known as 'Huttonian' geology.

1 What type of events would change the Earth's landscape?
2 How could you convince someone that the Earth was very old? What evidence would you use to persuade them? Look through the chapter so far for some ideas.

EXTENSION **3** Hutton believed that the present was the key to the past, and he was the first person to describe the rock cycle. What do you think he meant by 'The present is the key to the past.'?

Time to think Check through the work you have done in this chapter so far. Devise a test with ten questions that you feel would test the knowledge and ideas covered. Try out your test on others in your group. Decide together which were good questions and which were weak ones. Make a list of the best questions and their answers. Make up a loop game to try out on another group.

Metamorphic rocks

While you are reading this book:

- volcanoes are erupting and earthquakes are shaking
- mountains are being pushed up and are being worn down
- rivers are carrying sand and mud to the sea
- huge slabs of the Earth's surface called **tectonic plates** are slowly moving, about as fast as your fingernails grow.

Earth movements can push all types of rock deeper into the Earth. These rocks are then subjected to extremely high temperatures and pressures, causing their crystalline structure and texture to change. This is how metamorphic rocks are formed.

All rock can be heated. Inside the Earth there is heat from pressure (push your hands together very hard and feel the heat). There is heat from friction (rub your hands together and feel the heat). There is also heat from radioactive decay of unstable elements in the rocks.

Heat bakes the rock. Baked rock does not melt, but it changes. It forms crystals. If it has crystals already, it forms larger crystals. The change is called **metamorphism**. Metamorphism can occur in rock that is heated to 300–700 °C.

Some common metamorphic rocks

Slate is formed from mudstone or clay and is the most common kind of metamorphic rock in Britain. Pressure causes the new minerals to grow in parallel sheets. This makes slate split easily to make roofing tiles.

4 The fact that the heat and pressure cause minerals to grow may suggest that slate is alive! Convince your group that the slates on their roof are not going to grow up and leave the roof!

Slate sometimes contains fossils that have been badly squashed. The results of the squashing give clues about the directions of the forces that have squeezed the rocks. These may be from top to bottom, from side to side, or **shear** pressures.

Key words
* tectonic plates
* metamorphism

Key words
* slate
* shear
* marble
* schist

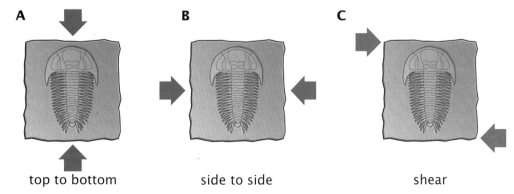

A top to bottom

B side to side

C shear

5 The drawings below show trilobite fossils, found in slate. For each, say in which direction the pressure was that distorted the image (see the diagram on page 225). Note that one fossil has not been distorted.

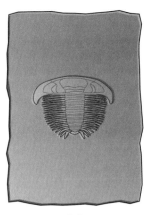

(a)

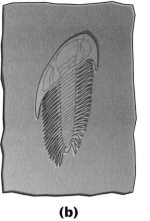

(b)

(c)

(d)

Marble is formed from limestone that has been squashed and heated. The calcite shells in the structure of the limestone break down and recrystallise into crystals of differing sizes. Marble is chemically the same as limestone but it is much harder. Some of the finest marble comes from Italy and it is used for sculptures and as a fine building material. It is very expensive.

The Taj Mahal, built between 1632 and 1654 in India, is made entirely of marble.

Schist (pronounced 'shist') is formed from mudstones that are heated to very high temperatures over long periods of time. Schist has layers of banded crystals. Did you identify it correctly using the rock key in Chapter 2 (page 42)?

Research

1 Find out about the following metamorphic rocks:
   - gneiss
   - quartzite.

   For each type, say:
   a) what the original rock was before the metamorphism
   b) what factors caused the change
   c) how the new rock is different from the old rock.

2 **a)** Why would the temperature and pressure increase as rocks get pushed deeper underground?
   b) What would happen to any fossils if the pressure became too great?

Word play

The word metamorphic has two parts:

- _meta_, meaning change or alter
- _morphic_, meaning shape or structure.

During the life cycle of a butterfly we say that 'metamorphosis' happens when a caterpillar changes to become a butterfly. Why do you think this term is used?

→ Igneous rocks

Key words
* magma
* molten
* lava
* extrusive
* basalt
* intrusive
* granite

Many kilometres below the surface of the Earth the temperature gets high enough to melt some of the rock. **Magma**, which is a hot liquid of melted minerals, is produced. It is **molten** rock. Magma rises up because it is less dense than the solid rock. It may rise to the surface and erupt as **lava**, or it may cool down while trapped within the Earth's crust. Igneous rocks are formed when the magma cools and solidifies. Lava that pours out of volcanoes cools down to form **extrusive** igneous rock. **Basalt** is an extrusive igneous rock. It has cooled quickly in the air and is characterised by small crystals.

Magma that cools down within the Earth's crust forms **intrusive** igneous rock. **Granite** is an example of an intrusive igneous rock. It has been trapped under the Earth's surface and is characterised by having large crystals. Igneous rocks contain minerals randomly arranged as crystals and are usually tough and hard.

DID YOU KNOW?

Basalt is considered to be the most common rock on Earth.

6 A pupil has tried to summarise the information about igneous rocks but has got the details mixed up. These sets of words have been mixed up. Discuss in your group which words fit together and make a sentence from them.

Set 1	Set 2
EXTRUSIVE	INTRUSIVE
COOLED QUICKLY IN AIR	COOLED SLOWLY UNDERGROUND
BIG CRYSTALS	SMALL CRYSTALS

7 Look at these two examples of igneous rocks.
   a) Which one do you think is granite? Why?
   b) Which rock could be extrusive? Explain your choice.

8 Pumice is another type of volcanic rock. It is a very unusual rock: it floats in water. Look at the pictures of pumice carefully. Can you explain why it floats?

Pumice.

Word play

Copy the word spiral and use the clues to complete it.

1 This rock is made from calcium carbonate (calcite). (9)
2 The molten rock inside the Earth. (5)
3 This type of rock forms when molten rock cools and solidifies underground. (7)
4 The name of the molten rock that flows out of volcanoes. (4)

Enquiry Volcanic eruption

Key words
* viscosity
* catastrophe

In January 2002, there was a powerful volcanic eruption in the Democratic Republic of Congo, Africa. The Nyiragongo volcano erupted and it took the inhabitants of the nearby town of Goma by surprise because of the speed of the lava. It quickly flowed down the hills and destroyed thousands of homes. This was due to the low **viscosity** of the lava. Viscosity is a measure of how runny liquids are: the lower the viscosity, the more runny the liquid.

1 a) Make a list of liquids that have low viscosity.
  b) Think of liquids that are very viscous (have high viscosity).
  c) What can you do to a liquid to make it more runny (less viscous)?

Lavas can be very sticky and slow-flowing or they can be runny and fast-flowing. This **catastrophe** had a real impact on a group of pupils and they wanted to understand more about how lavas flow. They couldn't bring lava into the laboratory (1000 °C is a bit too hot!), so they needed to use something that would act like lava in their enquiry.

Suki's team decide to use syrup as their 'lava' and they wanted to investigate how the runniness (viscosity) of the lava affected how quickly it flowed. Ben's team decided to use treacle as their lava.

Both teams decided to investigate the effect of temperature on the runniness of the lava. Each team timed how long the lava took to flow down through a filter funnel. Here are their results:

Table A

Temperature of lava (°C)	Time for lava to flow through filter funnel (s)
20	58
30	42
40	30
50	19
60	11

Table B

Temperature of lava (°C)	Time for lava to flow through filter funnel (s)
20	128
25	110
30	88
35	70
40	62

2 In each case, name:
  a) the input variable
  b) the outcome variable
  c) the fixed variables.

3 a) What measuring equipment did they need?
  b) What else would they need to carry out this investigation? Discuss in your group, make a list and then compare your list with those of other groups in the class. Can you decide on a final list?

4 Plot both sets of results on the same piece of graph paper.
  a) Which set of results shows a wider range? What is the advantage of this?

b) What sort of relationship is there between the input and outcome variables? Choose from one of these three:
   A The values of the two variables increase together.
   B The value of one variable increases as the other variable decreases.
   C There is no relationship between the variables.

5 Which table of results do you think was produced by the team using treacle? Give a reason for your choice.

EXTENSION

6 To keep the tests fair, each team must use the same amount of syrup or treacle each time. How would you measure out either of these substances? How much (what value) would you use?

7 In practice, their choice of lava was very messy. To alter this investigation:
   a) What would be your choice of liquid? Give reasons for your choice.
   b) How else could you measure the lava flow? Describe how you would do this. Draw a diagram if it helps your explanation.

The rock cycle

The rock cycle is a group of changes that occur to rocks over long periods of time. Igneous rock can change into sedimentary rock or into metamorphic rock. Sedimentary rock can change into metamorphic rock or into igneous rock. Metamorphic rock can change into igneous or sedimentary rock.

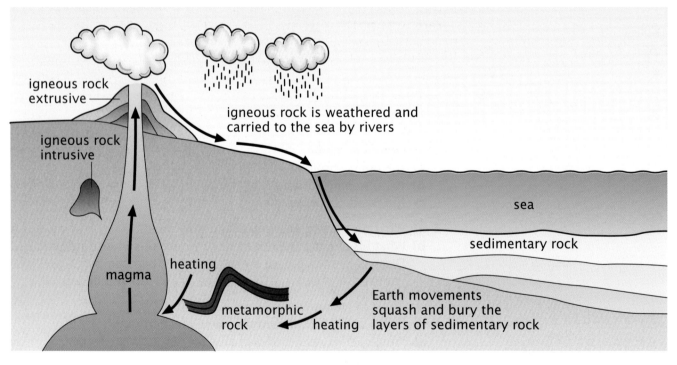

The rock cycle.

Read the passage below carefully and match up each part of the story with the rock cycle diagram. Try to work out what is happening to the rock at each stage.

ROCK AND ROLL *Part 2*

The pressure grows and you begin to get very, very hot. You change colour and many hard crystals form inside you. What sort of rock are you now?

You keep getting pushed farther down. It is boiling hot! Everything begins to melt and you are part of a hot mass of melted rock called magma deep underground. It seems like forever that you are part of this big melted sea of rock. It is really uncomfortable deep underground. You really want to be back on that warm, sunny hillside in the fresh air. Suddenly you're being pushed up and the Earth is shaking and rumbling again. You can feel yourself rising higher and higher. There is fire, ash, dust and steam everywhere and, with a loud explosion, you burst up out of the top of a volcano. You are a scalding, steamy piece of red-hot lava shooting through the air when, suddenly, you land on a high point of the volcano away from the hot flow of lava below.

Slowly the volcano begins to quieten down and you cool and harden. What sort of rock are you now? When all the dust settles and the ground has stopped rumbling you find yourself resting high on the side of a huge volcano and down below is the sea. You are now living on a beautiful, sunny volcanic island.

EXTENSION

Key word
* meteorites

The rocky history of an idea

If you had asked a well-informed European in 1700 how old the planet Earth was and asked him to give an account of its history, he would have said that it was about 6000 years old and that its ancient history was given by the biblical account in Genesis. In 1654 the Irish Archbishop James Ussher had added up all the ages of the people in the Bible and came to the conclusion that the Earth was created on 26th October 4004BC, at 9:00a.m. That made the Earth about 6000 years old.

If you asked the same question of a well-informed European in 1900, you would have received a quite different answer! In 1897, Lord Kelvin assumed that the Earth was originally molten and calculated a date based on cooling through conduction and radiation. The age of Earth was calculated to be between 24 million and 40 million years.

In 1860 scientists had tried to measure the thickness of sedimentary rocks in the Earth's crust, and had divided this number by how quickly sediments formed (in mm per year). They calculated that the Earth was 3 million years old. In 1910 this estimate was changed to 1.6 billion years!

So far, the oldest dated Earth rocks are 3.96 billion years old. Older rocks include **meteorites** and Moon rocks with dates of the order of 4.6 billion years. So, how old is the Earth? The current answer is 4.6 billion years (4 600 000 000 years).

1 Why do you think the estimated age in 1910 was so different from that calculated in 1860?

2 What might have improved in science during those 50 years?

Sedimentation data

1 This table shows the sedimentation rates of a typical ocean bed:

Depth of layer (cm)	Number of years
1	500
2	1000
4	2000
6	3000
9	4000
10	5000

a) Plot this data as a line graph.
b) What is the usual rate of sedimentation shown by the data?
c) During what time period could there have been volcanic activity in the region? What difference has it made?
d) What depth of sediment would you expect after a million (1 000 000) years?

2 Not all layers take this long to form; some take a few months and some just a few days! Make up a table with these headings:

Many years	Months	Days

Decide under which heading each of these layers should be placed and add them to your table:
- a layer of ash from the eruption of a volcano
- a layer of mud after some serious flooding
- a layer of shelled creatures as a result of a gradual change in temperature of the ocean
- a layer of silt produced by erosion from river banks.

→ Cross-section through the Earth

Key words
* crust
* mantle
* outer core
* inner core

The Earth is composed of four different layers. Many geologists believe that as the Earth cooled the heavier, denser materials sank to the centre and the lighter materials rose to the top. Because of this, the outer layer, the **crust**, is made of the lightest materials (basalt and granite rock) and the core at the centre consists of heavy metals (nickel and iron).

The crust is the layer that we live on, and it is the most widely studied and understood. It is less than 10 km thick in places.

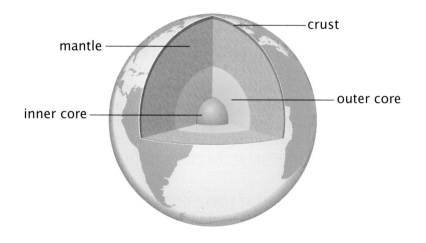

The **mantle** below is much hotter and has the ability to flow. The **outer core** and **inner core** are hotter still, with pressures so great that you would be squeezed into a ball smaller than a marble if you were able to go to the centre of the Earth!

Sometimes the structure of the Earth is compared to an egg: the thin, hard shell, the egg white and the yolk.

The Earth's continents

Alfred Wegener on a polar expedition.

Close examination of a globe often results in the observation that most of the Earth's continents seem to fit together like a jigsaw puzzle: the west African coastline seems to snuggle nicely into the east coast of South America and the Caribbean Sea; and a similar fit appears across the Pacific. This is not a new idea. Francis Bacon wrote about it in 1620.

Alfred Wegener (1880–1930) suggested that there had once been only one continent, which he called Pangaea, and this had gradually split up and moved to form the present continents. He did not provide an explanation as to how these continents had moved. This was left to Arthur Holmes in 1928, who suggested that the land movement was caused by convection currents (see pages 70–71) in the liquid mantle below the Earth's crust.

9   *Pangaea* means 'all lands'. Why do you think Wegener gave it this name?
10 a) Pangaea has sometimes been called a 'super continent'. Suggest why.
   b) Look at a modern map of the world. How many of the continents can you spot in Pangaea?

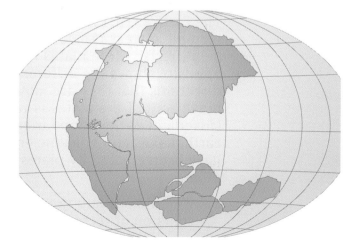

The super continent Pangaea, 225 million years ago.

Our 'egg' model has to be modified (changed) now. The shell is not complete but actually contains lots of cracks. Not only that, but the different pieces are on the move!

Wegener was also puzzled by the similarity of unusual rock structures and of plant and animal fossils found on the matching coastlines of South America and Africa, which are now widely separated by the Atlantic Ocean. He reasoned that it was impossible for most of these organisms to have swum or have been transported across the oceans.

11 Why do you think that these organisms could not have managed to cross the oceans?
12 How did the discovery of matching rocks and fossils support Wegener's theory of moving continents?

In the most recent one-tenth of the Earth's time scale, fossils became much more common. Animals began to develop hard shells and outer skeletons around their soft bodies.

13 Why would shells and outer skeletons be an advantage to animals?
14 Why do you think that shelled creatures were more easily preserved as fossils?

How the continents move

Key word
* plate tectonics

The mobile molten rock beneath the Earth's crust is believed to be moving in a circular manner, rather like a pot of thick soup when heated to boiling. The heated 'soup' rises to the surface, spreads and begins to cool, then sinks back to the bottom of the pot where it is reheated and rises again.

15 What is this type of heat transfer called?
16 What happens to the particles of molten rock as they get heated? How does this explain why they rise upwards? (Look back at Chapter 3.)
17 What is the source of heat that causes the 'soup' to rise?
18 Draw a diagram of a pot of thick soup. Draw arrows showing how the soup circulates as it heats and cools.

The Earth's crust is made up of rigid slabs of rock called tectonic plates. The convection currents in the liquid rock below cause these plates to move about. The diagram opposite shows the different tectonic plates and the directions that they are moving in. The study of this movement of the plates is called **plate tectonics**. Movement at the boundaries of these plates causes earthquakes and volcanic eruptions. Huge mountain ranges have been created by plates slowly colliding with each other.

19 Which mountain ranges may have been formed by the collision of tectonic plates?

key

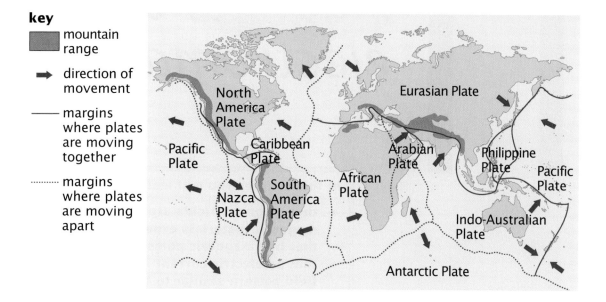

mountain range

➡ direction of movement

—— margins where plates are moving together

········ margins where plates are moving apart

Time to think

1 The oldest rocks on Earth cannot be sedimentary rocks. Can you explain why? Use the rock cycle (page 230) to help you.

2 Stages in the rock cycle are very slow. It can take hundreds and sometimes millions of years for changes to take place. Imagine that sediment is settling on the sea bed at the rate of 3 cm per year.
   a) How long will it take to form a bed of sediment half a metre deep?
   b) What problems might this cause to shipping in the area?

3 This is a photo of a fossilised seashell found in slate. Some fossils look odd because of the way they have been squashed. Explain how the direction of the pressure can alter the fossil's shape.

4 Make up your own rock cycle diagram. Here are some words to include. Discuss in your group which other words you will use.

   heat   pressure   weathering
   transport   melting   cooling

5 Someone in your group says: 'To understand the rock cycle, you have to understand about changes of state.' Look at the rock cycle you have produced for question 4. Add to it all the changes of state that are taking place.

11 Magnets and electromagnetism

In this chapter you will learn:

➡ that magnetic fields are regions in space where magnetic materials experience forces
➡ that like magnetic poles repel and unlike poles attract
➡ that an electric current in a coil produces a magnetic field pattern similar to that of a bar magnet
➡ how to make an electromagnet
➡ about uses of electromagnets

You will also develop your skills in:

➡ plotting graphs which are not straight lines
➡ making predictions about magnets and magnetic materials
➡ making and presenting observations
➡ drawing conclusions

➡ ➡ ➡ WHAT DO YOU KNOW?

1 Look at the photos below and opposite, then in your group discuss anything that you know about magnetism from the photos or from doing experiments yourselves. For example:
- Which materials are magnetic?
- What type of force is there between magnets?
- How does a compass work?
- What is a magnetic field?
2 Write two or three sentences containing some information about magnets and magnetism.

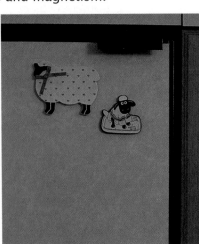

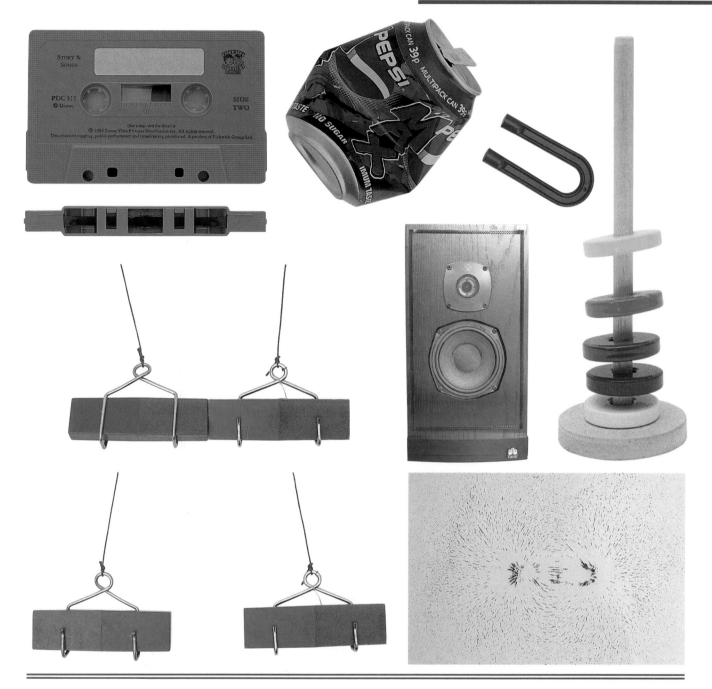

➡ *Properties of magnets*

The properties of magnets have been known for hundreds of years. The ancient Chinese knew of the properties of **lodestone**. This is a rock containing iron. They discovered that it would attract pieces of iron and if it was freely suspended it would set in a particular direction. They used pieces of it as a simple compass.

Today we use a variety of materials to make magnets. Those that are **magnetised** and stay magnetised are called **permanent magnets**. Those that do not stay magnetised are called **temporary magnets**.

Not all metals are magnetic. We can find out which are magnetic by bringing a permanent magnet up to different materials. The table shows some results:

Material	Magnetic?
iron	yes
steel	yes
aluminium	no
cobalt	yes
copper	no
nickel	yes
Magnadur	yes

1 Write a sentence to summarise which metals are magnetic and which are not.
2 Use a magnet to find out if a 1p coin produced in the early 1990s is magnetic and whether one produced in 2000 is. Which other coins are magnetic? What does this tell you about the materials they are made from?

EXTENSION

Key words
* domains
* microscopic
* magnetically hard
* magnetically soft

William Gilbert (1540–1603) recorded the results of many experiments with magnets.

The domain theory of magnetism

Ever since William Gilbert wrote about magnetism in 1600 (see page 244), scientists have put forward theories about why some materials are magnetic. Today we explain why materials such as iron are magnetic in terms of the particles from which they are made. We think that neighbouring particles are arranged in small groups called **domains**. A domain, though **microscopic**, contains millions of particles. Each domain acts like a very small magnet within the material. Normally the domains are randomly arranged. When we magnetise the material, the effect is to make these domains all line up in the same direction. It is a bit like pupils talking in groups in the playground. Suddenly there is a loud bang and they turn to face the direction from which the noise comes.

domains in
unmagnetised material

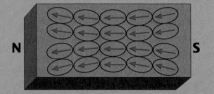

domains in
magnetised material

The domain theory explains why there is a limit to how strongly a particular material can be magnetised. If none of the magnetic domains are lined up, then it is unmagnetised; as more and more become lined up it becomes more strongly magnetised. When the domains are all lined up the material is fully magnetised. It cannot now be any more strongly magnetised.

We can also explain the difference between **magnetically hard** and **magnetically soft** materials. A magnetically hard material is hard to magnetise but once it is magnetised it stays magnetised. The magnetic domains are hard to align and hard to disarrange. A magnetically soft material is easily magnetised, even in a weak field (see page 242). As soon as the magnetising field is removed the magnetically soft material loses its magnetism. The magnetic domains are easy to align and easily get disarranged. The magnetism is temporary.

Permanent magnets, made from magnetically hard materials, gradually lose their magnetism. This could be due to a variety of causes, such as dropping them, hitting them or heating them. Magnets need to be stored carefully to keep their magnetism. 'Soft iron keepers' can be used, as shown in the diagram, to keep the magnetic domains lined up.

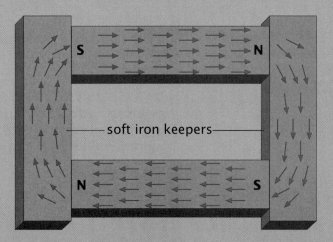

— soft iron keepers —

Complete the following passage using the words below.

- domain theory
- magnetism
- force
- particles

- alignment
- materials
- attracted
- magnetic

Certain substances are _____**A**_____ to a magnet. These substances are called magnetic _____**B**_____ and are those that contain the elements iron, nickel or cobalt.

The area around a magnet where a magnet material experiences a _____**C**_____ is known as the magnetic field.

How the _____**D**_____ are arranged in a material determines its magnetism. Groups of particles in a _____**E**_____ material can be lined up in a single direction like tiny magnets. This is known as the _____**F**_____ of magnetism. Heating, dropping or hammering a magnet can disarrange the _____**G**_____ of the domains (groups of particles). Consequently, the magnet will lose its _____**H**_____.

➡ *Magnets and forces*

You saw in Book 1 how two ring magnets could **repel** or **attract** one another. These photos show a bar magnet floating in a dish. As a second bar magnet is brought towards the dish, one of two things will happen. Either the floating magnet will be attracted to it as here, or it will be pushed away (repelled).

The region where this magnetic force is strongest is called the **pole** of the magnet and it is usually found near the end of the magnet. However, some special magnets have their poles on the sides. All magnets have two poles. One is called the north pole and the other the south pole. Some examples are shown in the diagrams.

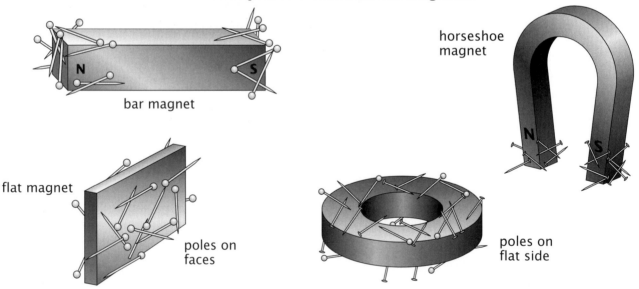

horseshoe magnet

bar magnet

flat magnet

poles on faces

poles on flat side

The poles exert the strongest magnetic force.

When two like poles are brought together they repel each other. So two north poles will repel each other and two south poles will repel each other. A north pole and a south pole will attract each other. However, an unmagnetised piece of iron will also be attracted. This means that the only sure test of whether two materials are magnets is if they repel each other.

Information processing · *Forces between magnets*

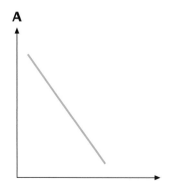

It is possible to demonstrate the repulsion of like magnetic poles using a top-pan balance. In the diagram, one bar magnet is fixed onto the top-pan balance. A second bar magnet is brought down towards the first magnet.

1 Explain what you think will happen. What will happen to the reading on the balance? If one of the magnets was turned round to face in the opposite direction, how would this affect the reading?

The table shows some readings that were taken using similar apparatus:

Height above top-pan balance (cm)	Reading on balance (g)
10	7
8	11
6	20
4	45
3	80
2	180
1	700

Remember that when we plot a graph of results like these, what we change (the input variable) goes along the horizontal axis. What we measure (the outcome variable) goes up the vertical axis.

2 What is the largest reading that has to go on the horizontal axis? What is the largest reading that has to go on the vertical axis?

3 Plot a graph of the results.

4 Which of these graphs does your graph look most like?

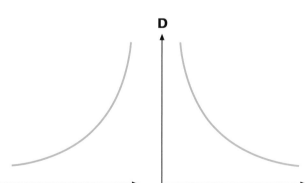

A   **B**   **C**   **D**

5 If the magnet was placed 5 cm above the balance, what do you predict the reading on the balance would be?

6 If the reading on the balance was 110 g, how high above the balance would the magnet be?

7 How does the size of the repulsive force change with distance?

➡ *Making magnets*

One way in which magnets used to be made is by stroking an unmagnetised steel bar using one pole of a permanent magnet. You could try stroking a screwdriver. The steel has to always be stroked in the same direction, as shown in the diagram. This method, called **magnetic induction**, does not make a very strong magnet. Nowadays magnets are made electrically.

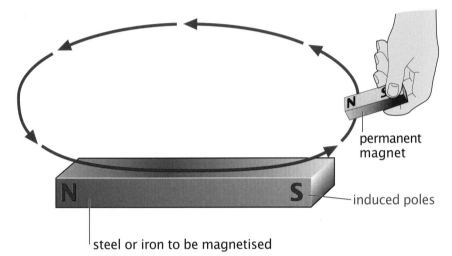

permanent magnet

induced poles

steel or iron to be magnetised

3 Magnets can be found in many places around the home. How many examples can you think of?
4 Some screwdrivers are magnetised. Why might this be useful?

➡ *Magnets and fields*

The region around a magnet where magnetic forces can be detected is called a **magnetic field**. Magnetic fields can be demonstrated in various ways. One common method is to use iron filings. In the photo iron filings show up the magnetic field around a bar magnet. Another way to map the magnetic field is to use a **plotting compass** (see opposite). This is a small, magnetised steel needle that is freely suspended. It lines itself up along the direction of the magnetic field.

We can draw a magnetic field using **field lines**. These are not real lines, but are a way of helping us picture the magnetic field. We put arrows on the lines to show the direction of the field: away from north, towards south. A strong magnetic field is shown by drawing the field lines close together. The field lines near the pole of a bar magnet are shown in the diagram opposite.

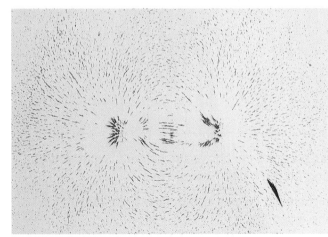

Mapping a magnetic field with iron filings.

Mapping a magnetic field with a plotting compass.

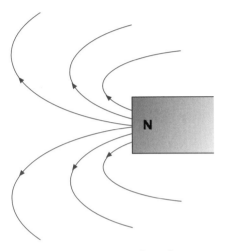

Field lines near a north pole.

5 Look at the photos **(a)**–**(c)** below, showing magnetic fields produced by different arrangements of magnets. Can you identify the type of magnet and where the poles are in each case?

(a)

(b)

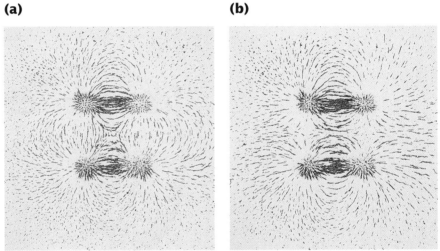

(c)

6 Draw the magnetic field around the whole of a bar magnet. Be sure to label the poles and put arrows on the field lines.

Word play

- Sometimes a person is described as having a 'magnetic personality'. What does this mean?
- Sometimes two people are described as having ideas that are 'poles apart'. What does this mean?

William Gilbert's discoveries

In 1600, William Gilbert, later physician to Queen Elizabeth I of England, published his book on magnetism, '*De Magnete*' or 'On the Magnet'. At that time you could have bought the book for seven shillings and sixpence (about 40p). It was written in Latin, as all science books were in those days. It is important because it gave the first explanation of why a compass needle points north–south: Gilbert was the first to suggest that the Earth itself acted as a magnet.

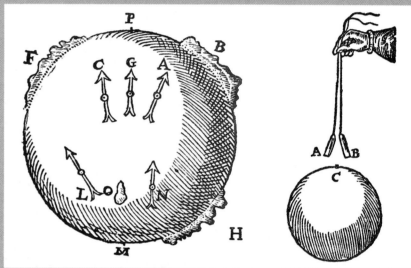

A drawing from Gilbert's '*De Magnete*'.

Imagine that you were the captain of a ship in Elizabethan days. Write a letter to William Gilbert, thanking him for his book '*De Magnete*' and explaining the usefulness of compasses in sailing.

➡ *The Earth's magnetic field*

Key words
* north-seeking pole
* south-seeking pole

The magnet floating on a dish of water described earlier will always settle with its pole pointing in the same direction. Any magnet that is free to move will do this. The diagram shows a bar magnet suspended in a paper stirrup. One end will always point towards the Earth's geographical north. This end of the magnet is called the **north-seeking pole**. We generally shorten this to the 'north pole' of the magnet. Similarly, the other end is the **south-seeking pole** or the 'south pole' of the magnet.

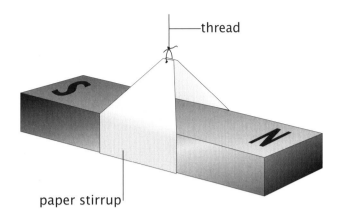

Scientists think that the reason for this is because the centre of the Earth is made mostly of molten (liquid) iron. This iron acts like a giant magnet. The Earth's magnetic poles are not stationary but move around the geographical poles. The difference between magnetic north and geographical north is often shown on maps such as Ordnance Survey maps. A compass will always point to the magnetic north pole and this then allows you to set your heading, or direction you want to go, more accurately. Even more surprising is the fact that scientists believe that every 200 000 years, or thereabouts, the Earth's magnetic field reverses.

DID YOU KNOW?

The Aurora Borealis or 'Northern Lights' sometimes seen in the northern sky are caused by the action of the Earth's magnetic field on electrically charged particles in the atmosphere. There are similar lights visible in the southern hemisphere. These are called the Aurora Australis.

Aurora Borealis.

→ *Magnetic fields around current-carrying conductors*

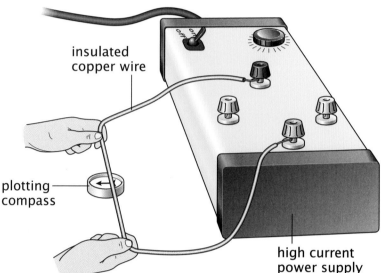

Hans Christian Oersted (1777–1851) performing his demonstration.

Demonstrating the magnetic field around a current-carrying wire.

The first person to demonstrate the link between an electric current and a magnetic field was Hans Christian Oersted. He conducted an experiment similar to the one shown in the diagram above. You may have seen such experiments demonstrated or even done them yourself. The magnetic field has a circular pattern around the wire.

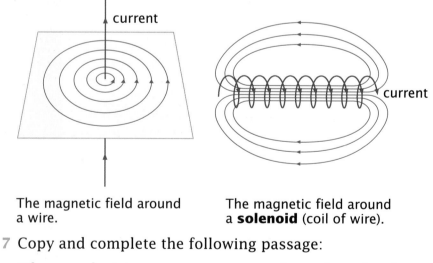

The magnetic field around a wire.

The magnetic field around a **solenoid** (coil of wire).

7 Copy and complete the following passage:

When an electric _____ passes through a wire, it creates a _____ _____. If you sprinkle _____ _____ in the area around the wire, you can see the magnetic _____. Another way to check where the magnetic field is would be to use a _____ _____. The _____ of this would move to line up with the field.

→ *Electromagnets*

Key words
✳ electromagnet
✳ core

When an electric current flows in a wire it can produce an **electromagnet**. A solenoid with an iron bar inside it makes a strong electromagnet. The bar of iron is called the **core** of the electromagnet. Such an electromagnet can easily be made by wrapping a number of turns of wire around a large iron nail. As soon as the electric current is switched off, the magnetism disappears. This is very useful.

Time to think

Write down all the key words in the chapter so far. In pairs, choose one key word and write down a question for which the key word is the answer. Try it out on another pair. If necessary alter your question so that it is clearer and try it out on another pair. If you have time, do the same for other key words.

Information processing ## Testing an electromagnet

The diagram shows an experiment using an electromagnet.

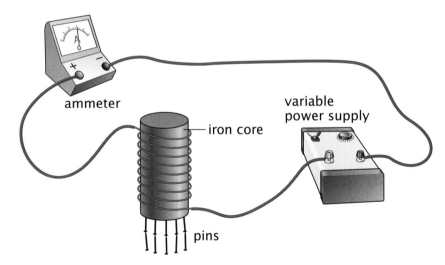

ammeter — iron core — variable power supply — pins

Current (A)	Mass of pins (g)
0	0
0.3	2
0.6	8
0.9	16
1.2	30
1.5	54
1.8	100
2.1	136
2.4	146
2.7	150
3.0	150

1 What variables could you change in the experiment shown?

2 What variables could you measure?

The table gives some results that were obtained using the apparatus shown.

3 Which is the input variable?

4 Which is the outcome variable?

5 Plot a graph of the results.

6 What would be the effect of increasing the number of turns of wire in the coil?

7 How does the strength of the electromagnet change as the current increases?

8 Explain this in terms of the domain theory.

Word play

Write clues for the word quiz below:

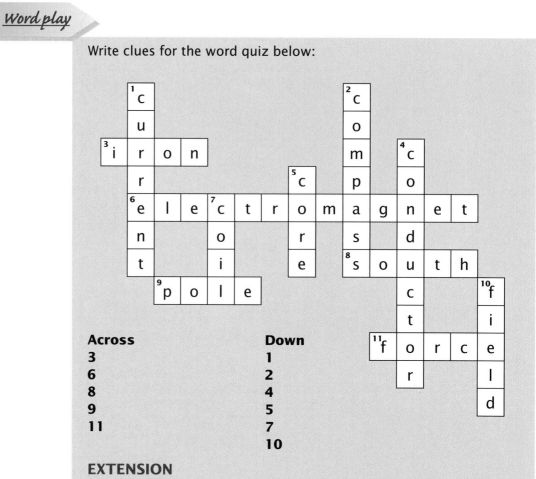

Across
3
6
8
9
11

Down
1
2
4
5
7
10

EXTENSION
Think back to your work on electricity in Year 7. Use the ideas from that plus the ideas in this chapter to make up your own word quiz.

Creative thinking My hero

Produce a comic strip about a hero who has electromagnetic powers whenever he clips his belt buckle together. Use your knowledge of electromagnetism to create a plot in which his enemies try to remove his powers.

Uses of electromagnets
The photo shows an electromagnet being used in a scrap yard. They are also used in doorbells and chimes.

8 List some uses of permanent magnets. Can you think of any toys that use magnets?

9 a) Why is an electromagnet more useful than a permanent magnet in a car scrap yard?

   b) What materials can be sorted by magnets?

10 The diagram shows a circuit for an electric bell. It uses an electromagnet. Can you identify the parts labelled **A**, **B**, **C** and **D**? Choose from the following:

bell push   hammer   contact   springy metal strip

Can you explain the purpose of these four parts and their role in how the bell works?

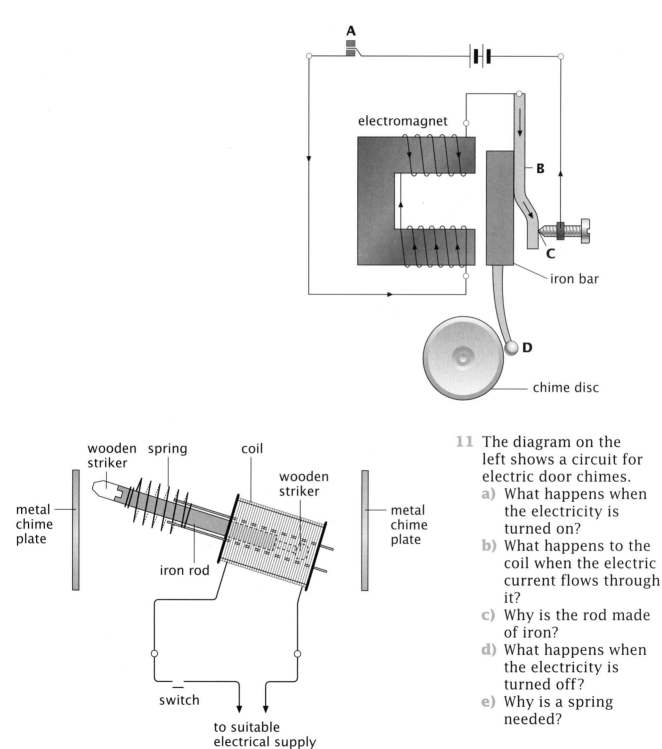

electromagnet

iron bar

chime disc

11 The diagram on the left shows a circuit for electric door chimes.
   a) What happens when the electricity is turned on?
   b) What happens to the coil when the electric current flows through it?
   c) Why is the rod made of iron?
   d) What happens when the electricity is turned off?
   e) Why is a spring needed?

wooden striker   spring   coil

wooden striker

metal chime plate

iron rod

metal chime plate

switch

to suitable electrical supply

Enquiry ## Making an electromagnet

Design and make the best electromagnet you can. You will be provided with the following materials:

- insulated wire
- an iron nail
- iron filings
- a balance
- a power supply
- some paper clips
- an ammeter.

Evaluation ## Which is best?

Key word
* precision

Here are extracts from two pupils' investigations.

Pupil 1

Method
I used a 200 cm length of green wire and wrapped it 30 times round an iron core. Then I connected it to the power supply, including the ammeter in the circuit. I switched the power supply on and counted how many paper clips it would pick up. I then increased the current and noted how many paper clips were now attracted.

Evaluation
I found that as the current increased the number of paper clips that stuck also increased, up to a maximum value. If I increased the current any more it made no difference. This shows that, to start with, the greater the current the greater the magnetic field. But once all the magnetic domains line up, the magnetic field cannot get any stronger.

Pupil 2

I performed two experiments. In the first experiment I varied the current but kept the number of coils of wire fixed at 50. In the second experiment I kept the current constant and changed the number of coils from 10 to 100 in steps of 10 turns. In both experiments I poured iron filings over the electromagnet with the power on. I gently shook it until no more filings fell off. I then cleared the bench of filings, turned the power off and weighed the iron filings that then fell off.

In the first experiment I plotted a graph of current against weight of iron filings. In the second experiment I plotted a graph of number of turns against weight of iron filings. As the number of turns was increased, the weight of iron filings increased.

I would need to do a further experiment to see whether it is the total number of turns that affect the strength of the magnet or whether it is how closely the coils are pushed together. Also I would need to find out whether the diameter of the turns of the coil makes any difference.

1 Which pupil performed the best experiment? Why do you say this?

2 Which pupil produced results with the greatest **precision**? Why do you say this?

3 Which variables did the first pupil consider?

4 Which variables did the second pupil consider?

5 Which pupil used their scientific knowledge and understanding to explain their observations? What was the scientific explanation that they gave?

6 Which pupil suggested improvements to the method used?

7 How would you have improved the first pupil's investigation?

8 How would you have improved the second pupil's investigation?

Time to think

Produce a Key Facts card. An example is shown here. Make your own to explain one of the key points that have been discussed in this chapter. You could choose one of the following topics:

- uses of magnets
- types of magnets
- the Earth's magnetic field
- using a compass
- plotting magnetic fields
- the construction of an electromagnet
- how an electric bell works.

Compare your Key Facts card with others in your group. Check that the ideas are explained well and the correct scientific terms are used.

KEY FACTS

An electromagnet

To make an electromagnet you need some wire, a battery or power pack and an iron nail. Wrap about 20 turns of wire around the nail and then connect it to the power source. If you bring a compass near the nail you will see that it is attracted towards one end and repelled from the other end. The nail acts like a magnet. One end is a north pole and the other is a south pole. The nail will also attract objects such as paper clips.

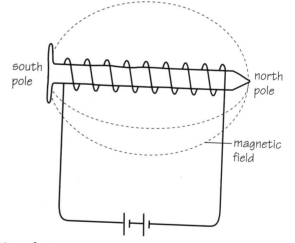

south pole

north pole

magnetic field

In industry, electromagnets are used in scrap yards to sort and lift the iron material.

Electromagnets are used in electric bells and chimes. The advantage of an electromagnet over a permanent magnet is that when you switch off the electricity, the magnet loses its magnetism.

Links: compass, magnetic fields, electric bell

12 Ecology

In this chapter you will learn:

➡ **how communities of organisms interact within a habitat**
➡ **how to identify some organisms**
➡ **the importance of fieldwork in ecological investigations**
➡ **about habitats, populations, communities, ecosystems, biomes and the biosphere**
➡ **about pyramids of number and pyramids of energy**

You will also develop your skills in:

➡ **modelling feeding relationships quantitatively**
➡ **modelling environmental changes in a habitat**
➡ **using sampling techniques**
➡ **collecting, presenting and interpreting data**
➡ **making predictions**

WHAT DO YOU KNOW?

Key words
* producers
* consumers
* herbivores
* predator

Look at the picture opposite of a woodland habitat.

These questions are to help you recall your Year 7 work about the environment. Work in your group to answer them together.

1 Name three **producers** in the picture.

2 What **consumers** can you see?

3 Which of these consumers are **herbivores** and which is the **predator**?

4 What is the difference between consumers and producers?

5 Classify all the animals you can see in the picture.

6 Each person in your group is to choose one of the consumers in the picture and describe how it is adapted to its environment. You should each make your own notes about what everyone describes.

What is ecology?

Key words
* organisms
* species
* ecology
* population
* adaptations
* hypothesise

All **organisms** (living things) need energy and materials to live. The life of each organism affects other organisms (within and between **species**) as well as the environment. Although people have always been interested in other organisms around them, it is only fairly recently that this has become a scientific study called **ecology**. Ecologists study organisms in their natural environment – 'in the field'. As well as fieldwork, they carry out laboratory investigations. They look for the links between **population** numbers, diet, size, behaviour, and the **adaptations** of organisms to their environment. Ecologists also study the physical environment, finding out about the soil, rocks, air and water. They look for patterns and trends in the data so that they can **hypothesise** about causes and effects.

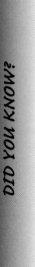

DID YOU KNOW?

In 1866, Ernst Haeckel, a German biologist, used the word 'oecology' to describe the study of organisms and their interaction with the world around them. The word is based on a Greek word '*oikos*' which means 'household'. This is also the origin of the word 'economy'. The modern spelling of the word ecology was first used in 1893.

Producers, the green machines

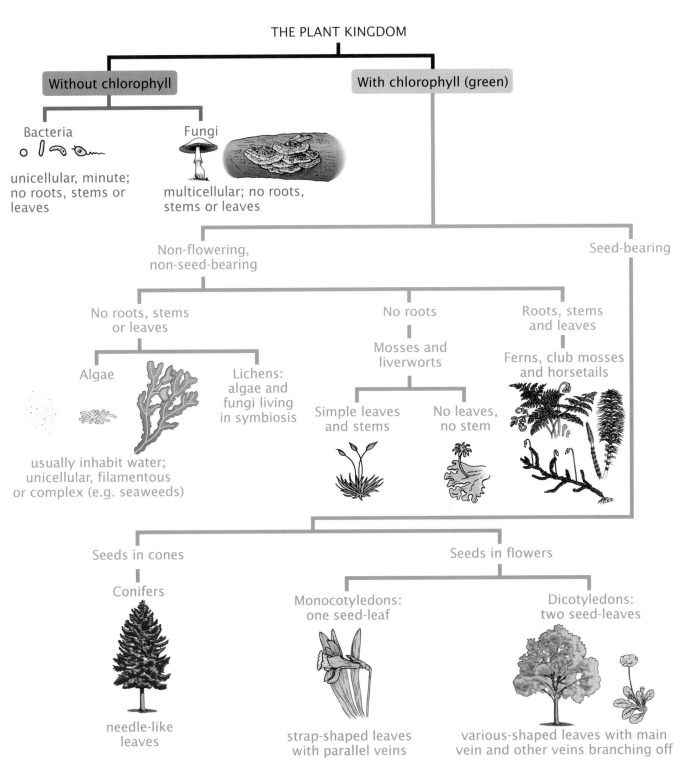

THE PLANT KINGDOM

Without chlorophyll

With chlorophyll (green)

Bacteria

unicellular, minute; no roots, stems or leaves

Fungi

multicellular; no roots, stems or leaves

Non-flowering, non-seed-bearing

Seed-bearing

No roots, stems or leaves

No roots

Roots, stems and leaves

Algae

Lichens: algae and fungi living in symbiosis

Mosses and liverworts

Ferns, club mosses and horsetails

Simple leaves and stems

No leaves, no stem

usually inhabit water; unicellular, filamentous or complex (e.g. seaweeds)

Seeds in cones

Seeds in flowers

Conifers

Monocotyledons: one seed-leaf

Dicotyledons: two seed-leaves

needle-like leaves

strap-shaped leaves with parallel veins

various-shaped leaves with main vein and other veins branching off

Use this classification key for green plants to classify the three producers that you identified in the woodland picture.

Decomposition

Do you remember thinking about the compost heap as a habitat in Book 1?

Key words
* decomposers
* secreting
* enzymes
* absorbed
* cytoplasm
* nutrient cycle

1 Which micro-organisms break down and decompose dead plants and animals?

Fungi do not feed like green plants. They are **decomposers**. They feed by **secreting enzymes** onto dead materials to digest them. Then the nutrients are **absorbed** (taken in) into the fungus. There is more information in Chapter 9 about the other types of micro-organisms that cause decay.

A rotting cow pat

* Microbes in the soil and air invade the cow pat and feed on it. Nitrogen-loving bacteria break down the proteins in the dung and release nitrates and other minerals into the soil.
* Fungi live on the surface of the dung as well as on other dead material. Their digestive enzymes break down and rot away the cow pat.
* Some insects and slugs also eat cow pats, as well as leaves, twigs and other organic matter.

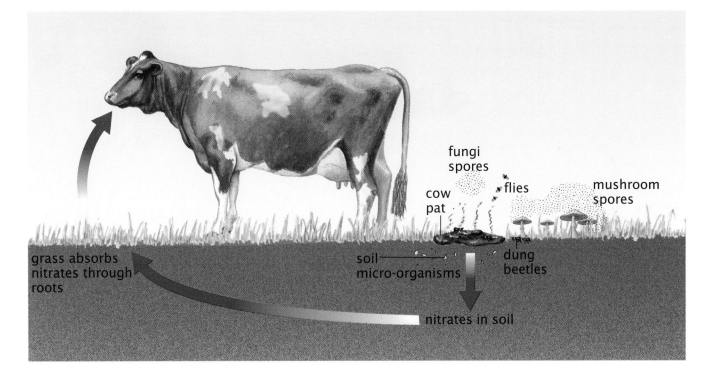

Green plants absorb the nitrates from the soil and use them to create protein. This protein is used to make new **cytoplasm** in cells. The plants grow, reproduce and die. They are then decomposed by fungi and bacteria and the **nutrient cycle** continues, as shown on the next page.

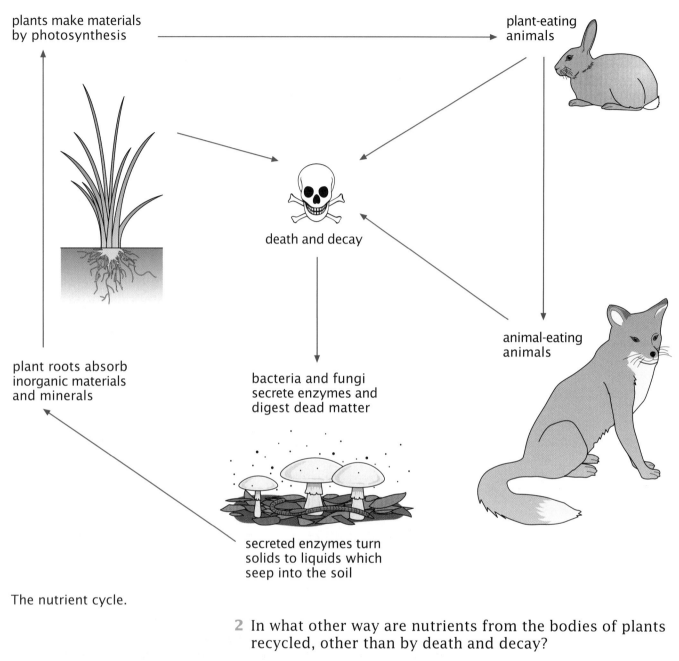

plants make materials
by photosynthesis

plant-eating
animals

death and decay

plant roots absorb
inorganic materials
and minerals

bacteria and fungi
secrete enzymes and
digest dead matter

animal-eating
animals

secreted enzymes turn
solids to liquids which
seep into the soil

The nutrient cycle.

2 In what other way are nutrients from the bodies of plants recycled, other than by death and decay?

3 Imagine you were making a film about how cow pats rot away. What film shots would you select?

4 Why do gardeners buy horse manure for their gardens?

→ *Complicated classifying*

Some plants have cones and some have flowers.

5 Divide the plants shown here into two groups:
cone-bearing and flower-bearing.

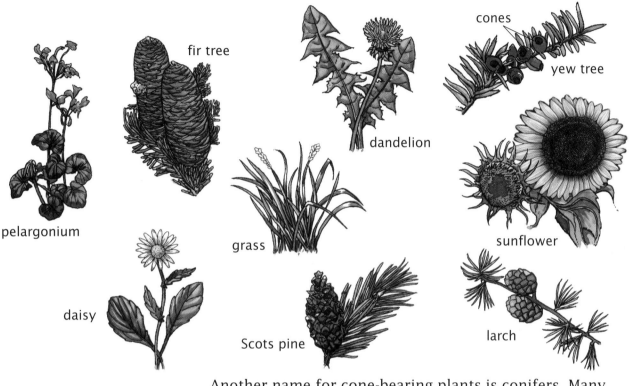

Another name for cone-bearing plants is conifers. Many conifers do not lose their leaves in winter so we call them 'evergreens'. Conifers are good at surviving in cold or dry climates because they have tiny leaves which we call needles. Water loss is very low through these needle-shaped leaves, so they help keep moisture inside the plants.

Flowering plants can be further classified into smaller groups. Some are called **monocotyledons** and others are **dicotyledons**. Cotyledons are the first leaves a seedling grows. 'Mono' means one and 'di' means two.

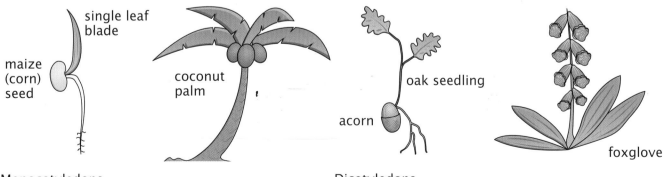

Monocotyledons.

Dicotyledons.

The study of classifying organisms into groups based on their similarities and differences is called **taxonomy**.

Enquiry Growing seeds

1 Look at the seeds of some peas and maize. Draw them to scale: make them twice as large as life. Label the features you can see. Refer to the drawings below for some help.

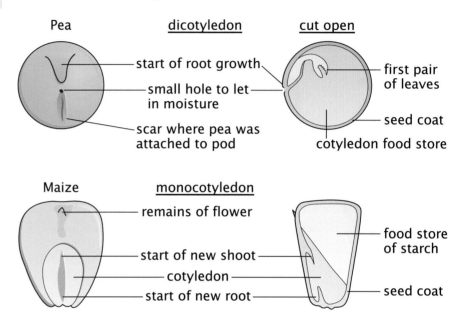

Pea   dicotyledon   cut open

- start of root growth
- small hole to let in moisture
- scar where pea was attached to pod
- first pair of leaves
- seed coat
- cotyledon food store

Maize   monocotyledon

- remains of flower
- start of new shoot
- cotyledon
- start of new root
- food store of starch
- seed coat

Sammy decided to investigate what conditions you need to make seeds **germinate**. He planted seven pea seeds and seven maize seeds. Each seed was put in a different flowerpot, and each was given different growing conditions. He recorded information over the next 3 weeks about the number and shape of the first leaves, the stems of the seedling, and the root structure.

Here are the notes and drawings that he made:

Summary of bean growth

Bean	Treatment	root length	shoot length	leaves
1	2 days fridge	2 cm	2 cm	just starting, white
2	3 weeks fridge	3 cm	4 cm	1 pair, white
3	2 days windowsill	3 cm	4 cm	1 pair, green
4	2 days cupboard	3 cm	4 cm	1 pair, white
5	3 weeks windowsill	8 cm	10 cm	2 pairs, green
6	3 weeks cupboard	8 cm	14 cm	3 pairs, white
7	3 weeks no water	nothing, shrivelled, dead		

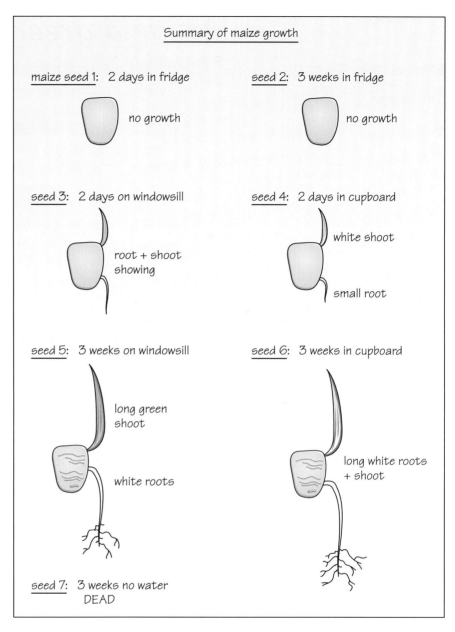

Summary of maize growth

maize seed 1: 2 days in fridge

no growth

seed 2: 3 weeks in fridge

no growth

seed 3: 2 days on windowsill

root + shoot showing

seed 4: 2 days in cupboard

white shoot

small root

seed 5: 3 weeks on windowsill

long green shoot

white roots

seed 6: 3 weeks in cupboard

long white roots + shoot

seed 7: 3 weeks no water
DEAD

2 Do you think Sammy has recorded enough information?

3 What do you think Sammy **inferred** about the conditions needed for germination?

4 Sammy did not make a plan of his investigation. Make a plan for him. Add any new instructions that you think he should include the next time he does this investigation, so that it is more scientific.

Research Think of some seed-based foods that you eat. Collect together some wrappers from these products or do some drawings, and make a display.

Do all the seed-bearing plants in your examples come from Britain? If not, where do they come from? What type of climate do these countries have?

Inside a green machine

Plants cannot move around to get their food, so how do they make it?

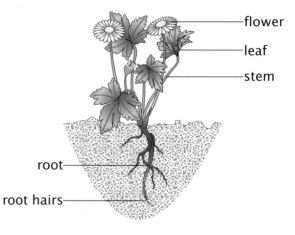

Look at this picture of a flowering plant.

6 What are the leaves for? Why are they green?

7 How does the plant get water?

8 What is the stem for?

Plants, just like animals, must transport substances around inside their bodies. Their transport system is made up of two different types of tubes – for food and water to travel through. The **phloem** tissue has tubes for transporting food; the **xylem** tissue has tubes (or 'vessels') for transporting water. Sections of these can be viewed under a microscope.

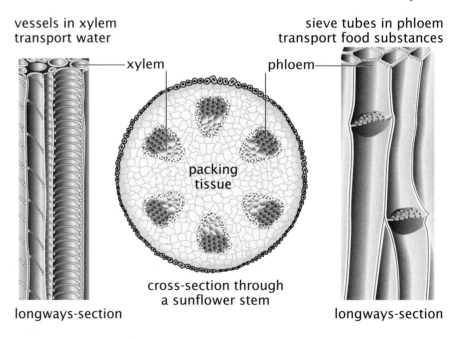

9 What is the transport system of vertebrate animals called?

Below are some photographs of cross-sections of a stem, a leaf and a root, magnified by a microscope. The slides have been stained to show up the different tissues. See if you can identify the phloem and the xylem in the slides that your teacher shows you. Make a few sketches of what you see. Make sure you write down the magnification by each of your drawings. (Remember, this is the product of the magnification of the two microscope lenses.)

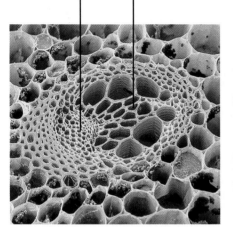

phloem   xylem

Part of a stem section (×130).   Leaf section (×120).   Root section (×30).

Reasoning *Controlling the water*

Mohammed and Leah investigated water loss from leaves. They set up an experiment like this:

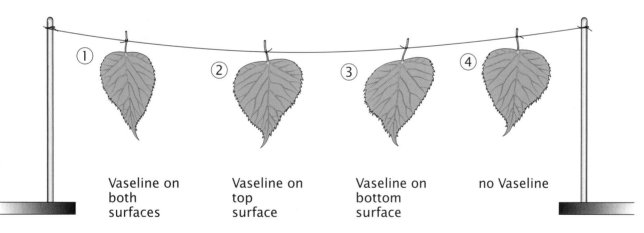

① Vaseline on both surfaces

② Vaseline on top surface

③ Vaseline on bottom surface

④ no Vaseline

Here are their results, after 3 days:

Leaf	1	2	3	4
Appearance	fresh, green	shrivelled, brown	a bit crinkled, still green	shrivelled, brown
Mass (g)	0.7	0.2	0.5	0.1

1 What do you think they might infer from these results about water loss from leaf surfaces?

2 What protects a leaf from losing too much water?

Looking at the surfaces of leaves

If a leaf is torn roughly in two, you can peel off some of the **epidermis** (outer layer) and look at it under a microscope. You will see holes in the epidermis. These are called **stomata** (one is a stoma) and they control water loss from the leaves.

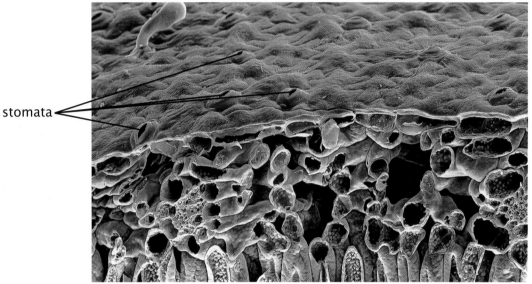

stomata

Stomata in the lower epidermis of a leaf (×225).

The diagrams show cross-sections through leaves from two different plants.

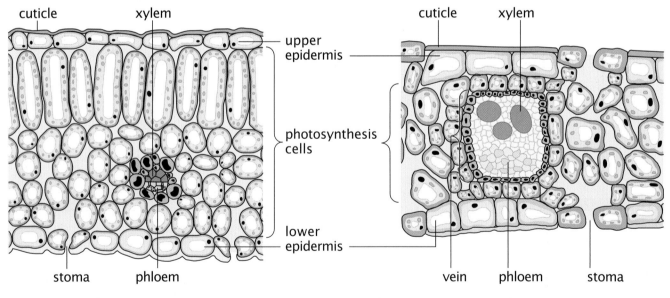

cuticle   xylem

upper epidermis

photosynthesis cells

lower epidermis

stoma   phloem

Typical dicotyledon leaf section.

cuticle   xylem

vein   phloem   stoma

Typical monocotyledon leaf section.

10 Do you notice any differences between the leaf surfaces of the monocotyledon and the dicotyledon?

11 Why do you think some leaves, like holly, look shiny?

12 a) What sort of leaves do cacti have? Why?
    b) Why are their stems so thick and fleshy-looking?
    c) Where do cacti make their food? How do you know?

Some plants are called **succulents**. Look up the word succulent in a dictionary.

13 Cacti are succulents. Where do you think these types of plant would grow? Why do you think that?

Information processing

Comparing leaves

Professor Green compared leaves that grew on elderberry bushes in the middle of an oak wood with elderberry bush leaves from the edge of a field. This is what he found:

	Woodland	Field
Biomass (dry weight) of 10 leaves	5.3 g	12.6 g
Total leaf surface area of 10 leaves	720 cm²	201 cm²

How do you think he explained these results? Think about the different environmental conditions in the wood and at the field edge.

Time to think

In Year 7 you found out what 'adaptation' means. Look back over the work you have done so far in this chapter. Find some examples of plants and animals that you think are adapted to suit their environment. On a large poster ask each person in your group to explain at least one example in turn until you think all the examples have been listed.

➡ *The carbon-based world*

All life on Earth is based on the element carbon.

14 What is meant by 'element' here?

Think back to your work on food chains in Year 7. Like energy, carbon is passed from organism to organism through a chain of producers and consumers.

In the Earth's atmosphere, carbon combines with another gas to form carbon dioxide.

15 What is the other gas?

In plants, carbon becomes **carbohydrate** and is a source of energy for growth.

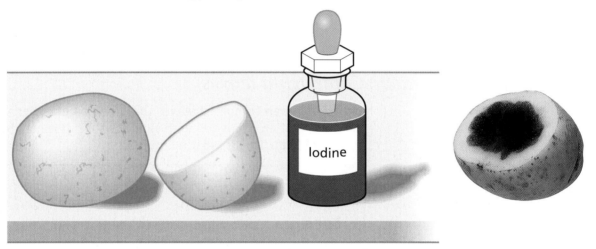

Iodine shows up the carbohydrate starch in plant material.

Plants are the main exchange agents for carbon, using atmospheric carbon dioxide to produce carbohydrate through **photosynthesis**. Animals that eat plants break down the plant carbohydrate to give them energy and to remake their own body's carbohydrates to store energy.

16 What is the process of breaking down food in animals called?

In the ground, and in the bones and shells of animals, carbon is found as calcium carbonate. Decomposition eventually returns most of the carbon to the atmosphere as carbon dioxide. Under certain conditions, some parts of dead and decaying plants and animal bodies become coal, peat, oil and gas. These are the fossil fuels.

17 Why do you think they are called 'fossil fuels'? You may need to look back to the work you did in Year 7.

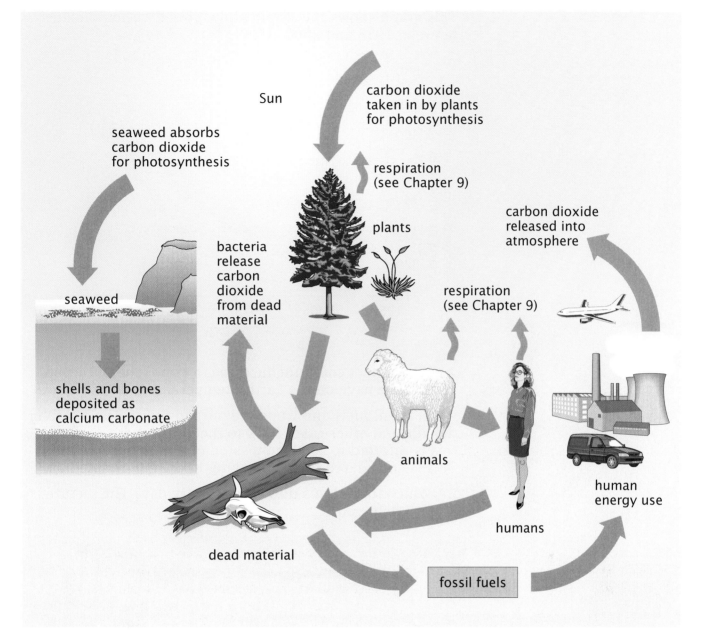

The carbon cycle.

This diagram shows how carbon is cycled through the world. You will find another type of natural cycle in Chapter 10.

18 What is being cycled in the cycle in Chapter 10?

The greenhouse effect

Carbon dioxide in the atmosphere prevents the Earth's heat radiating out into space. This is the 'greenhouse effect'.

19 What does 'radiate' mean here?
20 If all the heat released by living things escaped into space, what do you think would happen to the temperature of the Earth over time? What would be the consequences of this?

This graph shows the rise in atmospheric carbon dioxide between 1958 and 2000.

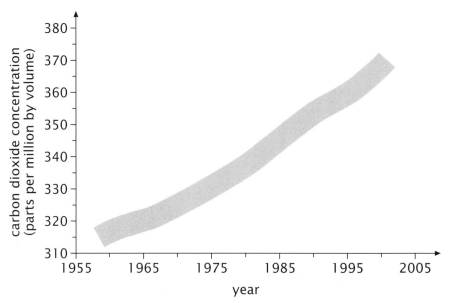

21 What effect could the increase in atmospheric carbon dioxide have on the Earth's temperature? Why?

When fossil fuels and wood are burned they release carbon dioxide and other gases back to the atmosphere. Sometimes this is referred to as 'the emission of greenhouse gases'. This is considered to be damaging to the environment.

22 Which fossil fuels do we burn every day? The picture will help you.

Information processing ## The greenhouse effect

In your group 'brainstorm' your ideas about what the greenhouse effect means to you. (Look back to Chapter 3, page 74.)

1 Put your ideas into a concept map.

2 Draw a poster to show how a greenhouse is a model for this environmental effect.

Research

Find out more about the greenhouse effect from the internet and from books in the library. Try to answer these questions:

- Does the Government issue any advice on reducing the emission of greenhouse gases?
- What do conservation bodies such as Friends of the Earth and Greenpeace think are the dangers of the increase in the greenhouse effect?
- What other conservation issues are current news?
- What do you and your friends think are the biggest dangers to our environment and how would you reduce these threats?

Creative thinking ## Conservation

Find out what the word 'conservation' means. Is it different to 'preservation'?

Here is some publicity material from a conservation group. Imagine that you are a member of that group.

1 Decide on a name for your group, and redesign the poster to include more details about your group's purpose. For example, you might want to indicate why you think tree planting is important.

2 How would your group raise funds to buy trees to plant? Think of some fundraising activities. Make sure they have a positive environmental impact and image.

→ # The transfer of energy

Key words
* ecosystem
* trophic level
* pyramid of numbers
* pyramid of energy

In every **ecosystem**, energy is trapped and stored by green plants – the primary producers. When animals eat plants they take in some of this energy. When predators in turn eat those animals some of their energy is transferred, and so on along a food chain.

At each stage of the food chain energy is passed on and some is stored as plant material or animal flesh. Ecologists call each stage a **trophic level**.

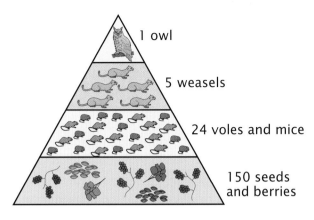

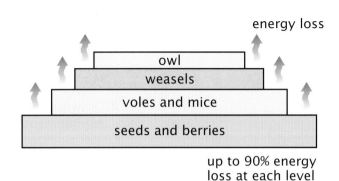

energy loss

up to 90% energy
loss at each level

Pyramid of numbers for a food chain.

Pyramid of energy for the same food chain.

Some energy is always lost as it passes from one trophic level to another. This is because the plants or animals need energy for all their living processes and so only some of the energy is used to make new cells. In most ecosystems only about 10–20% of the energy from each trophic level reaches the level above.

Look at the **pyramid of numbers** above:

23 What do you notice about the numbers of organisms at each of the trophic levels as you move towards the top of the pyramid?

24 Name the producers, consumers, predators and prey in this example.

Look at the **pyramid of energy** above:

25 What happens to the energy at each trophic level?

26 Why does it take so many weasels to feed one tawny owl?

EXTENSION Here are some more pyramids of energy:

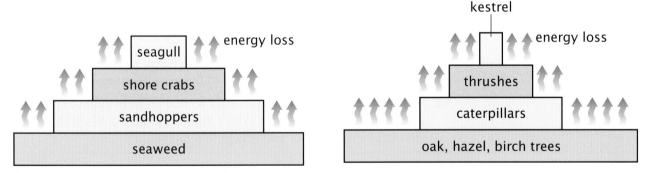

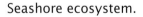

Seashore ecosystem.

Woodland ecosystem.

27 Why is there less energy lost at the first level in the pyramid of a seashore ecosystem than in the woodland ecosystem? Think about the type of plant matter growing in each ecosystem.

28 Some scientists use the term 'pyramid of biomass' for a pyramid of energy. Explain whether you think this is a good name or not.

Mathematicians can use the data that ecologists collect to create mathematical models about how energy flows through ecosystems, based on energy pyramids. These tell them something about the feeding relationships between plants and animals in that particular ecosystem. This link between maths and science could provide solutions to the problem of shrinking energy supplies in the future.

All the energy entering an ecosystem is eventually released back into space as heat. It cannot be recycled as useful energy.

Insecticides

Key words
* insecticides
* toxic
* concentrated

Insecticides are chemicals that kill insects. After the Second World War, a new range of chemical insecticides was developed. One of these was called DDT. Scientists believed they had solved the huge problem of insects destroying crops. The Government encouraged farmers to use these insecticides to increase crop yields. In 1962, Rachel Carson published a book called '*Silent Spring*'. She made people realise that killing insects with chemicals that were **toxic** was dangerous to other organisms in the food chain, in particular, birds. These insecticide chemicals were not breaking down. They remained toxic and were passed on to other animals that ate the dead insects. At each step in the food chain the chemicals became more **concentrated**. The concentrated insecticide killed some birds and weakened the egg shells of others.

1 What problem did scientists believe DDT would solve?
2 Why does the insecticide get more concentrated in each link of the food chain? Think about pyramids of numbers.
3 Why do you think Carson gave her book the title '*Silent Spring*'?

A hierarchy of life

Key words
* community
* biome
* biosphere
* hierarchy

Living things can be studied at six different levels.

* The first level is the individual organism.
* The second level is the population of that organism. Ecologists study one specific population to collect data about their feeding relationships, adaptations and reproduction.
* At the third level several populations of different species that link together in a food web make up a **community**.
* Several different communities found close to each other create an ecosystem.
* Different types of ecosystem are grouped together in a single geographic zone to create a **biome**. A biome has one particular climate.
* All of Earth's varied biomes make up the highest level of organisation, the **biosphere**. This is the layer above, on and below the Earth's surface that contains all living things.

These six levels form a **hierarchy**.

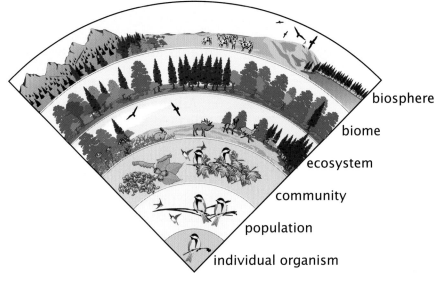

The hierarchy of living things.

The Eden Project

> '... it was important to keep reminding ourselves why we had begun this journey. We had started with the idea of four conservatories representing some of the key climate zones of the world, and one further conservatory that would demonstrate the widest possible range of productive plants from these regions. This then evolved into four conservatories containing both their wild and productive flora. By December 1999 we were looking at three conservatories: the Humid tropics (broadly rainforest), the Sub-tropics (islands) and the warm Temperate (Mediterranean climate), with an external designed parkland that would tell the story of our own temperate climate.'
>
> Tim Smit, from '*Eden*' (Bantam Press)

The Eden Project is in Cornwall. Over a million people have visited since it opened in 2000. It is a huge and ambitious conservation and education project. At its heart is the largest greenhouse ever built, an artificial biome.

Word play

Read again what Tim Smit says about the intentions of the project. Find out what these words mean:

conservatory humid temperate zone

29 Think about the artificial biomes – what variables need to be controlled to provide the right climates for the plants in each of the conservatories Tim Smit writes about?

30 Why do you think it is called the 'Eden' Project?

EXTENSION The Earth's major biomes are shown on this map. You will study these in more detail in Geography.

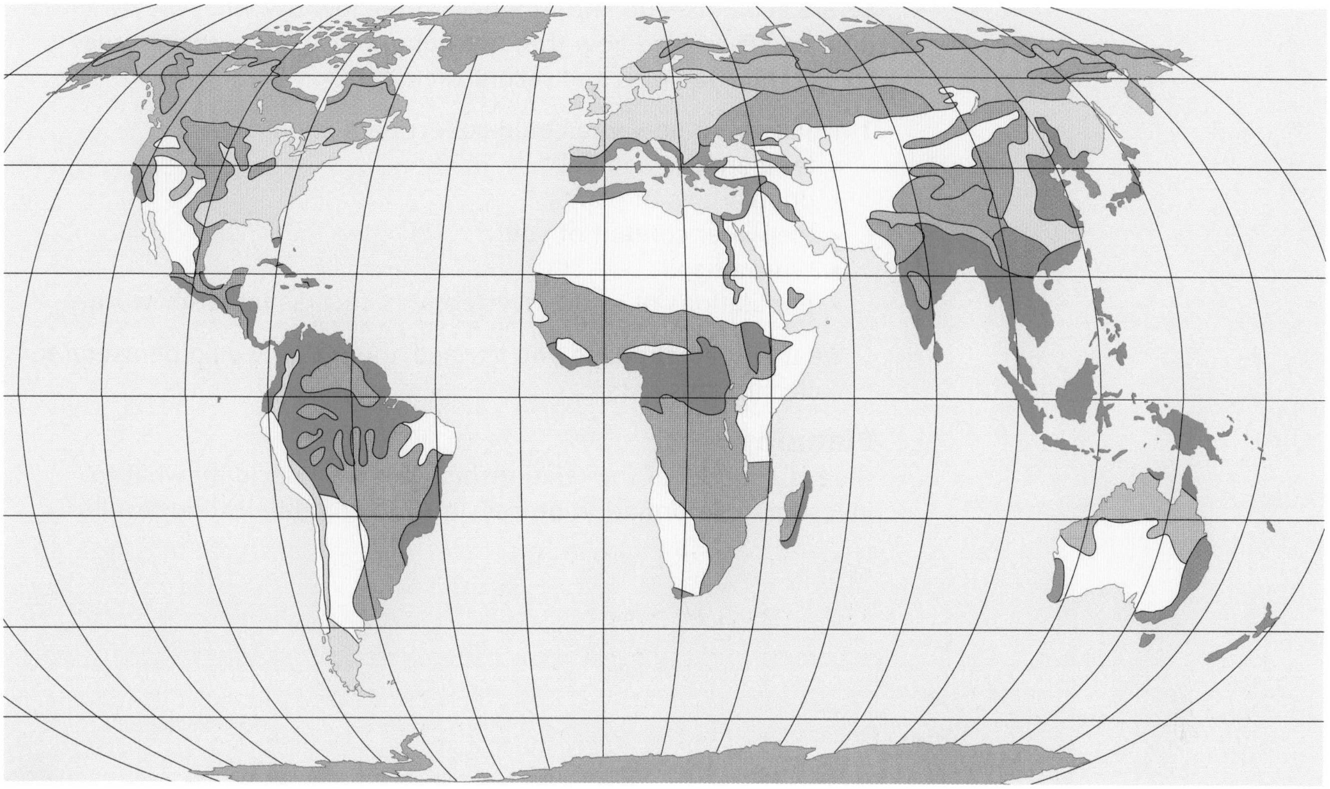

key

■	tropical rainforest
■	temperate rainforest
■	temperate deciduous forest
■	boreal coniferous forest (taiga)
■	Mediterranean scrub forest
■	grassland and savanna
□	desert
■	ice and tundra (treeless plains of marsh and stones)

The world's biomes.

31 Make a table that will help people to see where in the world different biomes are found.

Word play Work in pairs to make up a crossword puzzle where the following words are included as either part of the clue or as an answer. There are internet sites where you can find help.

- predator
- consumer
- carbon dioxide
- decomposer
- prey
- DDT
- adaptation
- toxic
- greenhouse
- oxygen
- conservation
- ecosystem
- biome
- pyramid

You may want to add some more words to the list.
See if another pair in your class can solve your 'ecopuzzle'.

Enquiry *Fieldwork*

Before ecologists go 'into the field', they identify what they want to find out. They plan how they are going to carry out their surveys, collect their samples and record their data.

1 Think about how you could collect data about:
- temperature and light
- populations of plants
- the water content of soil
- types of soil
- populations of small invertebrates such as insect or worms.

What equipment have you learned about that would be useful for collecting this data?

Planning

Here is a model of the relationships between deciding what to investigate, information processing and communicating results:

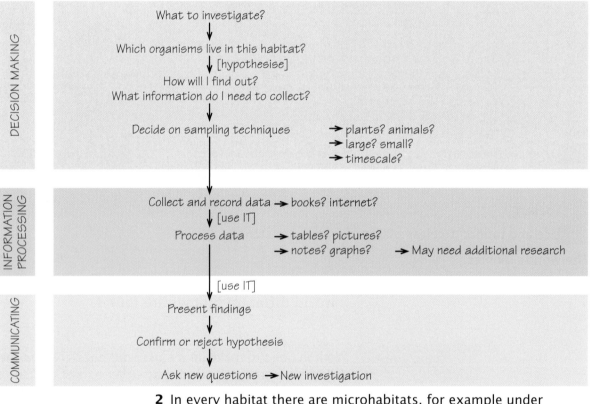

DECISION MAKING

What to investigate?
↓
Which organisms live in this habitat?
↓ [hypothesise]
How will I find out?
What information do I need to collect?
↓
Decide on sampling techniques → plants? animals?
→ large? small?
→ timescale?

INFORMATION PROCESSING

Collect and record data → books? internet?
↓ [use IT]
Process data → tables? pictures?
→ notes? graphs? → May need additional research

[use IT]

COMMUNICATING

Present findings
↓
Confirm or reject hypothesis
↓
Ask new questions → New investigation

2 In every habitat there are microhabitats, for example under stones, beneath tree bark, in leaf litter. Here are a few ideas for creating your own microhabitats to study:

Which organisms would you expect to find in these microhabitats?

3 In your group make a plan of how you would survey the ecological microhabitats around your school. You need to think about what you could do in just 2 hours, so make sure your plan is realistic, as well as safe.

4 Make some tables ready to fill in with the data you want to collect.

Going large-scale

To study larger habitats you need team work. A lot of information is needed to create a picture of the relationships between organisms in one habitat. Your class will be doing some fieldwork. Each group will collect information about a different part of the habitat and all this information will be combined in some way.

EXTENSION Class 8 in Greenville School did some ecology work in a park near their school. Here are some of their records.

Group 1 made this sketch map to scale:

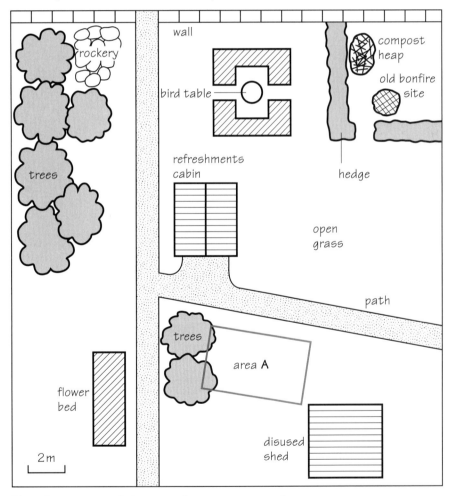

5 Make a copy of the map for your group. In your group, use coloured pencils or crayons to indicate where you think there will be most:
  a) light
  b) damp conditions
  c) warmth.

6 What sort of animals would you expect to find in the areas you have indicated? Name some.

7 **a)** How would you capture some of these animals for closer study?
  b) What precautions would you take to make sure you and they are not harmed?

Group 2 put a tape measure down from under the trees in area **A** on the map to the open grass space. They used a quadrat every $\frac{1}{2}$ metre to estimate the percentage cover of grass, daisies, plantains and clover in each square. Here is the data they collected (they estimated to the nearest 10%):

Quadrat number	Percentage cover			
	Grass	Daisy	Plantain	Clover
1 (under trees, where mower cannot reach)	40	50	10	0
2	50	30	10	10
3	60	20	20	0
4	70	10	10	10
5	80	10	10	0
6	80	0	10	10
7	90	0	0	10
8	80	10	0	10
9	90	10	0	0
10 (in open area of park)	90	0	0	10

8 What do you notice about the percentage of grass cover under the trees compared with the open area?

9 **a)** Where are daisies most abundant – near or far from the trees?
  b) Where are plantains most abundant – near or far from the trees?

10 The Class 8 teacher told group 2 that they had to be careful in the assumptions they might make about the effect of light on plant distribution. She said: 'This is a survey, the variables are not controlled'.
  a) Discuss what you think she means.
  b) Plan a simple controlled investigation that group 1 could carry out. First decide what they might hypothesise about light and plant growth. Make sure you plan a 'fair test'.

11 What inferences can you make about the relationship between light and plant growth?

Group 3 studied the 'lie of the land'. They wanted to find out how the land slopes. They used a map with contour lines, as shown opposite.

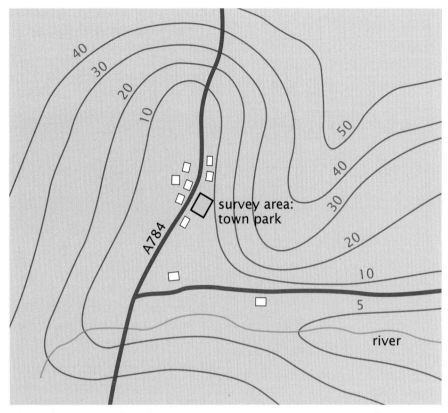

They also used a height measurer to get a more accurate description of the variations in the land level over the study area.

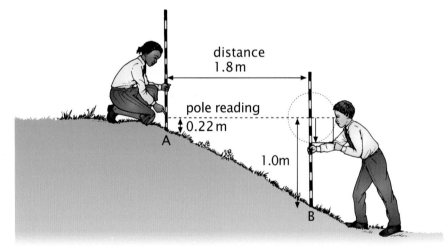

Here is their results table for the area:

Poles at	Distance (m)	Pole reading (m)	Difference of level (m)	Up or down
AB	1.8	0.22	0.78	down
BC	1.6	0.53	0.47	down
CD	0.8	0.37	0.63	down
DE	0.7	0	1.00	up
EF	0.6	0	1.00	up
FG	1.0	0.23	0.77	down

12 Use graph paper to draw an accurate profile of the land from the data in the table drawn up by group 3.

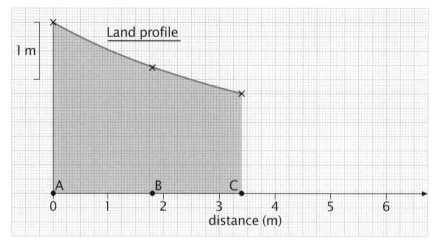

13 The teacher told group 3 that it would have been simpler to take height measurements at 1 metre intervals. Why would this have been easier?

14 a) What other information should group 3 record to provide more detail about this particular ecosystem?
   b) Is there any information from the other two groups that could help them?

EXTENSION

The Gaia hypothesis

In 1972 James Lovelock, a British scientist, put forward a new theory of life. In his 'Gaia hypothesis' he proposed that the Earth is a self-regulating organism itself. It responds to changes in the environment so that conditions for life are maintained. He suggested that life on Earth will continue, no matter what humans do to it. The Earth will somehow compensate and adapt, creating new environments and habitats. However, the forms of life that survive and evolve may not be human!

1 In your group, discuss whether you think Lovelock was right in considering the Earth itself as an organism. Does it show the seven characteristics of living things?
2 Imagine about a thousand years into the future, when the increase in the greenhouse effect has raised the temperature of the Earth so that in Britain the climate is similar to the present climate of Africa.
   a) What do you think would be the effect on water supply?
   b) What new habitats might have appeared?
   c) Think of some animals and plants that grow and live locally. How might they have adapted to the new environmental conditions?

Population studies

The study of the reasons why populations of particular species increase and decrease is called **population dynamics**. Computer models can **simulate** the way in which a change in one species' population can affect all the populations of other species that are linked through the food web. Lemmings are a good example. These small rat-like creatures live in cold northern regions. Every 3 to 4 years their numbers get very large and whole populations must move to find enough food to live on. Tales of their mass suicide by jumping off cliffs into the sea are based on the fact that they will swim across rivers to find food. When they reach the sea they probably think it is a river and they attempt to swim across.

Factors that can affect the size of a population include:

* predation
* seasonal changes
* environmental disasters, for example an oil spillage at sea or a forest fire.

'Algal blooms' are another example. Large amounts of nitrates can drain from land that has been spread with manure or fertilisers. Nitrates from the manure or fertilisers can reach ponds and lakes. This causes 'blooms' of algae – a sudden increase in the population of microscopic algae. They cover the water surface, preventing light from reaching plants below. This causes the death of plants, which begin to rot. This uses up the oxygen in the water and in extreme cases all life in the water dies.

Algal blooms on a pond.

Sampling populations

To study populations, ecologists need to find out the numbers of individuals in a population, and also the area of the land, water or air that the population lives in. This gives the **population density**. It can take many years to collect enough data to show patterns in population density.
  Here are some examples:

- the population density for periwinkles on a shore line might be 98/1 = 98 periwinkles per metre square
- the population density for kelp might be 5/100 = 0.05 kelp plants per metre square

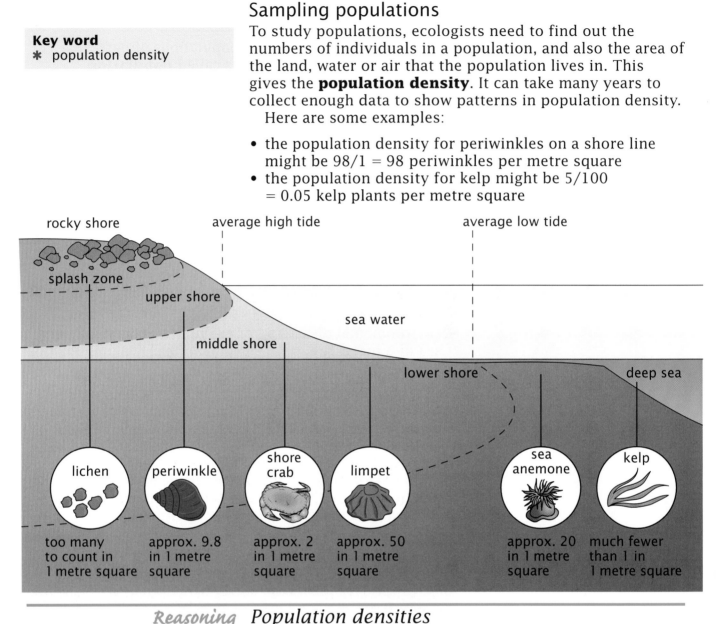

Reasoning *Population densities*

1 Find the population density of each of the organisms in the table.

Organism	Number of individuals in a population	Area for the population
daisy	1030	field, 1000 × 100 metres
fox	2	woodland and fields, 2000 × 100 metres
vole	160	field, 1000 × 100 metres

2 Make a food chain including daisies, foxes and voles. You may need to add other organisms to complete it.

3 Explain why you have chosen to add those organisms to the food chain.

Information processing *Predators and prey*

Charles Elton was a biologist in the early 1900s. His work earned him the title 'father of ecology'. He collected data about the snowshoe hare and the lynx in the Canadian part of the Arctic circle. Here is a graph of his data:

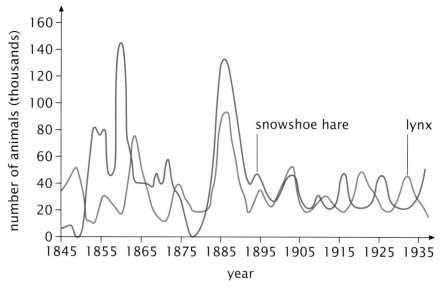

1 Which is the predator and which the prey?

2 For how many years was the data collected?

3 When is the population of the snowshoe hare at its greatest? When is it at its lowest?

4 When is the population of the lynx at its greatest? When is it at its lowest?

5 Why did he draw line graphs rather than bar charts?

6 The peaks in the population numbers of the hare and the lynx do not always occur at the same time. What reason would you give to explain this?

Time to think

- Review this chapter. The process of 'reviewing' is an active mental attempt to put information into your long-term memory. The more senses you involve in trying to remember things, the more likely you are to succeed. That means visually, aurally (using your ears) and physically. So you could repeat something out loud, picture it in your head, jot down a few notes.
- In your group identify the most difficult parts of this chapter for you all. Split into pairs. Each pair should discuss and review one section that you found difficult until you are sure you understand and remember it. Now get another pair to test you. Do the same for them.

Index